Counting the Many

Supermajority rules govern many features of our lives in common: from the selection of textbooks for our children's schools to residential covenants, from the policy choices of state and federal legislatures to constitutional amendments. It is usually assumed that these rules are not only normatively unproblematic but necessary to achieve the goals of institutional stability, consensus, and minority protections. In this book, Melissa Schwartzberg challenges the logic underlying the use of supermajority rule as an alternative to majority decision making. She traces the hidden history of supermajority decision making, which originally emerged as an alternative to unanimous rule, and highlights the tensions in the contemporary use of supermajority rules as an alternative to majority rule. Although supermajority rules ostensibly aim to reduce the purported risks associated with majority decision making, they do so at the cost of introducing new liabilities associated with the biased judgments they generate and secure.

Melissa Schwartzberg is an associate professor of politics at New York University. She previously taught at The George Washington University and Columbia University. She received her A.B. from Washington University in St. Louis in 1996, and her Ph.D. in 2002 from New York University. She is the author of *Democracy and Legal Change* (Cambridge, 2007) and of articles in leading journals including the *American Political Science Review*, the *Journal of the History of Ideas*, the *Journal of Political Philosophy*, and *Political Theory*. She is a 2013 recipient of the Me... ...New H... ...m 2010 to 2013, she serve... ...tion for Political Theory.

Cambridge Studies in the Theory of Democracy

General Editor
Adam Przeworski *New York University*

Other Books in the Series

Robert Barros, *Constitutionalism and Dictatorship: Pinochet, the Junta, and the 1980 Constitution*

Jon Elster, ed., *Deliberative Democracy*

Roberto Gargarella, *Constitutionalism in the Americas, 1776–1860*

José María Maravall and Adam Przeworski, eds., *Democracy and the Rule of Law*

José María Maravall and Ignacia Sánchez-Cuenca, *Controlling Governments: Voters, Institutions, and Accountability*

Adam Przeworski, *Democracy and the Limits of Self-Government*

Adam Przeworski, Susan Stokes, and Bernard Manin, eds., *Democracy, Accountability, and Representation*

Adam Przeworski et al., *Democracy and Development: Political Institutions and Well-Being in the World, 1950–1990*

Melissa Schwartzberg, *Democracy and Legal Change*

Counting the Many

The Origins and Limits of Supermajority Rule

MELISSA SCHWARTZBERG
New York University

CAMBRIDGE
UNIVERSITY PRESS

CAMBRIDGE
UNIVERSITY PRESS

32 Avenue of the Americas, New York, NY 10013-2473, USA

Cambridge University Press is part of the University of Cambridge.

It furthers the University's mission by disseminating knowledge in the pursuit of education, learning, and research at the highest international levels of excellence.

www.cambridge.org
Information on this title: www.cambridge.org/9780521124492

© Melissa Schwartzberg 2014

First published 2014

Printed in the United States of America

A catalog record for this publication is available from the British Library.

Library of Congress Cataloging in Publication data
Schwartzberg, Melissa, 1975–
Counting the many : the origins and limits of supermajority rule / Melissa Schwartzberg.
   pages cm. – (Cambridge studies in the theory of democracy)
ISBN 978-0-521-19823-3 (hardback) – ISBN 978-0-521-12449-2 (paperback)
1. Majorities – Cross-cultural studies.   2. Representative government and representation – Cross-cultural studies.   3. Constitutional law – Cross-cultural studies.   4. Democracy – Cross-cultural studies.   I. Title.
JF1051.S386   2013
324.6'3–dc23   2013007634

ISBN 978-0-521-19823-3 Hardback
ISBN 978-0-521-12449-2 Paperback

Cambridge University Press has no responsibility for the persistence or accuracy of URLs for external or third-party Internet Web sites referred to in this publication and does not guarantee that any content on such Web sites is, or will remain, accurate or appropriate.

For David, who abides

Contents

Acknowledgments

This book was written and rewritten during my years at Columbia University, though its inception dates to my four wonderful years at The George Washington University. Conversations with Sarah Binder, Forrest Maltzman, and the late Lee Sigelman convinced me that a book analyzing supermajority rules from a normative perspective needed to be written, and that I was probably the person who ought to write it. I have occasionally regretted having taken that advice, but my gratitude for their friendship – and that of many other colleagues from my time at GW, especially Nathan Brown, Ingrid Creppell, Henry Farrell, Steven Kelts, Eric Lawrence, Kimberly Morgan, Elliot Posner, John Sides, and Erik Voeten – has never wavered. I hope Lee would have liked this book; it has been shaped by his memory.

A distinct benefit of undergoing a multi-year, iterated tenure process is that one has the opportunity to receive advice from a captive audience of brilliant scholars, both at one's own institution and elsewhere. At Columbia, I am especially grateful for detailed comments on the entire manuscript from Michael Doyle, Jon Elster, David Johnston, and Ira Katznelson as well as to Page Fortna, Tim Frye, Andrew Gelman, John Huber, Macartan Humphreys, Robert Lieberman, Isabela Mares, Victoria Murillo, and Greg Wawro for thoughtful and constructive advice. Jean Cohen and Nadia Urbinati provided critical feedback on Chapters 5 and 6 that led me to sharpen my argumentation. Tanisha Fazal read this manuscript both in parts and in its entirety; her intellect and friendship have been invaluable. I am also very thankful for many helpful substantive (and frivolous) conversations with Lucy Goodhart, Turkuler Isiksel, Kimuli Kasara, Jeffrey Lax, Justin Phillips, Pablo Pinto, and Tonya Putnam. I benefited from research assistance from two extraordinary former Columbia students: then–graduate student, now–assistant professor Jeffrey Lenowitz, and then-undergrad, now–Harvard history Ph.D. student Charles Clavey. A third wonderful graduate student, Kevin Elliott, created the index and provided substantive help in the final stages of the project. Friends at Columbia outside of the Department of Political Science also helped in myriad ways. I am grateful to Sam Moyn for allowing me to learn from him and to tax his patience for more than twenty years; to Rachel Adams, Bob Amdur, Christopher Brown, Eileen Gillooly, Olati Johnson, Hagar Kotef, Molly Murray, Fred Neuhouser, and Katja Vogt for encouragement during my years at Columbia; and to Jim Zetzel for his support in the Department of Classics.

Outside of Columbia, I would like to thank Jack Knight and Bernard Manin for their sustaining friendship and their invaluable comments on the project, as well as Corey Brettschneider, John Ferejohn, Russell Hardin, Jim Johnson, Dimitri Landa, Jacob Levy, Eric MacGilvray, John McCormick, Josiah Ober, Pasquale Pasquino, Philip Pettit, Adam Przeworski, Andrew Rehfeld, Rogers Smith, and Bernard Yack. Ryan Pevnick and Peter Stone offered insightful and critical comments on the entire manuscript for which I am greatly indebted. One of the greatest privileges of my life has been to participate in a writing group with Bryan Garsten, Karuna Mantena, and Annie Stilz, from whom I always learn, and to whom I will never be fully capable of repaying my debts. I thank them for shaping the work in innumerable ways, from the title to the bibliography, and for their sustaining friendship. Andrew Murphy's extraordinary service as co-president of the Association for Political Theory enabled me to neglect my duties when necessary. Conversations with my beloved friend Jennifer Gandhi continue to shape my work and the contours of my life.

Lewis Bateman has been an extraordinarily patient and supportive editor. I deeply appreciate his forbearance. I am honored and moved by Adam Przeworski's willingness to include this second book in his Theory of Democracy series. I would also like to thank Ann Jamison Loftin for her exceptional editing during the final stage of the project.

Chapters from the book were presented at political theory or related seminars at Brown University, Princeton University, Rutgers University, University of Pennsylvania, and Yale University, as well as at the NYU School of Law, the Remarque Institute at NYU, and the classics department at Columbia; and at conferences at Yale University, Moritz College of Law at Ohio State University (2011, 2012), the Midwest Political Science Association, the American Political Science Association (2005, 2007, 2009), the Association for Political Theory (2005, 2007), and the European University Institute. I am grateful to the discussants and participants at all these sessions. I would like to thank the faculty of the Department of Government at Georgetown University in particular for its feedback, as well as for its support for my scholarship more generally.

Finally, I thank the faculty of the Department of Politics at New York University, especially David Stasavage, for welcoming me home. I am thrilled to be back.

I had two children – Isaiah ("Izzy") and Leah Schwartzberg Jones – while writing this book (more literally than my obstetrician or I would have liked). I am grateful for the generous parental leave provided by Columbia, but this book simply could not have been completed without the wonderful childcare provided by Basic Trust. I thank the late Peggy Sradnick for making us at home at BT, and Mary Biggs, Rafiyah Coaxum, Cassie Alicea, Andrew Doucet, Joy Harden, E. J. Otero, John Parker, Martina Proctor, Julia Rundbaken, Lena Sradnick, and the rest of the remarkable staff for caring for Izzy and Leah every day, and the community of parents at BT for helping my children flourish among their own.

For their love and support for both my career and my family, I thank Rosalyn and Barry Schwartzberg, Debbi Schwartzberg and

Mark Pecoraro, and Nina and Howard Jones. My dear friends Michael Adler, Dana Burde, Kristin Karner, Nalo McGibbon, Nerina Rustomji, Takumi Sato, Lina Umylny, Barry Vasudevan, Wendy Woodford, and Ivan and Karla Zeitz have helped keep me relatively sane over these difficult years.

David Jones weathered the slow-moving storm system and even slower recovery effort that surrounded the writing of this book. For that, I thank him most of all and dedicate it to him with love.

I am grateful to publishers for permission to reprint the following material: Much of Chapter 2 was first published as "Shouts, Murmurs, and Votes: Acclamation and Aggregation in Ancient Greece," *Journal of Political Philosophy*, 18:4, 448–468 (2010), published by Wiley-Blackwell. Sections of Chapter 4 first appeared in "Voting the General Will: Rousseau on Decision Rules," *Political Theory* 36:3 (2008), 403–423, published by Sage. Brief passages from Chapter 5 were first published in "Should Progressive Constitutionalism Embrace Popular Constitutionalism?" 72 *Ohio State L.J.* 1295 (2011). Chapter 6 draws on material first published in "The Arbitrariness of Supermajority Rules," *Social Science Information* 49:1 (2010), 61–82, published by Sage.

I

Introduction

Today we encounter supermajority rules in most elements of our social lives. If we choose to purchase a home in a residential community, we are likely to be bound by covenants, rules, and regulations enforced by community associations and secured by strenuous supermajority rules. The school boards that oversee our children's education may be obliged to use a supermajority rule for issues including the discontinuation of a recently adopted textbook, or standardization of equipment or supplies,[1] and our children's athletic clubs may have their bylaws subject to a supermajority amendment clause.[2] University professors encounter supermajority rules at many levels, from the initial hiring of faculty to tenure decisions and other decisions made by the board of trustees. Employees of other corporations, both nonprofit and for-profit, abide by decisions implemented by corporate boards that use supermajority rules for governance.

If these norms are common in our private and associative lives, they are nearly ubiquitous in the political realm. In the United States, on both the state and federal levels, laws are regularly subject to supermajority rules for enactment and abrogation. In sixteen

---

[1] See, for instance, New York General Municipal Law §103.
[2] See, for instance, the bylaws of the Palm Beach Garden's Youth Athletic Association:http://www.pbgyaa.com/

states, supermajorities are required to raise taxes.[3] In the Senate, the use – or threat – of filibuster, requiring a three-fifths vote for cloture, rose dramatically in recent years. Constitutions around the globe almost inevitably have recourse to supermajority rules for adoption and amendment.

These norms have profound consequences for the justice of the political universe in which we live. Consider three stylized examples:

- It is June 30, 1982, and an advocate for the Equal Rights Amendment (ERA) just learned that her efforts have been in vain. Ten years prior, Congress approved the ERA by an overwhelming margin, considerably more than the two-thirds majority required. The ratification process went smoothly in its early stages: thirty states ratified the proposed amendment by the end of 1973, followed by three more in 1974, and an additional two states in 1975 and 1977. However, even after the time limit was extended from March 22, 1979 to June 30, 1982, the amendment remained three states short of the thirty-eight necessary for approval. In total, merely seven votes stood in the way of the passage of the ERA: three in the Nevada senate, two in the North Carolina senate, and two in the Florida senate (Steiner 1985).[4]
- It is May 17, 2005, and a participant in the British Columbia Citizens' Assembly just learned that the ballot measure he helped craft, failed. The Citizens' Assembly was convened in response to widespread dissatisfaction with the dispropor-tionality of a single-member plurality electoral system. Its members were assigned the responsibility of recommending electoral reforms and of creating a proposal to be subject to

---

[3] http://www.fiscalaccountability.org/supermajority

[4] For a systematic and rigorous account of the political factors contributing to the defeat of the ERA, see Mansbridge (1986). Whereas the time limit on the ERA led to its formal defeat, because of the absence of a time limit govern-ing the proposal of the Madison Amendment, a.k.a. the Congressional Pay Amendment, 203 years passed before the thirty-eighth state ratified it on May 7, 1992 (Held, Herndon, and Stager 1997).

referendum. The participant, chosen through a process of near-random selection, spent six weekends learning about the electoral system. He attended public hearings and then spent six more weekends from September to November 2004 deliberating with 159 others about the question of electoral reform. On the basis of these hearings and deliberations, the Citizens' Assembly ultimately proposed a single-transferable vote system, and the measure was placed on the ballot during the provincial elections. The government had set a double supermajoritarian threshold: 60 percent of the province-wide vote and a majority in 60 percent of the electoral districts. The measure satisfied the latter criterion (seventy-seven of seventy-nine districts) but received only 57.7 percent of the province-wide vote.

• It is November 4, 2008, and a gay couple in California has just been forced to cancel their wedding, scheduled for Thanksgiving. On May 15, the California Supreme Court had ruled that the state constitution permitted same-sex marriage, striking down a state law restricting marriage to opposite-sex couples. In response, opponents of same-sex marriage launched an expensive campaign to amend the constitution, and Proposition 8 passed by a vote of 52.3 percent. The couple are dismayed by the cancellation, but they are also furious that what the state supreme court had recognized as their constitutional right to wed could be struck down by a mere simple-majority vote.

These examples illustrate modern uses of supermajority rule, with its attendant liabilities and possible benefits. Those who lose under supermajority rule often lament the excessively stringent bias toward the status quo it protects; similarly, those who believe their rights have been violated under majority rule often turn to the promise of supermajority rule as a means of guaranteeing their protection. It might seem, then, that nothing inherent in supermajority rules ought to generate any serious normative concerns: The complaints of the ERA advocate and the member of the Citizens' Assembly, purely contextual, are no more valid – indeed, perhaps less so – than the frustrations of the same-sex couple. In this work, I hope to demonstrate that in all three cases, the losing parties have a reason to object to the procedures under which their preferred alternatives were defeated.

Legislators, citizens, and political theorists alike identify three core problems generated by majoritarian decision making. The first is institutional instability: A majoritarian system would encourage political actors to revise their laws, including constitutional provisions, each time the composition or preferences of the majority change. This would introduce uncertainty into law and leave the consequences of actions and investments insecure. Second, because a bare majority would be sufficient to enact such changes, the majority would have no incentive to consult with the minority or to take their interests into account; fundamental laws would not necessarily reflect social consensus. Third, because the majority could act without the support of a minority, a simple-majority rule would not protect vulnerable minorities from abuse or neglect.

For at least two centuries, the view that supermajority rules effectively solve these defects of majority rule has proven compelling to legislatures, constitutional framers, and corporate bodies around the world. Even as critics of the filibuster, of the political conditions of the State of California, and of the barriers to amendment under Article V of the U.S. Constitution grew increasingly vocal over the past several years, their objections to supermajority rule in these contexts have not typically been theorized more broadly. The problems of supermajority rule are usually thought to be local rather than general. Objections are raised against excessively partisan politicians who abuse their power to block changes, or the "dead hand of the law" under constitutionalism, not against supermajority rule as such.

In contrast, I argue that supermajority rule has distinctive liabilities of its own that make it incapable of remedying the defects of majority rule. My central aim in this book is to challenge the view that supermajority rules are necessary for normatively attractive and stable democratic decision making, and to demonstrate the inadequacy of supermajority rule to many of the tasks with which it has been charged in modern history. This deficiency is in part because supermajority rules were originally designed not to remedy the problems of majority rule, but to address the issue of persistent disagreement under unanimous-decision rules. This book is written, in a sense, to try to justify the procedural objections to supermajority rules raised by the ERA advocate and the Citizens' Assembly member, and to caution vulnerable minorities, such as the gay couple in California, against relying on supermajority rules to protect their interests. But to justify these objections I must tell a story about the origins of supermajority rules in the premodern era, and the way in which modern constitutionalism appropriated these rules for different purposes. As I hope to show, this story begins with the origins of the counted vote.

Originally designed to accommodate human error and persistent disagreement under unanimity rules, supermajority rules are a weak solution to the challenges of majoritarian decision making. The deceptive ease of raising a vote threshold have helped supermajority rules become the default response to the problems of instability, partisanship, and vulnerable minorities in contemporary democracies. After all, supermajority rules seem to require no derogation from the normal mechanisms of vote aggregation; a higher threshold appears to be an obvious solution when the number of votes in favor of an outcome is the dispositive factor in resolving disputes. Yet this very simplicity – their crudity, I shall suggest – is their major liability. A blunt instrument, a supermajority threshold cannot ensure that only the right institutions are secured or that only vulnerable minorities are protected. Addressing the problems of majority rule in modern democratic societies requires far finer tools.

Voting and Judgment

In this book, I seek to explain and assess the significance of supermajority rules within the context of democratic decision making. I argue that the counted vote is aristocratic in origin, restricted initially to an elite possessing special and superior faculties of judgment. The mass did not have judgments worth counting separately, and so it merely acclaimed rather than voted. Only in the context of democratic Athens did the belief emerge that the many made judgments worth counting individually and independently – at least in certain contexts. Even there, in domains where there was a desire to demonstrate communal commitment, the Greeks used acclamatory mechanisms to avoid what I term an enumerated minority.

Supermajority rules, virtually from inception, reflected ambivalence about the use of aggregation instead of acclamatory or consensual mechanisms. Among their earliest uses, supermajority rules constituted an alternative to medieval *unanimitas* ("oneness of spirit"), in which the divine spirit suffused the electors of the pope. Only after losing the hope of transcendent resolution through acclamation were votes counted. Even then, the relative quality of the judgments of the cardinals played an important role in shaping the voting rules that emerged to replace acclamation. Ultimately, supermajority rule emerged as a mechanism designed to reflect the distinctive wisdom of the individual voters while accommodating their fallibility, both moral and epistemic. In turn, through acknowledging the inevitability of human fallibility, supermajority rules reduced the coercive potential of unanimity rules and helped quell discord. As we shall see in the first half of this book, arguments for supermajority rule traveled far from the context of papal elections, playing a pivotal role in the development of modern political thought about the institutional design of assemblies and juries. Even today, supermajority rules (also termed qualified-majority rules) replace unanimity rule to avoid potentially ruinous disagreement, particularly in confederations, transnational bodies, and multinational organizations. In general, however, supermajority rules are no longer regarded primarily as a solution to the problems of unanimity rule, but instead as a remedy for the deficiencies of majority rule – a task to which they are ill-suited.

Majority and Supermajority Rule

Though originally devised as an alternative to the unyielding demands of unanimity rules, supermajority rule has in the past two centuries acquired a different set of justifications. The aim of the modern use of supermajority rules is ostensibly to curb the abuses of unfettered majoritarianism. Yet in the second half of the book, I suggest that to weigh judgments unequally in a given domain, as supermajority rule does, is an affront to the members' dignity; it fails to treat members with equal respect. In a democracy, I shall suggest, citizens' judgments – which include, but are not restricted to, judgments of their interests[5] – should be presumed to be of equal merit.

From antiquity, democrats have been committed to the view that ordinary citizens possess sufficient capacity for judgment for political decision making; this distinguishes them from aristocrats. To presuppose that some citizens possess less valuable judgments – to establish institutions that systematically weigh judgments unequally – is to treat such citizens disrespectfully. If respect for individual and independent judgment are central commitments of democracy, and if equal respect for citizens entails the presumption that citizens' judgments – again, including their judgments of their own interests – are of equal merit, then the default voting rule within democracies should be majority rule. As I shall argue, this does not mean that expertise cannot play a role in political decision making. Representative institutions

---

[5] Throughout this work, I intentionally elide the common distinction between judgments and preferences; my view is that the arguments on behalf of aggregation in general and majority rule in particular hold regardless of whether voters assess what is in their own interest or that which is in the common good. For my purposes, the relevant issue is whether we take *individual* judgments – of their interests or the common good – as the basic component of democratic politics, or some judgment that seems to emerge from the whole via acclamatory or consensual mechanisms. For discussions of the judgment-versus-preference ideal, see Coleman and Ferejohn (1986), Cohen (1986), and Brennan and Pettit (1990). More recently, see Goodin's (2003) account of a way in which a model of democracy for which the aggregation of preferences is fundamental can nonetheless attend to the construction of these preferences through what Goodin terms "democratic deliberation within."

reflect in part the importance of eliciting expert judgments in certain domains, although respect for representatives' judgments (which include judgments of their constituents' interests) within legislatures also means that they ought to be given equal weight through majority rule. My view also does not entail the claim that fundamental decisions about our lives in common ought to be made by immediate recourse to referendums or by a swift vote of the legislature; constitutionalism is surely beneficial to political communities. But this is because judgments worth counting individually and independently require careful development through deliberation and over time. Counter to conventional wisdom, constitutionalism does not depend on supermajority rule. At the end of this work I sketch and advocate a set of "complex-majoritarian institutions." These could take different forms, but they must help citizens develop the sort of reflective judgments worth counting.

No doubt the defense of majority rule from equal respect for judgment will elicit skeptical responses of the sort that have met Jeremy Waldron's *Law and Disagreement*,[6] an important work offering a similar justification of majority decision making from a different set of vantage points. Two significant objections arise in response to any assertion that majority rule can or should be justified by reference to the equal treatment of citizens. The first is that formal equality in the vote may generate, or fail to remedy, substantive inequalities among citizens. The second, related objection targets more sharply the claim that majority rule is respectful of citizens' judgments. This view holds that the substantive outcomes of majority decision making may disrespect the fundamental interests of minorities; as such, liberal rights, rather than any voting procedure, constitute the proper institutional manifestation of equal respect for citizens.

It is impossible to dispute these objections; majority rule may usher in injustice or exacerbate distributive inequalities. Yet my primary aim here is to suggest scholars and citizens alike have misplaced their faith in supermajority rule as a remedy for

---

[6] See, for instance, Christiano (2000); Eisgruber (2002).

the deficiencies of majority rule. The minority veto created by supermajority rule increases the capacity of powerful actors to thwart efforts at redistribution, and may as readily hamper the expansion of fundamental rights as prevent their eradication. A case in point is the shameful historical use of the filibuster against civil rights legislation in this country. Supermajority rule introduces a generally unwarranted bias in favor of the judgments (including, again, the judgments of the interests) of some citizens against others, rendering decisions that may generate and secure adverse distributive consequences without providing an effective remedy to the primary liabilities of majority rule. I hope that even if readers reject equal respect for judgment[7] as a justification for majority rule – or even if they reject majority rule on other normative grounds entirely – they may find my critiques of supermajority rule compelling.

The best argument for supermajority rule as an alternative to majority rule is that in some restrictive circumstances, the bias it introduces may in fact have moral or epistemic warrant, as in jury decision making, or as with a restrictive set of civil and political rights designed to protect the capacity for critical engagement judgment. As we shall see, however, in most cases this bias is not merited. Further, supermajority rules are today defended on different grounds. Conventional wisdom assumes that requiring a supermajority (1) helps ensure institutional stability; (2) promotes consensus-building; and (3) grants protection to vulnerable minorities.

First, institutional stability is ostensibly attractive because of the "security of expectations" such conservatism affords. The cost of major policy changes is so high, it is thought, that

[7] The argument from equal respect is, of course, not the only possible justification for majority rule (Risse 2004; Beitz 1989). Among the most famous are claims from utility maximization, the Condorcet Jury Theorem, and May's Theorem (proving that majority rule is the only threshold satisfying the key conditions of anonymity, decisiveness, neutrality, and positive responsiveness). The argument for majority rule I develop here, I shall suggest, is broadly compatible with these justifications in many respects; it does not claim to override or supersede them, although I shall argue that it is both historically significant and has substantial normative appeal.

the supermajority thresholds are necessary to ensure that the investment will not be squandered once a new party takes majority control of the legislature. Further, it is often thought that only if strenuous supermajority rules secure the "rules of the game" (i.e., fundamental legislative and constitutional matters) against easy amendment can constitutionalism enable ordinary politics to occur (Holmes 1995). We can get the hard, messy work of politics done only if we ensure that we are not always tinkering with the rules governing political life. Such arguments support the use of supermajority rules themselves, as well as serving as a basis to defend the ongoing existence of supermajority rules against efforts at change. That is, supporters of Article V of the U.S. Constitution argue that its strenuousness and durability constitute the means by which the constitutional system operates. To alter it would be to risk eviscerating American constitutionalism as a whole, and in any case to harm the clause's intrinsic value as a legacy of the American founding and its constitutional history.

The second purported justification is that critical political changes, such as sweeping health care reform or constitutional amendments, ought to receive widespread and bipartisan support before adoption. When confined – as it is often, if erroneously, thought to have originally been (Binder and Smith 1997) – to fundamental matters of national importance, the filibuster ensures that narrow partisan majorities cannot enact their will at odds with the general interest. More generally, the requirement that more than a narrow majority of voters or representatives support a proposed law ostensibly lends an extra degree of legitimacy to the decision, which may be important if the proposed change is relatively dramatic.

Third, without supermajority rules such as the filibuster, the interests of the minority in particular would be overlooked. Granting the minority the power to veto ensures that the majority takes their concerns into account, and promotes compromise and consensus-building across the aisle. In the constitutional context, a supermajority rule helps ensure that key protections for minorities are not eviscerated by majority decision making.

Although these arguments have substantial force, they do not withstand close scrutiny. The benefits ascribed to supermajority rule can be realized through other institutions, ones that do not generate adverse distributive consequences or unequal respect for citizens' judgments.

The Normative Analysis of Supermajority Rule

Throughout this work, I emphasize three key normative values that a democratic society ought optimally to instantiate in its decision rules. As already mentioned, the first is *equal epistemic respect*; the second is *fallibility*. That an institution is designed to cope with the inevitability of human error surely counts in its favor, especially in a democratic society. Because the assumption of fallibility enables the critical perspective necessary to check political authority and to improve beliefs and institutions, it is a core democratic value. It surely trumps unanimity rules on this score. But it does not outstrip majority rule in most circumstances, which quite readily accommodates the possibility of error, as Habermas and other democratic theorists have noted. Thus there is no reason to prefer supermajority to majority rule strictly on the grounds of fallibility.

The third value is *minimizing coercion*. As I hope to show, supermajority rule generates less coercion in the form of social pressure during the moment of decision than does unanimity rule, at least in public contexts (where unanimity rule is typically used), but it does not improve upon majority rule. Supermajority rule ostensibly reduces the risk of the substantive coercion of minority members. It reduces the chance that they will be forced to obey laws harmful to their interests. But those concerned especially with the status of minorities under majoritarian decision making have taken false comfort in supermajority rules. These rules are at best unreliable as a means of ensuring protection for minorities because they do not guarantee that the minority group in danger will preserve a vote share sufficient to reliably achieve the veto point secured by a supermajority rule. Nor can a supermajority rule ensure that a vulnerable minority, rather than a powerful one, wields the veto. More obviously, even if at the moment of an original contract unanimity ensures that members obey only those laws to which they consent, and supermajority reduces the number coerced into obedience in comparison to majority rule, this logic does not endure after the initial stage. Once the question of revising the terms of agreement emerges, a requirement of a supermajority or unanimity for amendment increases the number of those who must live under laws they oppose.

In sum, the aim of this work is to explain and analyze supermajority rules from a distinctly normative perspective. Broadly speaking, political theorists have not been preoccupied with the historical origins and moral significance of different voting rules as such. To be sure, unanimity has great moral significance for scholars working in the social-contract tradition, notably including John Rawls and his followers. And indeed, as already suggested, there is a substantial literature on the justification of majority rule, if perhaps not its history (at least not in the English language). But largely this literature seeks to limn the contours of legitimate decision making: the constraints that unanimity places on agents' choices, the extent to which majority decision making ought to be limited by rights, the necessity of deliberation prior to the vote, and so forth. Even those democratic theorists who have specifically examined vote thresholds, perhaps most importantly the late Brian Barry and Robert Dahl, gave supermajority rule little sustained attention. Instead, theorists tend to bundle it with a set of countermajoritarian mechanisms (such as judicial review or constitutionalism) designed to protect minority rights and interests, and assess its value indirectly.

The evaluation of the normative implications of supermajority rule has been largely relegated to social-choice theorists, who focus on the capacity of supermajority rules to break cycles.[8] As Caplin and Nalebuff (1988) demonstrated, under certain conditions of "social consensus," a threshold of 64 percent makes

---

[8] The *locus classicus* of the social-choice study of supermajority, or "δ-majority," rules is Black (1958).

vote cycles impossible. Yet as Partha Dasgupta and Eric Maskin demonstrated, simple majority rule is more robust than any other voting rule. It satisfies the conditions of Pareto, anonymity, neutrality, independence of irrelevant alternatives, and decisiveness over a larger domain of preferences than any other voting rule (Dasgupta 2008). Moreover, the circumstance in which supermajority rules are most widely thought to be not only defensible but indispensable is that of constitutional amendment. Because constitutional amendment is typically presented as a binary choice between the status quo and some alternative, cycles will not arise. The justifications of supermajority rule must therefore lie beyond the narrow bounds of social-choice theory, in the wider scope of normative democratic theory. A key goal of this work is to provide a historical and analytical account of what these justifications might be, and to emphasize their limitations.

Finally, supermajority rule poses a distinctive and overlooked analytical problem for institutional design. The use of a supermajority rule presupposes a decision to count individual votes. This may seem obvious or tautological. Yet both majoritarian and unanimous decision making may take forms that are not strictly aggregative, relying on heuristic devices rather than a formal mechanism. In voice votes and other acclamatory mechanisms, the aim is to assess preponderance. Any counting that occurs takes the form of rough estimation to assess which side has "more" rather than "fewer." Likewise, unanimity may be expressed in terms of apparent consensus or the absence of expressed disagreement; it need not consist in a formal vote. But a supermajority threshold does not have a straightforward informal variant; "most" generates indecision in a way that "more" does not. Why is this?

A formal voting rule is necessarily aggregative; that is, it presumes that the inputs are quantifiable or countable, and it specifies the precise proportion necessary to adopt a particular measure. Supermajority rule is selected when "more" is deemed insufficient support: we do not just want more votes in favor of an alternative; we want "most" of the community to be in accord. Yet "most" resists any such quantification or the specification of a formal boundary: it is essentially fuzzy (Solt 2011). There is no precise upper or lower boundary for "most," and it resists quantification – unlike "more," which has a clear lower boundary and translates directly into a majority vote threshold. Applying the logic of "most" to a voting rule entails a basically arbitrary choice among alternatives in a range between 50 percent plus two and 100 percent minus two: two-thirds, three-quarters, three-fifths. The intuition that we want the policy supported by "more" voters to prevail translates readily into a majority rule, whereas the intuition that we want "most" voters to support a policy before adoption does not generate a determinate supermajoritarian threshold. As such, supermajority rules depend on this decision to count in the first place and then the selection of some threshold within this wide range to indicate "most." From a normative perspective, the fuzzy logic of "most" may render supermajority rule more susceptible to strategic behavior in its enactment than either majority or unanimity rule. Thus, apart from the normative logic of epistemic dignity that justifies majority rule, this work places supermajority rule in the context of the counted vote because of its ineliminably aggregative character.

Overview
The book is divided into two parts. Part I traces the original use of supermajority rule as an alternative to unanimity rule. Part II questions the contemporary logic of using supermajority rule as a remedy for the deficiencies of majority rule. Again, an important thread throughout the work is the way in which voting rules reflect conceptions of political judgment, in particular the means by which institutions may or may not indicate respect for its citizens' capacity to render good decisions. A key claim is that the individual, counted vote – weighed equally through majority rule – recognizes the dignity of citizens as judges of political matters. Chapter 2 provides the historical basis in the ancient world for this claim. It also sets up an important distinction between "aggregative" and "acclamatory" mechanisms: those that sum

the distinct and independent judgments of citizens versus those that seek to capture the view of the community as a whole. Supermajority rules are necessarily aggregative, as I have suggested, but often are chosen to serve acclamatory ends. Chapter 3 focuses on the medieval use of supermajority rules in papal elections and beyond. This chapter demonstrates that supermajority rules were used after *unanimitas*, oneness of spirit, had broken down: the weaker threshold of a supermajority rule could accommodate moral and epistemic fallibility while generating a decisive outcome. The argument for supermajority rule as a solution to the problem of human fallibility proved compelling for centuries, shown in Chapter 4. Seventeenth- and eighteenth-century social-contract theorists developed a defense of supermajority rule as an alternative to unanimity rule so as to mitigate the risk of an individual veto. In response to two major criminal trials, eighteenth-century theorists (notably the Marquis de Condorcet) also established a defense of supermajority rule as an alternative to majority rule on the grounds that it would bias collective decisions against the paradigmatic injustice of false conviction in a jury trial.

Part II, beginning with Chapter 5, turns to modern defenses of majority rule as a mechanism that preserves not only the independent and individual quality of judgment, but also the rough equality of the capacity for judgment. Chapter 5 then focuses on the reasons why supermajority rules appear to serve as a remedy for the purported risks of majoritarian decision making – which are tied to the perceived risks of weighing judgments equally. It also introduces three core justifications for supermajority rules: they help stabilize fundamental political institutions, ensure that proposed changes receive widespread support among the population, and protect vulnerable minorities. In Chapter 6, I demonstrate that even in the hard case of the constitutional context, supermajority rules are not necessary to achieve these aims, nor are they the optimal means. Instead, in Chapter 7, I suggest that "complex majoritarianism" – institutions designed to improve the judgment of decision makers, while preserving a majority voting rule – can accomplish the aims of supermajority rule with fewer normative liabilities. In conclusion, I suggest that only when there is very good reason to believe that the moral and epistemic risks of a decision are distributed highly asymmetrically ought we to bias decision making against one outcome. Such circumstances are quite rare in most political contexts, and targeted remedies designed to minimize the effects of predictable and entrenched biases are likely to be less risky and more effective.

PART I

A REMEDY FOR THE PROBLEMS OF UNANIMITY

2

Prelude: Acclamation and Aggregation
in the Ancient World

It may seem surprising to begin a study of supermajority rule in ancient Greece. Athens did not use supermajority rules,[1] and the earliest documented use of such norms does not seem to be until the second century BCE in Rome. Although inquiry into many democratic institutions rightly begins in the great laboratory of democracy that was classical Athens, supermajority rules seem to be an important exception. Why turn to Greece, and to the circumstances in which the counted vote emerged?

The choice among majority, supermajority, and unanimity rule only emerges after a prior decision to count votes – and so the development of the counted vote in ancient Greece is the subject of this chapter. Here I shall argue that the assignment of a "counted" or "aggregated" vote conferred dignity on those rendering decisions: it was originally an "aristocratic" institution,[2] designed to assess the independent votes of those, and

---

[1] There were indeed rules such as the requirement that a prosecutor must receive one-fifth of the vote of the jury to avoid the charge of frivolous prosecution (i.e., no more than four-fifths of the jurors can vote to acquit the defendant), but these are better understood as "submajority rules," a distinctive category including the Supreme Court's "rule of four." Adrian Vermeule (2007) has provided the most sustained analysis of these rules.
[2] This formulation is intended in part as homage to Manin's (1997) Aristotelian claim that elections are an aristocratic mechanism.

only of those, who possessed a special and superior faculty of political judgment. In contrast, acclamation was a mechanism for the masses, lacking such developed faculties and not worthy of having their judgments counted discretely. Only with the rise of democracy in Athens did the view emerge that ordinary citizens merited a counted vote.[3]

The concept of "epistemic dignity" that underlies the assignment of the counted vote anchors much of the normative logic of this book. In particular, it helps to support the arguments on behalf of an equally weighted vote via majority rule, and the objection to supermajority rule, that will emerge most sharply in the second half of the book. Whereas acclamatory mechanisms effectively capture the notion of a community speaking univocally, an aggregative voting rule, regardless of threshold, emphasizes the importance of the members' individual and independent judgments. Majority rule captures the equal dignity of these judgments; supermajority rule is biased against one set of these judgments, often without good reason. Thus, investigating the origins of the counted vote provides a set of arguments that will undergird the book's examination of supermajority rules.

Remarkably, although classicists have recognized the importance of the emergence of the counted vote – G. E. M. de Ste Croix argued that it was "by far the most important single step in the development of democracy" – and have marveled at how little attention the matter has received, the topic has remained largely unaddressed by historians and political scientists.[4] Even though my primary aim here is not historical reconstruction but analysis, given the relatively unfamiliar nature of the subject even for scholars well versed in the ancient world, a brief review of the emergence of the counted vote in archaic Greece

---

[3] Note that the question here is not of the expansion of the suffrage as such (having one's vote "count" in the usual sense), but in the analytical structure and normative significance of the shift to having individuals' particular judgments subject to aggregation.

[4] G. E. M. de Ste. Croix (1972, 348–349), for instance, writes: "It is extraordinary how both ancient and modern writers have neglected this development."

will situate the critical examination. First, I turn to Homeric councils and assemblies to challenge the dominant explanations for the emergence of aggregation, and I argue that perceptions of competence gave rise to different accounts of political behavior in these groups. Second, I trace the development of voting in the archaic period to highlight the coexistence of mechanisms of acclamation and aggregation, and to suggest that vote-counting constituted a means of showing respect for the quality of judgment possessed by members of the Spartan *gerousia* and Athenian *areopagus*. I then examine the circumstances under which both estimated and counted votes were used in fifth- and fourth-century BCE Athens. To provide some basis for comparison and further context, I turn to the contrasting uses of the counted vote and acclamation in ancient Rome. The chapter concludes with a discussion of the first use of supermajority rule, in second-century BCE Rome.

Such an inquiry illuminates the possibility that the use of aggregation reflects an attractive respect for individual members of a society as possessing *epistemic* dignity. But insofar as we wish to convey that a decision emerges from a body as a whole, mechanisms of acclamation or of estimation may be preferable. This logic underlying the choice to count votes presses against key justifications of supermajority rule – in particular, the desire to capture the consensus of a community, as later chapters argue. The ancient world helps us clarify the logic of counting votes, and in so doing enables us to unveil the deficiencies in the modern defense of supermajoritarian decision making.

Acclamation in Homeric Assemblies

The first accounts we have of decision making in the ancient world are those of Homeric councils and assemblies, in which decisions were made by acclamation. Although "[t]here is no formal vote hence no counting of votes, and no formal obligation to respect the people's opinion. ... it is clearly in the leaders' interest to heed the assembly's voice" (Raaflaub, Ober, and Wallace

2007, 28).[5] Yet the consensual mechanism famously broke down in the Homeric context.[6] The most influential accounts of the origins of the counted vote take this as significant; Glotz, in particular, held that the failures of acclamation necessarily caused the counted vote to emerge: "The vote is the prophylactic against civil war; where it does not exist there remains, in default of absolute power, only the alternatives of civil strife or anarchic inertia" (Glotz 1929, 56).[7]

It is surely the case that acclamation may under certain conditions fail to resolve disagreement. Yet this falls short as an explanation for the emergence of vote-counting on two grounds. It suggests that there is something fundamentally inadequate about the mechanism of acclamation for decision purposes, and it asserts that the counting of votes can effectively resolve these deficiencies. Indeed, Nicole Loraux argued that voting in an assembly in many Greek cities was called *diaphora* (in her translation, "dividing up" or "disagreeing"), and that victory in a vote was still disturbing insofar as *stasis* was always latent.[8] By the time of classical Athens, in Paul Cartledge's words, "every vote on a major policy issue threatened the outbreak of *stasis*" (Cartledge 2001, 166). In the case of widespread division, though, it is surely true that no decision may be taken (Glotz's "anarchic inertia"). Why a ballot would resolve matters marked by widespread disagreement more effectively than a voice vote, however, requires some explanation.

---

[5] Scholars today generally concur that the Homeric works provide valuable historical insights into the sociopolitical context of the late eighth and early seventh centuries BCE (Raaflaub, Ober, and Wallace 2007, 24).

[6] See book 2 of *The Iliad* (Homer 1990), in which Agamemnon tests the Achaeans' resolve; book 9, in which Diomedes counters Agamemnon's efforts to persuade the troops to return home; and book 24 of the *Odyssey* (Homer 1996), in which the assembly is divided on the question of whether or not to avenge the suitors.

[7] Further, Tsopanakis (1954) holds that the evidence Homer notes that certain matters were decided unanimously, or with the members in complete accord, in fact implies that dissent was not just possible but frequent.

[8] Loraux (1997, 101) holds also that in the case of equal division, the Greeks believed that it would be the worse opinion that would prevail, and thus longed for unanimity.

It is true that a ballot might resolve second-order disagreement about the relative strength of the support for each side. But it is not clear that uncertainty about this matter generally caused or exacerbated conflict. Further, the archaic Greeks, already relatively sophisticated institutionally, could not have believed that the problem of indecisiveness would be resolved through counting hands. There is no reason that a split vote would not lead to a minority's refusal to accept the outcome, leading as with acclamation to *stasis*. Finally, as we shall see in a moment, the ballot was not introduced first in large bodies, in which the immediate consequences of division might have been large-scale violence. Instead, it was used to resolve internal disputes among aristocrats. It is surely true that the relative difficulty of counting heads in a large rather than small body may partially explain its emergence in councils rather than assemblies. Yet given the remarkable level of technical organization among individuals in other mass settings – notably, the hoplite phalanx (Raaflaub, Ober, and Wallace 2007, 34–36) – it is hard to imagine that balloting would have constituted an insurmountable obstacle for the archaic Greeks.

So why, and under what circumstances, would the counted vote have been introduced? The evidence is necessarily suggestive, but even as early as Homer, there is evidence that the emergence of the vote in councils rather than assemblies may be attributable to the epistemic superiority of the council members. Recent work by Deborah Beck highlights this point. First, Homer presents speakers in councils and in assemblies differently. The example of Nestor in *The Iliad* is illustrative of this point. When Nestor speaks to the council – a body of *gerontas*, regarded as, if not old, then wise men – he is identified as "Nestor, whose advice had shown best before this" (Beck 2006, 198).[9] Compare this description with how Nestor is portrayed when he speaks to the assembly: "Nestor, he who ruled as a king in Sandy Pylos" (Beck 2006, 198).[10] Note here that whereas the salient feature

---

[9] Citing and translating Homer, *Iliad*, 9.94 (see also Homer 1990, 7.325).
[10] Citing and translating Homer, *Iliad*, 2.77.

of Nestor as a speaker in a council is his capacity to give good advice, his authoritativeness is what is highlighted in the assembly (Beck 2006, ch. 5).[11]

Second, the response of council members to speakers differs from the response of assemblies. In a council, the standard response is "so he spoke, and the word he spoke was pleasing to all of them." In contrast, Beck notes that the formulaic response of an assembly to a presentation is "and they were stricken to silence," and then after another person has taken his turn, the group responds positively: "they listened hard to him, and obeyed him" (Beck 2006, 196). Whereas an assembly obeys, a council considers whether or not the argument is pleasing. Both are acclamatory, but the faculty of judgment is more strongly emphasized in the council than in the assembly. Thus, in "wise councils," the speaker advises and the members listen reflectively. In assemblies, comprised of ordinary soldiers, the speaker offers an authoritative statement, which is obeyed passively by the assembly. Both are implicitly consensual – again, no vote is taken – but the council suggests the exercise of judgment, whereas the assembly's response is one of awestruck submission.

Finally, the judicial scene on the shield of Achilles also emphasizes the role of elders in giving their verdicts in a suit over the murder of a relative, with a responsive crowd before them:

> The crowd cheered on both, they took both sides,
> But heralds held them back as the city elders sat
> On polished stone benches, forming the sacred circle,
> Grasping in hand the staffs of clear-voiced heralds,
> And each leapt to his feet to plead the case in turn.
> Two bars of solid gold shone on the ground before them,
> A prize for the judge who'd speak the straightest verdict.
> (Homer 1990, 18.503–8, 586–592)

---

[11] *Pace* Finley (1979, 123), who argues that the council consists in authoritativeness rather than judgment. See also Borgeaud (1887, 7), arguing that in the ancient Homeric assembly the people did not so much vote as, without deliberation, shout or murmur their support for the proposals presented to them by those in positions of authority.

While the crowd cheers, the elders are physically set apart, their dignity as judges represented through their placement on stone benches and their orderliness in rendering their individual verdicts. Such a model of judgment is echoed in the *gerousia* of archaic Sparta and the *areopagus* of Athens.

The Origins of Counting Votes in Archaic Greece

The Spartan *gerousia* (council of elders) has generally been taken to be one of the first bodies in which the vote was introduced.[12] Although the dating of the *gerousia* and its powers relative to the *apella* (assembly) are both matters of serious contention, it is relatively well established that the *gerousia* rendered decisions through the vote. The *gerousia* was not itself chosen by vote. Lycurgus, Plutarch reports, appointed the first *gerousia*, but he also prescribed a procedure by which the most outstanding men over the age of sixty would be elected as members. The people would gather in the assembly, and a small body of judges would be shut in a nearby room, close enough to hear the cries of the assembly (these cries were the normal decision-making procedure in the assembly, Plutarch writes). In an order determined by lot, the candidates for the *gerousia* would pass through the assembly, greeted by the shouts of the crowd; the judges would evaluate which candidates had received the loudest shouts, and those candidates would be elected (Plutarch 2001, 26.1–3, 75–76). (Aristotle denigrated this procedure as puerile [Aristotle 1995, II.9, 1271a10, 71].) Note that the idea of expressly voting among multiple candidates – and the concept of election more generally – here retains its acclamatory character: the outcome is collective, or "clumped," rather than rendered by counting individual votes.

Yet though the *gerousia* was chosen by an acclamatory voice vote, its decisions do not seem to have been made by such a mechanism. It is believed instead that aggregation may have originated in

---

[12] See in particular Larsen (1949); Staveley (1972); Tsopanakis (1954, 44); Cartledge (2001, 35, by implication).

the *gerousia*, its votes governed by majority rule.[13] If the *gerousia* is likely one of the very first, if not *the* first, locus of political decision making by counting votes, why might it have been introduced in this context? Here I wish to suggest that voting emerged not in response to the threat of dissension – in which case we might have expected it to originate in the *apella* – but because of the individual merit of the members comprising the *gerousia*.

In selecting the *gerontes* (councilmen), Plutarch muses about the competition to determine "who of many wise and good was wisest and best, and fittest to be entrusted for ever after, as the reward of his merits, with the supreme authority of the commonwealth, and with power over the lives, franchises, and higher interests of all his countrymen" (Plutarch 2001, 26, 1, 75). Further, the composition of the *gerousia* suggests that each individual member might have had particular wisdom – Staveley refers to their "dignity," Forrest to their "prestige"[14] – that enabled each one to have special competence, and thus an individual "voice" worth hearing (perhaps literally in the form of deliberation, perhaps figuratively in the form of the vote).

Note also – although here we are on more controversial ground – the role of the *gerousia* in providing a corrective to the *apella*. The "Great Rhetra," the Spartan constitutional document ascribed to Lycurgus (2001, 6.1, 57–58), prescribes only that the twenty-eight elders and two kings, acting collectively

[13] What evidence do we have that votes in the *gerousia* were aggregated? Unfortunately, the two critical pieces of support are considerably later: the trial of King Pausanias in 403 BCE and the events, likely dating to the mid-third century BCE, described in Plutarch's *Agis* (2001, 9–11, 317–330). Although it is difficult to draw inferences from the fifth and third centuries BCE, Cartledge (2001, 35) argues that Sparta's archaic period was also its "classical epoch." The former case consists in a vote by a court consisting of the twenty-eight *gerontes*, the five ephors, and the other king besides Pausanias; the verdict for acquittal was fourteen *gerontes* and five ephors against the other fourteen *gerontes* and the king (Pausanias 1918, 3.5.2). The second case also describes a split among the *gerousia*, in which a decree is rejected by the *gerousia* with a one-vote majority (Plutarch 2001, 11.1, 324). Finally, a slightly more ambiguous passage from Aristotle in the *Politics* (1995, II.11, 1273a2–3, 77–78) seems to suggest that if the king and elders concur, they can decide whether or not to submit an issue to the assembly, whereas in case of disagreement, the assembly can address the issue.

[14] See Staveley (respectively, 1972, 30; 1980, 46).

as the *gerousia*, should put proposals before the assembly. The question of the relative power of the *damos* (the people *qua* Spartan citizens) to alter the proposals put before it need not concern us. Instead, let us turn to the "rider" (which we can accept, with most modern scholars, as part of the original text[15]): "if the *damos* speaks crookedly, the elders and kings are to be removers" (Cartledge 2001, 29). What matters for us here is simply that the reversal turned on the grounds of an *incorrect* decision, at least from the perspective of the *gerousia* and kings. As long as "crookedly" refers to the idea that a choice was made incorrectly, and that the *gerousia* (and kings) had some power to check the decision, this suggests that the function of the *gerousia* is to provide *good judgment*. There may well have been disagreements, and voting no doubt was designed to manage conflict-. But what voting offered, that shouting did not, was the ability of *each geron* to render his verdict on a given matter. Why would such power be of importance? To count votes is to implicitly affirm the weight of each individual's judgment on a matter. Whereas the masses' judgment could be shouted, the members of the *gerousia* deserved to be counted individually.

The Athenian *areopagus* is a second possible source for the origin of counting votes, although supporting evidence is scant.[16] Even the function of the *areopagus* prior to Solon – whether it served as a council or as a homicide court – remains unresolved.[17] A key source is the *Eumenides*, in which Athena establishes the

---

[15] But see Ogden (1997, 101).

[16] Staveley (1972) held that because the list of eponymous archons dates to 681 BCE, the establishment of a formal aristocratic Council that voted should be dated at Athens and Sparta to the latter half of the eighth century BCE. Larsen (1949) argues that either in electing magistrates or in functioning as a law court, formal votes must have been taken. Yet Larsen gives us little reason to think that formal votes were required, as opposed to acclamation, in the resolution of these sorts of matters in particular.

[17] The primary schism surrounds the question of whether Aristotle's *Constitution of Athens* is dispositive with respect to the powers of the pre-Solonian *areopagus* (Aristotle 1996, III.6, 212). Most scholars have held that the *areopagus* originally functioned as council to the king and then emerged as the major political body in its own right, but a few, most notably Wallace (1989), regard the account offered in the *Constitution of Athens* as spurious and argue that the *areopagus* was from inception a homicide court.

areopagus to decide the verdict between the Furies and Orestes; if the vote is equal, Athena declares that Orestes will win. Apollo reminds: "Shake out the lots and count them fairly, friends. Honor justice. An error in judgment now can mean disaster. The cast of a single lot restores a house to greatness," and the vote, once counted, is in fact equal (Allen 2000, 20). If the *areopagus* is indeed a key institution for the origins of counting votes, it is worth noting that either possible institutional role – homicide court or council – is a paradigmatic example of a body whose function is to exercise judgment. The composition of the body is suggestive on this score. At least in later days the members of the *areopagus* were ex-archons, chosen from the Eupatridai (the ancient nobility), but in general they are taken to always have been leading men. This is the sort of circumstance in which we would expect to encounter voting: members with a degree of dignity or standing and a view that they individually possessed a strong faculty of judgment. Their views ought not to be "clumped" together, either through acclamation or through the informal mechanism of "estimating votes" (which we shall encounter in a moment): these are the actors not only whose *independence* of judgment, but whose independent judgment of *an unusually high quality* ought to be counted rather than clumped. The origin of counting of votes with the Spartan *gerousia* and the Athenian *areopagus* highlights the fact that having one's vote count is a marker of distinction, one that was only expanded to the "mass" in democratic Athens.

Counting versus Estimating in Athens

In classical Athens, systems of counting and estimation largely displaced acclamatory decision procedures. There was still, as will be discussed shortly, a role for shouts and murmurs in the form of the *thorubos* (clamor, or tumult) of the crowds in the assembly (*ekklesia*) and the jury courts (*dikasteria*). But voting, rather than acclamation, constituted the decision mechanism in the classical Athenian jury and assembly.

Athenian democracy was predicated on the belief that citizenship conferred a certain epistemic dignity. In other words, to be a citizen meant that one was capable of exercising the faculty of judgment sufficiently well to serve in political life.[18] This is indeed closely reminiscent of Aristotle's account of a citizen as "one who is entitled to share in deliberative or judicial office" (Aristotle 1995, 1275b15–20, 87). But it is not fanciful to think that the Athenian conception of citizenship was akin to this view. Citizenship was a matter of desert, not simply of descent: as has frequently been noted, one's citizenship could be scrutinized and even revoked for failure to fulfill one's duties. Further, as Ober has suggested, the fifth century BCE witnessed the democratization of both *eugeneia* (high birth) and *kalokagathia* (imperfectly translated, beauty-and-goodness) (Ober 1989, 250–260). As such, there was no need to differentiate the population according to the criterion of judgment. For the Athenians, the concept of *ho boulomenos* – any ordinary person who wished could participate – was of central importance. Such an idea suggests a high level of confidence in the political judgment of the average person – that is, the sort of judgment that merited being counted individually.[19] While acknowledging the ongoing presence of an "elite," if we suppose that the citizen members of these various bodies were broadly, by mid-fifth century BCE, indistinguishable on epistemic grounds, how else might we explain the choice to count or to estimate in Athenian institutions?

The primary responsibility of the jurors in the people's courts (*dikasteria*) was to hear those private suits (*dikai*) that were not heard by an arbiter, and public prosecutions (*graphai*). The people's courts – typically held to be the quintessential democratic

---

[18] In his brilliant recent book, *Democracy and Knowledge*, Ober (2008, 162) elegantly describes the way in which Athenian democracy considered "[e]ach juryman and assemblyman as both an individual agent capable of learning and as a node in an extensive social network that was also a network of knowledge."

[19] As Bernard Manin (1997, 15–16) has argued, this concept helps explain the support for lotteries rather than election as the means by which most offices would be filled in Athens. Such an argument may also indicate – as Allen (2000, 44) implies – that there was a suspicion of *voting* as undemocratic. This, however, is hard to substantiate given the ubiquity of voting, if not of aggregation as such, in Athens.

institution – used ballots in the form of bronze disks, which were counted.[20] In contrast, most votes of the *ekklesia* (assembly) and the *boule* (council) were conducted by a hand count, *cheirotonia*, which was always estimated. The use of estimation extends both to the primary responsibilities of the assembly – the election of magistrates,[21] the establishment of treaties, and the ratification of legislation – and to the primary business of the Council of 500, notably setting the agenda for the Assembly, including the drafting of legislation. According to the *Constitution of the Athenians* (*Athenaion Politeia*), at least in the fourth century BCE, nine chairmen (*proedroi*) were to "judge" or "assess" or even "estimate" (*krinein*) the vote (Aristotle 1996, 44.3, 245). However, the assembly did not always vote via *cheirotonia*. In some cases in which an individual's status was at stake – considerations of ostracism, *adeia* (immunity), and the conferral of citizen rights – the *ekklesia kyria* (principal assembly) seems to have counted ballots. When conducting cases of *eisangelia* (public prosecution for political malfeasance), the *boule* voted first with ballots rather than hands (and secondarily with hands to decide on the penalty), and for internal votes of confidence, they first used a system of olive leaves (*ekphyllophoria*) and then ballots. Thus, when the assembly and council conducted their primary legislative and electoral functions, votes were estimated, and in most cases in which individuals were subject to judgment, votes were counted.

Let us consider possible alternative explanations for the origin of the counted vote. Was the critical question determining whether the vote would be counted or "clumped" whether an individual's fate was at stake? In cases such as the "vote on the magistrates," in which any magistrate could be subject to a vote of no confidence and removed from office, the *ekklesia kyria* used *cheirotonia*, suggesting that an individual's status as such

---

[20] I am indebted to Hansen (1991) for this discussion. Note that both Hansen and Staveley (1972) hold that because *psephismata* derives from "psephos" (pebble), it seems that the Assembly might at some point have voted in the same way as the courts.

[21] See Rhodes (1981, 129).

did not generate the choice to vote (Hansen 1991, 220–221). A second possible explanation might be that the estimation of the hand count was introduced for the sake of efficiency. Just as one might assume that the reason for the introduction of vote counting in councils, rather than assemblies, was owed to their relative size, one might also assume that the estimation of the hand count was introduced on practical grounds, a necessary move given the size of the body (attendance at the assembly numbered around 6,000). Along these lines, Staveley holds that the "multiplicity" of decisions rendered by the *ekklesia* encouraged the use of estimation rather than aggregation. However, the fact that in some cases the desire for an accurate count trumped efficiency demonstrates that the size of the body did not inhibit counting where deemed necessary. The number of jurors in the court could be more than 1,501, and the vote would still be counted. What of the hypothesis that counting might have been used instead of estimation in tight votes? The decision to count jury votes is independent of the margin of victory; later inscriptions from the Greek world provide the actual numbers of votes even when the decision is unanimous or very nearly so (Rhodes and Lewis 1997, 14).

Another possible explanation is offered by Mogens Hansen, who suggests that counting of votes was "doubtless" a mechanism to ensure a quorum was reached (Hansen 1991, 130). But given that the quorum requirement only pertains to a restrictive set of assembly decisions (those for which the *ekklesia kyria* used ballots), and does not make sense in the context of a jury for which a particular size is set, this cannot explain the choice to count votes as such. The question, "How many counted votes are necessary?" presupposes a positive answer to the question, "Should votes be counted?" In other words, the decision to count votes for certain matters is prior to the decision that a particular number of individuals ought to be present for such votes. Further, although there are different possible explanations for the choice of quorum rules – for instance, to ensure that a minority bloc of citizens could not enact their will because of low attendance (Vermeule 2007, ch. 4) – the explanation for the use of quorum rules, at least in this context, likely tracks the explanation for vote counting. If we believe that the Athenians counted votes to affirm the epistemic capacity of individual citizens, we might also think that the reason for specifying a quorum was to ensure that a sufficient number of such judgments had been brought to bear on a difficult matter. Aristotle's famous "Doctrine of the Wisdom of the Multitude" passage (as Jeremy Waldron [1995, 564] has termed it) hints at such an account:

> For when there are many, each has his share of goodness and practical wisdom; and, when all meet together, the people may thus become like a single person, who, as he has many feet, many hands, and may senses, may also have many qualities of character and intelligence. This is the reason why the many are also better judges of music and the writings of poets: some appreciate one part, some another, and all together appreciate all. (Aristotle 1995, 1281b4–7, 108–109)

A system of counting considers each voter's ballot discretely. Following a process of counting each vote separately, each individual could, in principle, identify the role she performed in a decision, whether as a member of a majority or a minority. This, it should be emphasized, does not mean that the citizen in a body even the size of the smallest ancient jury could expect to be decisive. But it does mean that he could know he had played *some* role – and an equal one, at that – in generating the outcome. There is, of course, a substantial literature in political science seeking to explain the supposed paradox of participating in a vote in which one cannot rationally expect to instrumentally affect the outcome. An important response to the paradox is that in a large body, the benefits to the voter are primarily expressive, because she cannot expect to be decisive.[22] One might believe, then, that participating in an acclamatory process would confer at least the same, if not greater, benefits as casting a ballot, given the excitement of shouting or hand-waving and the likelihood that one will be seen performing a socially beneficial act. But

---

[22] The *locus classicus* for both the discussion of the paradox and the expressive theory is Downs (1957, the latter at 48). See also: Hardin (1982); Brennan and Lomasky (1993); Schuessler (2000).

acclamation carries a risk that a fair system of voting does not: one's vote may be entirely neglected, simply because others were taller or louder.

In the jury system, as we have already seen, minority votes were recorded – for instance, Socrates in *Apology* expresses his surprise at the closeness of the vote, noting that a mere thirty votes would have tipped the balance (Plato 1975, 36a, 37). A convicted defendant could take some cold comfort in the fact that a minority believed his account. The clear, enumerated presence of such a minority, further, may have had little effect on the enforcement of the outcome. The decentralized nature of punishment in Athens – private citizens did most of the work of implementation alongside magistrates – meant that collective action was not even necessary to enforce penalties.[23] To estimate in a trial would have left both jurors and defendant to wonder about the accuracy of the outcome, leaving the fairness of the outcome subject to challenge on procedural grounds. In contrast, this very ambiguity about the proportion of the members in favor of a decision may be an affirmative benefit of a system of *cheirotonia*. Those in charge of assessing the vote can take the climate of the body as a whole without acknowledging the precise weight of the opposition. In an assembly setting, this action may be desirable, especially if the matter under consideration requires the coordination or compliance of thousands of citizens, as would adherence to a new law, or waging war. The presence of a formally counted minority could threaten the view that the outcome emerged from the community as a whole, and could lead to ongoing lobbying to reverse the decision.

Aggregation, by acknowledging the weight of each individual's vote on both sides of a decision, thus signals respect for the judgments of the distinct individuals who participated in the decision.[24] Estimation seeks instead to assess the dominant view

---

[23] See Allen (2000, 201–202, and passim)

[24] In this respect, aggregation is compatible with Thomas Christiano's argument that the principle of "public equality," which constitutes the moral basis of democratic decision making, requires that "institutions … be structured so that all can see that they are being treated as equals" (Christiano 2008, 2).

of the crowd *qua* totality, thus affirming the communal nature of the endeavor. The risk associated with estimation is that particular individuals – especially those in the minority – may not believe that their specific vote was counted; further, they may feel that the full weight of the opposition was not sufficiently acknowledged.[25] Even the winners of an estimated vote may wish to know that their *individual* votes constituted part of the margin of victory, rather than having been swept into a pile of faceless supporters. Estimation can give voters no such guarantees, and may, like acclamation, fail to signal the respect for individual judgment conveyed by aggregation.

Secrecy and the Vote

Another important objection to the explanation offered here may be raised at this point: the ostensible distinction between estimation and aggregation, it may be argued, depends on the publicity inherent in *cheirotonia* and the secrecy of the ballot. However, at least in the early part of the fifth century BCE, the voter would place the ballot in one of two urns, each representing guilt or innocence, and so the voter's decision was obvious to all.[26] This suggests that the decision to count votes in the classical world was at least initially independent of the desire for secrecy.[27] Further, in the case of *cheirotonia*, a practical reason for estimation might have been the difficulty of counting hands in a body comprised of people of different physical heights and levels of enthusiasm. Yet this does not fully explain the choice

[25] This may indeed leave room for the judges to distort the outcome, as Aeschines lamented. Yet there is little reason to believe, as we today know all too well, that vote counting is immune from manipulation. Aeschines, *Against Ctesiphon* [3.3] (cited in Hansen 1991, 210).

[26] See Boegehold (1963, 367).

[27] Boegehold (1963, 370) suggests that "early in the fifth century in the minds of some men who were living in Athens, viz. the painters, there could exist simultaneously and interdependently the notions of *psephoi*, a judicial decision, and a lack of secrecy." By the time Aeschylus wrote the *Eumenides*, the vote was secret; as ascribed to the *areopagus* by Aeschylus, secret ballots received the imprimatur of both ancient origins and of being a mechanism of the wise (Aeschylus 1977, 725–68, 263–265).

to estimate. Despite the logistical difficulties, in principle, hands *could* have been counted, particularly if, as is sometimes supposed, the citizens were organized into some set of groupings (perhaps tribal). In addition, because ballots, even once secret, were sorted into different urns, in many cases the outcome could have been estimated, although the ballots were always counted.

The presence of spectators (*hoi periesteikotes*, in Latin the *corona*) to the jury – a mix of elite members (there in part to hone rhetorical skills), citizens younger than thirty years of age, prospective jurors, other citizens in the agora, and sometimes foreigners – sheds light on this issue. At least some of the bystanders likely knew a litigant or had some other reason for caring about the outcome; litigants tried to fill the corona with their family and friends (Lanni 1997, 187). However, a concern about the pressure of bystanders may also have generated the norm preventing spectators to the assembly from observing votes concerning citizenship. Lanni calls attention to a passage sometimes attributed to Demosthenes on this point: "The law orders the *prytaneis* to set out the voting urns and to give ballots to the citizens, who enter before foreigners come in, and the barriers are taken away to insure that each citizen may be free to make an independent judgment concerning the man on whom he is about to confer citizenship."[28]

Given the potential influence of bystanders, and perhaps because of *thorubos* even among jurors, the Athenians may have thought that public voting on judicial verdicts could serve a sinister purpose. (Although if *thorubos* constituted a public activity among jurors, one might reasonably ask whether the Athenians did prize secrecy in judgment.) The risk was that jurors or spectators with a stake in the outcome would seek to distort others' judgments through the use of bribes or threats during the moment of the vote. Whereas in matters concerning all members of a society, such as warfare or legislation, every individual had to live with the consequences of a bad decision, a vote on a particular

---

[28] Demosthenes, *Against Neaera* (1949, 59.90), as cited and translated by Lanni (1997, 186).

individual's status in the community affected members of the society unequally, leaving some with an interest in influencing the verdict, regardless of the truth or fairness of the charge.[29] Note again that the fact that the jury had to judge an individual would not necessarily have dictated the choice of a mechanism, because elections and some prosecutions of magistracies were conducted by *cheirotonia*. Instead, the salient consideration may have been the grave consequences for the defendant's liberty and even life. Although the selection of an incompetent magistrate would have affected all citizens, a smaller proportion of the jury would have a specific interest in the verdict of a given case, and the *unequal stake* in the verdict would increase the chance of coercion among them.[30] The complicated procedure by which jurors were randomly assigned to courtrooms also suggests concern about the risk of bribery (Lanni 2006, 38).

Further, the jurors could be presumed to have equal information: they each heard the same presentations, and no juror, at least in principle was more likely than another to reach a superior conclusion. The absence of deliberation before voting in Athenian jury trials affirms this account: there is no need to share information or persuade others when each has equal capability to render a verdict independently. Thus, secret ballot may have emerged in Athens to preserve independent judgments

---

[29] From a perspective distinctly unflattering to jurors, Aristotle (1995) emphasized this in distinguishing between speeches in the assembly and in the jury-court in the *Rhetoric*:

In a political debate the man who is forming a judgment is making a decision about his own vital interests. There is no need, therefore, to prove anything except that the facts are what the supporter of a measure maintain they are. In forensic oratory this is not enough; to conciliate the listener is what pays here. It is other people's affairs that are to be decided, so that the judges, intent on their own satisfaction and listening with partiality, surrender themselves to the disputants instead of judging between them. (Aristotle 1995, I.1, 1354b29–1355a1, p. 2153)

[30] It seems jurors in Athens could not be excluded on the grounds of partiality; a day's jury panel was selected without prior knowledge of which cases the jury would judge. According to Hansen (1991, 197–198), daily selection by lot was likely introduced as a mechanism of control following bribery scandals in the late fifth and early fourth centuries BCE.

under conditions of *equal information but unequal stake*. The use of private *ostraka* in assembly decisions of ostracism may rest on similar grounds. Each citizen had equal opportunity to evaluate a political leader and thus presumably equal capacity to judge, although certain citizens might well have had private interests in retaining or excluding a given person.[31]

Secret ballot is so nearly ubiquitous today that the decision to retain the public form of *cheirotonia* may seem surprising. Public show of hands preserves the ability to alter votes in light of others' views – both through deliberation and even at the moment of voting – and may have been one of the attractive features of *cheirotonia* and of the system of estimation. This is because the public mechanism is not strictly simultaneous, enabling, as Elster has written, individuals to have some causal impact on each other. Although in principle, once the question is posed, those in support or opposed would raise their hands at the same time, the pause to allow the assessors to estimate the outcome would have permitted some to hesitate and then to raise their hands to accord with others' votes.[32] Each member could gain a sense of where he stood relative to others on a given matter: he could recognize when he was in the vast minority and alter his vote on the spot, or turn for guidance to those whom he considered knowledgeable. Whereas one might expect that jurors would have equal information, members of the assembly or council would not necessarily have had equal capacity to judge the best course of action, although in principle each would have had an equal stake in the outcome. [Aristotle held that the sort of political oratory necessary in the assembly was far more difficult than oratory in the courts because of the need in the former to address contingent future events, whereas the latter pertains to "what is or is not *now* true" (Aristotle 1995, III.17, 1418a1–5 and 1418a21–25, 2265).] Thus, the vote may have been public in cases of *unequal information but equal stake*.

---

[31] See Ober (2008, 180–181) for an ingenious discussion of ostracism as a means of aggregating social information about the probability that someone would constitute a threat to the city, akin in some respects to a prediction market.

[32] See Elster (2007).

The members' susceptibility to public pressure thus had epistemic advantages, insofar as one could defer to local experts at the moment of the vote, and perhaps also moral benefits. As Geoffrey Brennan and Philip Pettit have argued, the desire for social acceptance might have generated "discursive pressure" on individuals to vote in a way that could be defensible to others in terms of the common good. There are, of course, costs associated with open voting, notably the risks, as Brennan and Pettit discuss, of bribery, blackmail, or intimidation (Brennan and Pettit 1990, 329). Yet given the roughly equal stake each citizen has in the outcome, the incentive to coerce others will be mitigated. Although it is surely true that the bite of a given piece of legislation or the obligation to go to war may fall disproportionately on some members, the general nature of these norms suggests that the consequences will more equally distributed than they would be in the verdict of a jury trial, for instance. The more serious problem of open voting – that of threats – is more likely to arise in cases when a particular citizen or group has a special or personal stake in a matter, as in a trial, an ostracism, or a citizenship hearing. The incentive to bribe is greater in deciding an individual case than the creation of a general norm or widespread obligation to which all will be bound. Further, the public nature of the *cheirotonia* may ward against intimidation, as those seeking to coerce may easily be exposed for their behavior. When there was disagreement about the matter at hand, it is reasonable to expect that a coercer faced social opprobrium.

Finally, the physicality of *cheirotonia*, especially combined with the vocal expressions of *thorubos* in the assembly, must have contributed to a level of excitement (if not necessarily passion),[33] perhaps driving the sense of a communal outcome. Thucydides describes the way in which the acclamatory mechanisms of the Spartans in their assembly (which endured into the classical period) was manipulated for these purposes: the ephor Stheneliadas pretended that he could not tell which side – for

---

[33] See Elster (2000, 118–129) for a discussion of institutional checks on popular passion in Athens.

or against war – was louder, "because he wanted to make them show their opinions openly and so make them all the more enthusiastic for war," and then had them physically separate, so that the breadth of support could be demonstrated (Thucydides 1972, I.87, 86–87). Even once the capacity for good judgment was considered to be a faculty possessed by all native freeborn men, democratic Athens did not exclusively turn to aggregative mechanisms. Instead, it relied on acclamatory mechanisms when demonstrating unity would have been of paramount importance.

Acclamatory devices constituted the key means by which Athens as a political community spoke, as it were, univocally. Identifying the number of votes in the minority left no fiction of consensus in the community: the verdict was simply the judgment of the majority of the competent citizens comprising the jury. Though *cheirotonia* was a mechanism by which individuals waved their hands, and the *proedroi* estimated a majority, the absence of an identifiable and recordable minority and majority position helped convey the collective nature of the decision. Whereas assessing acclamatory shouts or estimating hand waves captured only the imprecise metric of preponderance, a threshold emphasized that a specific number of individual votes was necessary for passage.

From Athens to Rome: Acclamation to the Written Ballot?

Does evidence of the emergence and operation of counted votes in Rome support the theoretical account derived from the origins of counting votes in Greece? This is a particularly thorny question, because the records are very sparse; scholars have drawn strong inferences on the basis of little material. The dominant model is Staveley's: the first stage, acclamation, was replaced by the individual oral vote by the early fifth century BCE (stage 2), and then was replaced by a written ballot (stage 3) in the latter part of the second century BCE. The move from the oral vote to the written ballot is well established; we have a series of ballot laws supporting the shift: the *lex Gabinia* for elections in 139

BCE, the *lex Cassia* of 137 BCE for non-capital judicial decisions, the *lex Papiria* of 130 BCE for legislative decisions, and the *lex Coelia* of 106 BCE for capital trials (Lintott 1999, 46). Yet it is difficult to determine conclusively if decisions were ever taken by acclamation, and, even if we assume that they were, the circumstances under which individual voting came to replace it, and the original form that the individual vote took, remain opaque. Let us briefly assess the evidence for the emergence and significance of the individual vote in Rome.

The evidence for acclamation is slim, although scholars have taken for granted that it must have been the first stage. The direct textual support for acclamation during kingship is very limited.[34] According to Livy, efforts on the part of the senators to seize power during the interrex following Romulus's death generated popular resistance. To stave off revolt, the senate granted the people the power to elect a king (subject to senatorial ratification). The selection of Numa Pompilius was met with no opposition, "with the result that there was a unanimous decision to offer Numa the crown."[35] In Cicero, we do not see the language of a unanimous election until the selection of Lucius Tarquinius.[36] But it is difficult to discern from the language of Livy and Cicero whether this was *necessarily* an acclamatory procedure at inception. Given the weakness of the textual support, the primary piece of evidence adduced is from the etymology of *suffragium*; on this account, *suffragium* derives from the same root as *fragere*,

---

[34] Staveley argues that the *curiae* "no doubt greeted the appointment [of the king] with shouts of approval," but declines to support this claim (Staveley 1972, 157). Similarly, he argues without providing support that the early centuriate army used acclamation to accept their commanders, and that the plebeian masses used the same method to "voice their approval of particular courses of action which their leaders suggested." In Staveley's view, acclamation was replaced in the early fifth century BCE once the plebeians excluded patricians – arguing, without further explanation, that they could not have done so without a shift away from acclamation – and created an ordered plebeian assembly.

[35] Livy (1960, I.18.5 [*ad unum omnes Numae Pompilio regnum deferendum decernunt*]); see also Cicero (1928, De Republica 2.25).

[36] Cicero (1928, De Republica, 2. 35 [*cunctis populi suffragiis rex est creatus L. Tarquinius*]).

"to break," and fragor, "a crash of noise."[37] Even if we take that common root as plausible evidence, it is difficult to determine both the circumstances under which it was used and the circumstances under which it came to be replaced.

If we accept the etymology of *suffragium* as support for an acclamatory procedure, how might we trace its replacement by an individualized vote (stage 2)? Vaahtera holds that the effort to date or trace this mechanism is virtually impossible, but also suggests that the "reason for this innovation, however, must have been the desire for greater accuracy in judging the outcome of the votes," particularly in judicial decisions by popular assemblies (Vaahtera 1990, 164). But this argument is, again, purely speculative – the desire for precision in some contexts did not generate formal counts in Athenian acclamatory institutions. Further, the hypothesized move from acclamation to oral balloting has also come under recent criticism, because there is no direct evidence for the widespread view that in the early Republic the voter told his vote to a *rogator*, which was marked off on a tablet (*tabula*) with a point (*punctum*). Vaahtera has instead turned to Dionysius of Halicarnassus to propose the view that acclamation was replaced by *calculii* in the early Republic – the Latin version of the Greek *psephoi*, identified as a voting procedure by Dionysius.

We can, however, draw some inferences from the operation of institutions in the later republic, about which our evidence is considerably stronger. Roman assemblies, famously, voted by units: the *comitia curiae* voted originally by the 30 ancient *curia* (although in the later Republic these *curiae* came to be represented by lictors); the *comitia centuriata* voted by the 193 centuries; and the *comitia tributa* and *concilium plebis* voted by the 35 tribes. Yet the units' votes were determined by the majority vote of the individuals comprising each unit, and in light of this information we can try to tease out the significance of the individualized vote. Did the written ballot affirm the value and dignity of individual judgments? This is a difficult claim to support.

---

[37] See Staveley (1972, 157); Taylor (1966, 2); Vaahtera (1990, 173).

In fact, it is widely rejected because of the common view that voting by units in general emerged as a way to enable elites to efficiently manipulate the masses. Such an explanation may be functionalist, however; there is considerable variation among the assemblies as to the origin of the units and the voting structure. In the *comitia centuriata*, the argument that the system of voting by unit actually emerged to enable elite control is compelling. The *comitia centuriata* was ordered according to property classes (though originally derived from military organization), and the hierarchically superior classes voted first. Because the majority decision of the *comitia centuriata* could be determined prior to the voting of the latter classes, it is difficult to argue that this institution secured the equal participation, let alone the epistemic dignity, of all of its members.[38]

Whereas, on Staveley's view, the *curiae*[39] and centuriate organizations were explicable "in terms of the nature of early Roman society and the origins of voting itself," tribal voting originated when "in 471 BC the plebeians decided to conduct their business in a more orderly fashion than they had done hitherto" (Staveley 1972, 135). The critical move seems to have been the shift of the election of plebeian officers from the *curiae* to the tribes (Taylor 1966, 2), though the tribal organization was not without hierarchical features. In sum, there is scholarly disagreement about the effect voting by units had on policy outcomes, in part because of uncertainty about wealth distribution over time. To the extent that geography came to be severed from tribal membership, wealth may have been more evenly distributed among the tribes, and if attendance at the assemblies came

[38] Staveley suggests that this organization "almost certainly post-dated the institution of voting," but such a claim is not supported (Staveley 1972, 134). He argues that the original division of the army into century units was actually intended to provide, in an acclamatory system, a "very much more orderly sounding of opinion than would have otherwise been possible" (135).

[39] In contrast, the *comitia curiata* was thought to have emerged essentially unaltered from the original ancient *curiae*. We might ask, however, why the Romans chose to preserve such a structure, especially given that, according to Taylor, by the fifth century BCE many people did not know to which *curia* they belonged and thus celebrated traditional rites en masse (Taylor 1966, 4).

to be dominated by nonpropertied urban voters, policy decisions might have tended to benefit the less well off. Regardless, to the extent that group voting was designed to reduce the role of individual voters – and, perhaps, increase representation among rural voters who could not otherwise attend – it is difficult to reduce the vote by unit to a mere aggregation of the individual members of the society.

Evidence from the Senate is less ambiguous and, at first blush, seems to contradict the findings from Greece. In the Republic, vote in the Senate was by "division," an acclamatory/estimation system. Those in favor of a proposal, and all those thinking otherwise (*alia omnia*), would "divide" (*discessio*), each retreating to different sides of the chamber.[40] There is some uncertainty as to whether an individual could call for a precise count if he wished to challenge the determination of the presiding magistrate, because the cry of *numera* could be used to ascertain the presence of a quorum and perhaps for a headcount.

To the extent that we regard the Senate as an aristocratic body, it should seem surprising that the Senate would have used acclamation. The logic becomes clearer, however, when one considers the primary function of the Senate during the Republic and even during the kingship: *consilium*, which means giving advice, rather than concluding any matter. Strikingly, this advice was provided individually. The presiding magistrate would call upon each member sequentially by rank to speak, beginning with consuls, continuing to ex-praetors, praetors, and then other senators in descending orders. Each senator had to be given the opportunity to advise (*quid censes?*) – and was obliged to answer (even if simply noting agreement with a previous speaker) – before nightfall and the vote.[41] Thus the Senate constituted the most

---

[40] *Qui hoc censetis, illuc transite; qui alia omnia, in hanc partem.*

[41] Junior senators would often defer to those they viewed as possessing expertise on a particular matter (or, perhaps, to their patrons); rather than expressing a distinct opinion of their own, such a senator would move to stand behind a leading speaker, and, when called upon, would affirm the senior's view as his own. This may reflect a mode of decision making comparable to *cheirotonia*: the publicity of the deliberative process enabled a person to defer to those with greater expertise even at the advising stage.

robustly deliberative institutional body of the Roman republic. If, we believe, the true work of *consilium* is done here by the activity of calling upon individual speakers for their opinions, rather than through the estimation system of voting on a *senatus consultum*, it is possible that the Senate actually affirms rather than contradicts the findings from Greece.

In this case, although individual dignity (literally, the aristocratic virtue of *dignitas*) was secured through membership in the Senate and the ability to persuade other senators, the aim of the Senate was to provide authoritative (again, literally, *auctoritas*) counsel. In Cicero's words:

> For if it works out that if the senate is in charge of public deliberation (*publici consilii*), and if the remaining orders are willing to have the commonwealth guided by the deliberation of the leading order, then it is possible through the blending of rights, since the people have power and the senate has authority (*cum potestas in populo, auctoritas in senatu sit*), that that moderate and harmonious order of the state be maintained [....] (*Laws*, III.28)

Thus, consensus, rather than aggregation, may well have been the aim of the Senate; its authoritativeness may have been decreased in the presence of an enumerated minority. As in the Athenian assembly, the primarily deliberative function of the Senate may have given rise to the mechanism of decision. Their dignity affirmed through presence and speech in the Senate, the senators could vote publicly. At the same time, the outcome could be identified as that of the uncounted whole rather than a mere proportion of individual judgments.

The Origin of Supermajority Rules

Let us finally turn to the origins of supermajority rules, the earliest documented use of which is in the Gracchan *lex repetundarum* statute, approximately 123 or 122 BCE.[42] The law prescribed the means by which magistrates, senators, or senators' sons could be charged by foreigners for expropriating their wealth; it replaced

---

[42] For text and translation, as well as analysis, see Lintott (1992).

jurors from the senatorial class, who had failed to convict their colleagues, with jurors from the equestrian class. The "democratic" features of this law have been long attested, as the law checked the power of the senatorial class, and in general gave powers of scrutiny over judicial procedures to the *populus*.

For our purposes, the most important mechanisms are those by which the jurors rendered their verdicts. The praetor, or judicial magistrate, would draw up an annual list of 450 jurors and read it aloud at an assembly of the People; it would be widely publicized. The law barred many classes of people from serving as jurors, both for practical reasons (those outside of Italy) and perhaps for political reasons (those actively involved in provincial business affairs might be sympathetic to defendants); it also barred those younger than thirty and older than sixty. The law also specified that the praetor should select those "he believes will be the best and most capable judices," highlighting the importance of the faculty of judgment. For each trial, the plaintiff would select 100 jurors (barring those close to him and those ineligible on other grounds), among whom the defendant chose 50. Each juror took an oath to listen carefully to the witnesses and to not "act in such a way as to impair his judging of the matter" (line 37); when the trial was concluded, the jurors did not deliberate collectively, and each swore not to discover another juror's verdict.

The supermajority rule arose broadly in the context of the *ampliatio*, a mechanism by which jurors could request a further hearing if they were unable to render a verdict. Prior laws placed no limit on the number of rehearings, and constituted a means by which the defendant could prevail, in essence, by attrition; indeed, A. N. Sherwin-White (1982) termed it a form of filibuster. In this law, a rehearing was permitted only if more than one-third of the jurors – a submajority rather than a supermajority – held that the case had not been proven ("non liquet," that they were unable to decide), and then only two rehearings were permitted.[43] Jurors who still refused to render a verdict on more

---

[43] See Lintott (1992, 23).

than two occasions were to be fined the large sum of 10,000 ses-
terces. Once two-thirds of the jurors reported that the case had
been proven, however, those jurors who refused to give a verdict
were removed.

The remaining jurors each received a piece of boxwood with
A for *absolvo* on one side and C for *condemno* on the other,
and each deleted the letter he did not want. The juror then cast
his ballot in the voting jar in view of the public, concealing the
remaining letter with his fingers, with a bare arm to demonstrate
that there was no additional ballot up his sleeve (Lintott 1999,
47). Although a supermajority was necessary to demonstrate the
sufficiency of the case – the presence of adequate information to
form a judgment – a majority sufficed to convict.

The *lex repetundarum* provides for supermajority rule in a
quintessentially epistemic context, one of assessing the capacity
to render a judgment, given a body of evidence. The law more
broadly affirms not only the impartiality of judgment but its
independent and individual nature. It also captures, in a sense,
the view that most members needed to agree that they had
enough information to decide before the majority could vote,
suggesting that the absence of this shared capacity to judge indicated something amiss in the trial. Although later justifications
for supermajority rule in the context of juries affirm the importance of biasing judgment against conviction, it is nonetheless
remarkable that the earliest extant example of a supermajority
rule emerges in the context of judgment-formation.[44]

---

[44] An additional context in which Rome featured supermajority rules was in
the creation of new patrons – notably in the lex Colonia Genetivae Juliae
(the "Charter of Urso," 44 BCE) and also in the lex Municipalis Malacitana
(82–83 CE). The latter requires a two-thirds vote of decurions to create a
patron, whereas the former requires a three-quarters vote, explicitly by means
of voting tablets, to make a senator or his son a patron (thought to have
been a mechanism for checking senatorial power). In addition, the lex Colonia
Genevitae Julia prescribes a two-thirds quorum for decurions for decisions
pertaining to the fixing of days for festivals and sacrifices, and to decree lands
for aqueducts of sacrifices; only twenty or thirty of the fifty decurions constituted a quorum for routine business, and for an emergency measure a majority
of any number present was necessary.

Conclusion

Aggregation has a primary position in democratic theory as the ultimate decision-making mechanism for collective bodies, although both its potential for irrationality (because of the ostensible risk of cycling, for which supermajority rule ostensibly provides a solution) and its unreasonableness (because the vote does not need to be publicly justifiable) have been criticized in recent decades. Further, it seems that there is nothing intrinsically democratic about vote counting: any plural body, however hierarchical or elitist, may implement it, and, indeed, the evidence strongly suggests that it originated in aristocratic bodies such as the *gerousia* and *areopagus*. But the distinctiveness and appeal of counting comes to the fore once contrasted with acclamation: aggregation presupposes a positive view of the capacity for individual judgment among members, and in that sense confers dignity upon them. This move, we shall see in a moment, is echoed by the move away from a commitment to acclamation and *unanimitas*, toward a counted supermajority vote of cardinals, in the context of papal elections.

This very independence – collective decisions were merely the summation of particular individual judgments – was a liability in contexts when the Athenians wanted to convey that a decision was *theirs*. The variety of acclamatory mechanisms described here – the shouts and murmurs of Homeric assemblies, the *viva voce* mechanisms of Sparta, the estimations of hands in Athens, the *discessio* of the Roman Senate – are all means by which a collective body, *qua* mass, expresses its approval or disapproval as one. This expression could and did take an antidemocratic form, but the durability of the mechanism in Greece in particular underscores the fact that waving and shouting have their place in democratic decision making. Similarly, as we shall see in a moment, the acknowledgment that the oneness of spirit among cardinals had to be replaced by mechanisms that could accommodate disagreement was a cause for regret rather than celebration.

In recent years, scholars of the ancient world, among them Josiah Ober, have sought to affirm an epistemic account of the origins of democratic institutions.[45] Although aggregation may constitute a means of accumulating and sorting the dispersed knowledge of a *polis*, the decision to count votes has not typically been held to be an epistemic innovation. Yet respect for the epistemic quality of individual judgments is both presupposed and affirmed by the decision to count votes. Nonetheless the choice between aggregation and acclamation is not purely epistemic: it also must depend on the extent to which we want to imagine our democracy to be conceptualized strictly as a means of coordinating and assessing the judgments of individual citizens. Acclamation enables us to decide and to act *qua* community rather than via appeal to the majority of the citizens who comprise it. Such a capacity may be attractive. As we shall see in the next chapter, however, it cannot operate in a context in which disagreement persists and a minority refuses to capitulate. In such a context, there must be recourse to a counted vote.

In Rome, as we have seen, the initial use of supermajority rules reflected the importance of the distinctive judgments of individuals, while simultaneously capturing the value of agreement among jurors. As we shall now see, supermajority rules in the medieval era constituted an attempt to preserve the communal features of acclamation, and then the distinctive quality of individuals' judgments, in the face of important challenges.

---

[45] For instance, Kleisthenes' creation of the Council of 500, on Ober's (2005, 38) account, served to pool the knowledge of the various demes.

3

Unanimitas to a Two-Thirds Vote:
Medieval Origins of Supermajority Rule

Although supermajority rules originated in Rome, their true golden age began in the twelfth century. In many ways, the emergence of supermajority rule mirrored the development of the counted vote in the Greek world. In the preceding chapter, we saw that the counted vote replaced acclamatory devices in classical Athens where individual judgment was deemed paramount. Acclamation in the form of hand-waving was used when the presence of a minority was considered risky, and when a consensual outcome would have been highly desirable.

If there were one collective decision in which universal acclamation or unanimity might be expected to prevail regardless of the selection procedure or threshold governing it, it would seem to be the choice of a pope. The famous example of St. Ambrose evokes this vision of decision: prompted by the cry of an infant, a popular assembly is inspired by the Holy Spirit to choose him (Kantorowicz 1946, 118–120; Benson 1968, 36). Elections in the eleventh and twelfth centuries were religious occasions, events in which the electors would assemble so that the will of God might be expressed through them (Robinson 1990, 57). *Unanimitas* – oneness of spirit – was the hallmark of such bodies, by which power could be conferred upon a pope or bishop (or secular leader, for that matter). In other words, the means by which God could divinely ordain a pope or a bishop was through the "flock" to be governed (Burns 1988, 449).

Yet the hope of unanimous elections faded, resulting in schisms, and a set of institutional solutions emerged to avoid the costs associated with dissension. The decision mechanism that stuck, as we will see, was a supermajority rule: a two-thirds majority of the college of cardinals. But the change in threshold from unanimity to supermajority came indirectly, in large part because unanimity was not understood in strictly aggregative terms. *Unanimitas* was a marker of consensus rather than of perfect concord among individual judgments. The two-thirds majority rule adopted at the Third Lateran Council in 1179 was preceded by the *sanior et maior pars* doctrine, by which the choice of the "sounder and greater" share of the electorate would prevail.[1] But disagreement about whose judgment was "sounder," and the relative weight of "sounder" as opposed to "greater" (a quantitative metric), made this doctrine useless to resolve conflict. Further, as this chapter suggests, innovations associated with reformist movements enabled a strictly aggregative mechanism to take hold: merit-based distinctions among cardinals broke down. Once the cardinals were deemed equal in status, a shift to a strictly aggregative decision rule was both possible and, as a means of avoiding disagreement about relative merits, even necessary. A two-thirds majority rule democratized the concept of *sanioritas* – soundness of judgment – through investing an aggregative decision procedure with epistemic weight. The religious context in which the supermajority rule emerged, however, suggests that a moral aim was yoked to the epistemic purpose of discerning the true pope: preventing a few fallible cardinals in the minority from derailing an otherwise unanimous verdict. The supermajority rule would discourage would-be opponents from "sowing tares" and from the moral consequences that might attach to the majority in

---

[1] This doctrine will be familiar to political theorists in the form *"valentior pars"* in Marsilius of Padua's *The Defender of the Peace*; its meaning there is controversial, but the claim is essentially that the people, or its "weightier"/ "prevailing" part," possess the authority to legislate. See Marsilius of Padua (2005, 1.12.3–5); Nederman (2009, 108–109); Quillet (1988, 558–561).

seeking to suppress them. It would also reduce the likelihood of discord and its baleful effects on the community.

As in the religious context, the most noteworthy use of supermajority rule in the political context of the medieval city-states was to determine candidates' competence. Candidates for the magistracy were "scrutinized," and support of two-thirds of the "scrutineers" was required, prior to selection by lot. The political use of supermajority rule did have an epistemic function, insofar as it ostensibly served as a means of ensuring that candidates for the magistracies were sufficiently competent. However, the political deployment of supermajority rule in the medieval communes was neither purely epistemic nor strictly about moral agency. Instead, the political aims of supermajority rule in the medieval era tended to prefigure one primary modern use of qualified majority rule: they ensured that candidates had the wide support of the elites authorized to choose them, and in this way maintained a degree of political stability. This stability was reaffirmed insofar as the threshold itself enabled the elites to maintain control over the selection of candidates; at moments in the history of the republic in which popular movements were ascendant, the threshold typically fell.

It is unsurprising that the political institutions of Italian city-republics would mirror religious ones in important respects; the communes replaced episcopal rule. However, the inception of supermajority rule in the period is not clear: for instance, Alexander III, who introduced the use of supermajority rule for papal elections at the Third Lateran Council, is sometimes thought to have done so after observing them in Venice (although, as we shall discuss, this may be apocryphal). Sidestepping causation, the reasons for introducing supermajority rule and the development of such rules often ran parallel in the religious and the political contexts of the twelfth through fourteenth century. In this chapter, I trace the emergence of supermajority rule first in the context of ecclesiastical elections and then in the context of political institutions to highlight the epistemic and moral purposes it came to serve. I note in conclusion that supermajority rules in the medieval era also promoted recognizably modern ends.

Unanimity, Moral Fallibility, and the Sanior et Maior Pars

Although papal elections were in principle divinely inspired, culminating in *unanimitas* in a transcendent rather than aggregative sense, the capacity to reach such agreement began to deteriorate in the eleventh century. In brief, conflict grew partly because of Roman power struggles between aristocratic families, and partly because of the reformist movement (or movements). The reformists had multiple targets, but they focused on criticizing simony (payment for spiritual favors) and clerical marriage, and defending the separation of the clergy from laypersons, particularly with respect to the intrusion of laypersons into ecclesiastical matters such as papal and episcopal elections (the question of investiture) (Morris 1991).

In the wake of the disputed election of reformist Pope Nicholas II, the Papal Election Decree was promulgated at the 1059 Roman synod (an ecclesiastical gathering). The Papal Election Decree seems to have been designed to support the reformist agenda (Morris 1991): it located the right to elect a pope with the strongly reformist cardinal bishops, with assent from the other cardinals, and then from the clergy and the people as a whole. It also specified that when an election could not take place in Rome, it could be held elsewhere. However, the important collection of canon law, Gratian's *Decretum*, included a forged "imperial" version, situating power with the cardinals as a whole and granting the cardinals an equal role in the election of the pope, failing to provide a distinctive role for the cardinal bishops against the lesser-ranking cardinal priests and cardinal deacons. As we shall see, the *Decretum's* emphasis on the equality of cardinals may have influenced the emergence of a decision rule resting on a numerical majority.

The Papal Election Decree governed relatively few elections – perhaps only those in 1088 and 1099 – in part because it provided no guidance for disputed elections. In the wake of the Concordat of Worms, a papal election in 1130 led to an eight-year schism. In brief, two Roman aristocratic clams, Pierleoni and Frangipani, were engaged in a power struggle, and the Frangipani supported the election of Gregory of S. Angelo in Pescheria (Innocent II). As Honorius II lay on his deathbed, the cardinals established an electoral commission consisting of eight cardinals: two cardinal bishops, three cardinal priests, and three cardinal deacons. Each of the three orders in the college elected its own representatives, and five of the eight members – a majority – supported Gregory of S. Angelo: two cardinal bishops, one cardinal priest, and two cardinal deacons. Two of the three opponents withdrew immediately, likely in the hopes of derailing the commission. Against the protests of the remaining opponent, the majority elected Gregory of S. Angelo pope. Once the election became known in Rome, however, a majority of the cardinals proceeded to hold a new election, at which the cardinals chose Peter Pierleoni, one of the two who had withdrawn from the electoral commission, to become Anacletus II. The decree announcing this election states that Anacletus was "'elected by a majority of the college, by the lesser clergy of the Roman Church, and by the people of Rome'" (Robinson 1990, 75).

The most influential theorist of papal authority of the period, Bernard of Clairvaux, emphasized that the majority of the cardinal bishops, the sounder part, had supported Innocent's candidacy. The Anacletan party, however, held that the support of the cardinal priests and deacons was pivotal, claiming that they were both more numerous (greater) as well as sounder, and that the bishops should not play a decisive role. Given the uncertainty about which body formally possessed the authority to elect the pope, the debate shifted to the quality – the soundness – of those comprising the electors (Robinson 1990, 76).

This intermediate solution, by which both parties defended their respective claims to possess superior authority, was the doctrine of the *sanior et maior pars*, retrieved from the sixth-century monastic Rule of St. Benedict. Chapter 64 of the Rule of St. Benedict holds the following: "In choosing an abbot, the guiding principle should always be that the man placed in office be the one selected either by the whole community acting unanimously in the fear of God, or by some part of the community, no matter how small, which possesses sounder judgment."[2] We might note a few important dimensions of this rule for our analysis. First, the part is explicitly an alternative to unanimity, and at least not in this formulation an inferior one.[3] Second, the rule does not offer any guidance as to who possesses *sanioritas*; there are no criteria or categories to decide who among the community possesses this judgment in the context of papal elections. This has often been taken to be a deliberate act on the part of Benedict, either as a means of "leaving room for the will of God" rather than specifying the criteria in a juridical fashion,[4] or because of the standard and familiar nature of electoral procedures to Benedict's contemporaries.[5] Third, the rule as formulated here did not say anything about the role of a numerical majority except that a superior part "no matter how small" could be decisive, as the Innocentine party noted (Robinson 1990, 76). In the context of papal elections, the weaknesses of adopting the *sanior et maior pars* doctrine as decisive were evident from the start: the absence of agreement about the salient dimensions of seniority rendered it ineffective. The doctrine had an additional liability for episcopal elections, as the indecision it generated increased the risk of papal intervention in these elections (Peltzer 2008, 42).

The deficiencies of the Benedictine rule came to the fore in the 1130 election, because the absence of clear criteria left each party

---

[2] Fry 1981. RB 64.1. "In abbatis ordinatione illa semper consideratur ratio ut hic constituatur quem sive omnis concors congregatio secudum timorem Dei, sive etiam pars quamvis parva congregationis saniore consilio elegerit" (Fry 1981, 280–281).

[3] Note that this is at odds with the other cases from the medieval period, including the history of papal elections, in which unanimity was so desirable that "formulae are employed – in the decrees of councils, for example – to suggest a unanimity which was in fact not achieved" (see Lienhard 1975, 3).

[4] The status of *sanius consilium* as a juridical concept (a rendering of Justinian's *melior opinio*) (Lienhard 1975, 12).

[5] The most salient institutional account situates the *sanioritas* with the officeholders of the monastery (Hallinger 1965; Thier 2001), but as Lienhard suggests, Benedict specifically seeks to suppress the power of priors in chapter 65 of the Rule, rendering this account somewhat less plausible. Léo Moulin highlights earlier texts invoking a set of standard qualities – scholarship, age, good intentions (zelus), an exemplary life – but these were considered to be attributes of the moral quality of the electoral body as a whole, not a part of it (Moulin 1958, 500).

to construe it in its own favor. The Anacletan party, the first to invoke the *sanior pars* doctrine, argued that its seniority derived from the support of a majority of the priests and deacons, even though, as the Innocentine party noted, there was no *maior pars* doctrine in the Benedictine rule. Defending the Innocentine claim to seniority, Bernard of Clairvaux ultimately proved more persuasive: Innocent was worthier, as were his electors; he had been elected prior to Anacletus; and his papacy had been consecrated by the cardinal bishop of Ostia.

Twelfth-century canonists did develop a set of three criteria for episcopal elections: the number of voters, their "authority/dignity/merits," and their intentions (Peltzer 2008, 42). The canon lawyer Rufinus contrasted two sets of cases. The first cases yielded a numerical majority, but the two competing sides each possessed equal authority and each had been guided by good intentions. In this case, the numerical majority ought to prevail. If the minority possessed greater authority and was motivated by good intentions whereas the majority was motivated by ill, the minority ought to prevail. If the minority possessed greater authority and each side was motivated by good intentions, then the pope or archbishop should decide; in a case in which both candidates were equal, then he ought to choose a third party. In the second set of cases, the vote was split evenly or very nearly evenly. In those cases, the party possessing greater authority as well as good intentions ought to prevail. If both were equal in authority and had good intentions (or both had bad intentions), or if the side possessing greater authority was motivated by bad intentions, then the archbishop ought to decide (Peltzer 2008, 43). Stephen of Tournai, drawing on Rufinus, emphasized that authority was conveyed not only by the offices (*honores*) but by the merits, virtues, and knowledge (*scientia*) of the individual voters. Beyond that, he largely adapted Rufinus's determination of the cases in which the numerical majority ought to prevail. Ultimately, this led to the view that the party possessing two of the three criteria – dignity or authority, number, and good intentions – should win a split election (Peltzer 2008, 43).

The logic developed by the canonists for episcopal elections, though it could not be directly adopted for papal elections given the absence of a final authority, did end up helping solve the problem of indecisiveness. Although drawing on the general logic of the three criteria – dignity, number, and good intentions – and holding that if the number were evenly split the other two criteria could be used to decide the election, the *Summa Coloniensis*, a canonistic work of the French school dating to 1169, then introduced a final criterion: the size of the majority. If the numerical majority itself was two-thirds, it was decisive regardless of the other two criteria. According to Jorg Peltzer, it was this principle that was adapted for papal elections ten years later at the Third Lateran Council (Peltzer 2008, 44).

How supermajority rule came to govern papal elections awaits reconstruction. Before any purely aggregative rule could emerge for papal elections, however, each of the cardinals in the three orders in the college had to be capable of exercising this right as equals. The claim of the cardinal bishops to seniority had to be challenged before the formal voting equality of the two other orders could be assured.

How did equality in voting emerge? One hypothesis, deriving from the account of the link between voting and epistemic dignity examined in the previous chapter, is that the quality of judgment possessed by the cardinal-deacons and cardinal-priests became indistinguishable from that possessed by the cardinal-bishops. The cardinal-bishops remained superior hierarchically, and as such had invoked their status as the *sanior pars* when challenged. But the substantive basis for this superiority eroded in the twelfth century, in part because the recruitment of cardinals who were men of "letters," as well as of high moral standing, became important in the latter half of the twelfth century. Immediately prior to the Third Lateran Council, Alexander III had communicated with his legate in France, Peter, cardinal priest of S. Grisogono, regarding the pope's desire for names of French clerks of noteworthy "morality, knowledge or letters and religion" who would be attractive candidates for promotion to the college of cardinals (Robinson 1990, 46). Naturally, the pope would also have been concerned with their susceptibility to his influence – or their similar disposition – but the specific focus on education, a legacy of Gregorian reforms, is striking.

An alternative hypothesis relates to the reception of the *quod omnes tangit, ab omnibus tractari et approbari debet (q.o.t.)* ("what touches all should be considered and approved by all") rule in the twelfth century. This Roman principle is found in the Justinian Code of 531.[6] In brief, the code includes it as a maxim of private law operating in cases in which several persons had rights in common (e.g., for the use of water from a stream, as in Ulpian[7]). In such cases, each person had to consent – or at a minimum, the interests of each had to be taken into account – to changes affecting others' rights. *Q.o.t.* had become an object of interest for canonists as it pertained to the struggle for control over episcopal election.[8] Further, it was used frequently in ecclesiastical court procedures from the middle of the twelfth century (Monahan 1987, 103).

Although it was certainly an aggregative rule, for our purposes it is also relevant whether *q.o.t.* in the twelfth century exclusively constituted a unanimity rule, or whether it gave rise to the possibility of rule by a numerical majority even in the twelfth century. The evidence is highly suggestive: the *q.o.t.* appears in Gratian's *Decretum*, and at D. 50.17.160.1, from Ulpian, it is written: "Anything publicly done by the majority [*maior pars*] is ascribed to everyone" (Watson 1985, 480; Post 1964, 72). By the thirteenth century the provision was taken to permit a supermajority to act. In applying the provision to an Italian commune, Accursius drew on Ulpian to write that if the people are summoned by trumpet,

---

[6] As *ut quod omnes similiter tangit, ab omnibus comprobetur* (the formulation varies in both Roman Law and medieval canonist and civilian use). See Post (1964, 168–180); Monahan (1987, 100).

[7] D. 39, 3, 8; from Ulpian, *Edict*, book 53. In Watson's translation, "As a general rule, it is agreed that consideration must be given to the consent of anyone who has an interest in the land itself on which the water originates or in the rights pertaining to that land or in the water itself" (vol. 4, 300).

[8] D. 63 post c. 25; Monahan (1987, 99) (though with an ambiguous reference to Bernard of Clairvaux). St. Bernard had written in letter 260 to the clergy of Sens that the election of a pastor should be arranged as a "matter which concerns all with the help of all" (Bernard, *Letters*, 340–341).

bells, or crier, and "if all do not come, all seem to do what those who come do, provided that two-thirds respond to the summons, and the *maior pars* of these two-thirds consent" (Post 1950, 72).

While it is impossible to know for certain which of these factors generated the move to numerical majorities, and still less the shift to a supermajority as such, it seems clear that the ideas of equal participation by those affected – and equally *dignified* participation – emerged prior to the Third Lateran Council in 1179. The Council arose in response to the electoral schisms of the twelfth century, notably in the schism of 1159, which led to Alexander III's election. A minority of three cardinals refused to accept the candidate of the rest of the college of cardinals. As we shall now see, the Third Lateran Council "decided to use a strictly quantitative method and eliminate the qualitative method completely. ... All votes henceforth were of equal weight, regardless of the rank of the cardinals, that is, whether they were bishops, priests, or deacons" (Baldwin 1968, 188–189; see also Morris 1991, 211).

The formally equal dignity of the cardinals in the college, a necessary precondition for an aggregative rule to emerge, was insufficient to explain the emergence of a supermajority rule as such. Indeed, as we saw in Athens, such equality historically gave rise to majority rule. But the commitments both to unanimity and to the doctrine of the "sounder" meant that a simple majority rule would be unlikely to emerge as the substitute. The solution, then, was to place the threshold between unanimity and majority. The schism of 1159 showed that merely the obstinacy of a few cardinals could derail an election.[9] The aim, therefore, was to find a decision rule that would accommodate the fallibility or maliciousness of cardinals, and at the same time embody the sense of *unanimitas* necessary to legitimate the election's outcome.

---

[9] Fractious minorities had for centuries caused problems for episcopal elections, and efforts to solve the problem of moral fallibility had arisen. The Council of Nicea in 251 CE held that although the Metropolitan together had to elect a bishop, "if, however, two or three bishops shall from natural love of contradiction, oppose the common suffrage of the rest, it being reasonable and in accordance with the ecclesiastical law, then let the choice of the majority prevail." See also Gaudemet (1960, 152–153).

The Emergence of the Two-Thirds Rule

Canon 1, *Licet de evitanda*, of the Third Lateran Council in 1179 reads as follows:

Although clear enough decrees have been handed down by our predecessors to avoid dissension in the choice of a sovereign pontiff, nevertheless in spite of these, because through wicked and reckless ambition the church has often suffered serious division, we too, in order to avoid this evil, on the advice of our brethren and with the approval of the sacred council, have decided that some addition must be made. Therefore we decree that if by chance, through some enemy sowing tares, there cannot be full agreement among the cardinals on a successor to the papacy, and though two thirds are in agreement a third party is unwilling to agree with them or presumes to appoint someone else for itself, *that person shall be held as Roman pontiff who has been chosen and received by the two thirds.* But if anyone trusting to his nomination by the third party assumes the name of bishop, since he cannot take the reality, both he and those who receive him are to incur excommunication and be deprived of all sacred order, so that viaticum be denied them, except at the hour of death, and unless they repent, let them receive the lot of Dathan and Abiron, who were swallowed up alive by the earth. Further, if anyone is chosen to the apostolic office by less than two thirds, unless in the meantime he receives a larger support, let him in no way assume it, and let him be subject to the foresaid penalty if he is unwilling humbly to refrain. However, as a result of this decree, let no prejudice arise to the canons and other ecclesiastical constitutions according to which the decision of the greater and senior part should prevail, because any doubt that can arise in them can be settled by a higher authority; whereas in the Roman church there is a special constitution, since no recourse can be had to a superior.[10]

As the Cambridge Medieval History holds, *Licet de evitanda* constituted an effective means of resolving the disputes that had generated a dozen antipopes in 120 years; there were no such schisms in the two centuries that followed (although reaching a two-thirds majority was not always easy, as evinced by the contentious and protracted "Viterbo" election less than a century later) (Robinson 2004, 415).

---

[10] Translation from Tanner (1990, 211). Italics mine.

It is sometimes suggested that those voting in accordance with the qualified majority by definition constituted the *sanior pars*, or that the vote *revealed* who constituted a member of the *sanior pars* (Monahan 1987, 140). The rule did emerge, as we have seen, in response to the split elections of 1130 and 1159 and the claim of each side to be the *sanior pars* and therefore the decisive majority (Peltzer 2008, 22). But one ought to be careful here. The claim in *Licet de evitanda* pertaining to the *sanior et maior pars* doctrine is as follows: "However, as a result of this decree, let no prejudice arise to the canons and other ecclesiastical constitutions according to which the decision of the greater and senior part should prevail, because any doubt that can arise in them can be settled by a higher authority; whereas in the Roman church there is a special constitution, since no recourse can be had to a superior." This suggests a different interpretation: because the *sanior et maior pars* doctrine will be inconclusive in many cases, which can be resolved only by appeal to authority, it is not apt in the case of a papal election. A clear, decisive rule is required in this context, and thus a threshold provision is proposed as an alternative.

Even if the two-thirds rule was not originally intended to indicate the *sanior pars* as such (Moulin 1958, 388), we might think that its role was clearly to ensure the epistemic validity of the outcome. This is especially clear in light of Alexander III's commitment to enhancing the moral and intellectual merits of the college, and the preexisting *sanior et maior* doctrine for which it substituted. It aimed at identifying the true pope under conditions most likely to promote good judgment, given the desire to ensure a swift and decisive outcome.

Nonetheless, despite the remarkable salience of this norm, both historically and in terms of the effect on the history of the Church, the true source of the two-thirds threshold remains unclear. One possibility is, again, the two-thirds rule for episcopal elections in the Summa Coloniensis. The source of the threshold there is also uncertain, but the "two of three elements" logic of episcopal elections may explain it. An alternative possibility is that Alexander III learned of the threshold during a trip to Venice in 1177, although there is little evidence that Venice had such a threshold in any of its institutions prior to the thirteenth century (Colomer and McLean 1998, 9; Konopcyznski 1930; Baldwin 1968; Coggins and Perali 1998). Summa Coloniensis precedes this date, in any event. A further hypothesis, deriving the rule from the Roman *Lex Malacitana*, likewise has scant direct evidence in its support, as Léo Moulin argued (Ruffini Avondo 1925; Moulin 1958, 386). A final possibility is from the adage *tres faciunt collegium* ("three makes an association") (Foreville 1965, 144). We might note that if orders each possessed a single vote, the two-thirds rule would actually have constituted a simple majority rather than majority rule. Moulin seems to suggest as much when he highlights the potential role of a third as tiebreaker between two orders, and the physical power of two against one. Given the history of disagreement within orders and the absence of a corporate vote for each order, the intention must have been supermajoritarian rather than majoritarian. But the choice of a two-thirds rule among the various possible supermajoritarian thresholds (from 50 percent plus 2 to 100 percent minus 1) may well be ascribable to the *tres faciunt collegium* maxim.

So without access to the debates surrounding the adoption of the rule, what might we reasonably infer? First, the supermajority rule would have replaced unanimity. This was a necessity on pragmatic grounds, but note that it would have come at a cost: the acknowledgment that the divine spirit would not always suffuse the college and lead to a collective outcome. Thus a rule capturing the attractively communal nature of the unanimous decision while acknowledging human fallibility needed to be implemented. Once the orders were placed on equal footing, no particular order or any stable group of cardinals within the orders could necessarily be taken to be sounder in its judgment. The absence of a superior to determine the "sounder" side made the appeal to the *sanior et maior pars* doctrine impossible for the pope, as Canon 1 of the Third Lateran Council suggests; it was still authorized for other ecclesiastical appointments, as recourse to the judgment of a superior remained possible. Throughout much of the thirteenth century, the *sanior et maior pars* doctrine prevailed, and the side with seniority was not necessarily that possessing a numerical majority. However, at the council in

Lyons in 1274, it was decided that thenceforth the party obtaining two-thirds of the vote would be the *sanior pars*, finally marking the dominance of the "aggregative" model of episcopal as well as papal elections (Peltzer 2008, 48).

A supermajority rule would have ensured the elected pope the support of a wide consensus of cardinals (Colomer and McLean 1998, 9), signifying both that the decision was morally correct (in accordance with the divine will) and that it could command the allegiance of the vast majority of cardinals, reducing the likelihood of schism. For this reason, Canon 1 emphasizes that this rule is to be decisive. But the importance of the rule derived from the problem of moral fallibility among the cardinals. This is why the grave consequences associated with dissension were specified. Again, the canon holds that if the candidate supported by one-third should nonetheless assume the position of pontiff, he and his supporters will be subject to excommunication and, if they failed to repent, to damnation. Were someone elected by less than two-thirds but greater than a majority and assumed the papacy, he, too, would be subject to penalty. Nonetheless the aim was to achieve a degree of concord, if not true consensus, while acknowledging the likelihood of wrong judgment on the part of a few members. Doing so spared the members of the minority the full consequences of their dissenting judgments, while also ensuring that those in the majority were neither tempted to engage in coercion and nor subject to the harm of protracted negotiations. The moral stakes were less serious, but quelling disagreement was also the goal, at least in part, of the use of supermajority rule in the communes.

Supermajority Rules in the Italian City-Republics

Supermajority requirements operated in many contexts in the Italian city-republics: two-thirds for many quorum rules (Waley 1988, 63), two-thirds for decision making on the Florentine Great Council (Rubinstein 1997, 176), and on a sliding scale for important decisions as in Parma (Waley 1988). But the most important use of supermajorities in the city-republics, as in Florence, was to "scrutinize," or approve, candidates for office, where it constituted a locus of machinations and controversies (Rubinstein 1997, 5). Scrutiny operated in tandem with the use of lot for the selection of magistrates. Given that the lot would choose anyone within the pool to serve as a magistrate, the aim of the scrutiny was to ensure that the pool included only those deemed capable of holding office. In Bernard Manin's words, "The Florentines had no more desire than the Athenians to be governed by incompetent or unworthy citizens"; as such, they used the scrutiny to eliminate the incompetent, though the scrutiny also lent itself to partisan ends (Manin 1997, 57). As we have seen in the context of papal elections, the supermajority here served an avowedly epistemic purpose – ensuring that the prospective candidates were sufficiently worthy – but it also accomplished the political aim of ensuring that those eligible for selection had the support of a consensus of the elite.

The transition to complicated electoral procedures, of which the scrutiny constituted but one part, was not immediate or direct. In Jones's words,

From the later twelfth century the early and mismatched twin procedures of mass election (acclamation) and cooptation were gradually replaced by an indirect, two-stage or multi-phase system, of nomination by consuls, *podesta*, or more particularly electoral colleges or boards of *electors* – up to nine at Venice for the dogeship – a system then in turn widely superseded from the mid-thirteenth century by election by lot or sortition, the "extraction" from "bags" (*borse*, Florence; *sacchi*, Perugia) of pre-selected names. (Jones 1997, 411)

Voting was by majority rather than seniority, but nonetheless the principle of equal and expanded access to political offices coexisted with the logic of government by the fittest (*meliores, discretiores, prudentiores*), the *sanior et maior pars* revisited (Jones 1997, 411). As in the religious context, supermajority voting of members conducting the scrutiny for offices served to dignify the numerical majority.

As John Najemy has demonstrated, the corporate view of the Florence body politic was grounded in support for an electoral system based on guild autonomy and equality (Najemy

1982, 23). Such a system was already in the late thirteenth century identified with the popular challenges to oligarchic rule. Unsurprisingly, the oligarchs preferred procedures that protected their political power by restricting eligibility to the same families that had held the Priorate (*priores atrium*) – originally representatives of guilds and later the executive magistracy – since its creation in 1282. However, Florentine politics in the late thirteenth and fourteenth centuries were also marked by struggles over which guilds ought to receive political recognition, and the electoral form such recognition should take. Whereas the "socially inferior" guilds sought to be included on an equal basis and to promote rapid political turnover, a competing model seeking to ensure the rise to power of "men of experience and leadership" also emerged within the supporters of corporatism broadly construed (Najemy 1982, 52).

The reformist ordinances of 1328 aimed to select for magistracies competent candidates who could receiving and maintaining a consensus at least within the aristocracy, while also sought a more equitable distribution of offices among those deemed worthy. The election occurred in the following fashion. First, nominating committees identified capable candidates for magistracies. Next – and this is the mechanism of most interest– the candidates were subject to scrutiny (*scruptinium*). Two-thirds of the members of the scrutiny committee (fifty-seven of the eighty-five "scrutators") had to concur that the candidate was qualified for office before his name could be placed into a bag (*imborsatio*) for selection by lot. The selection of names occurred at designated intervals (*extractio*). There was also a mechanism (*divieti*) by which officeholders and their families were rendered temporarily ineligible for reelection.

The supermajority mechanism was initially an oligarchic mechanism; the composition of the scrutiny committee in 1328 was seven members of the Signoria, nineteen *gonfalonieri* (standard-bearers) of the companies, five members of the *mercanzia* (board of trade), two consuls from each of the twelve major guilds (twenty-four in total), and thirty Guelf representatives (five from each *sesto* or ward), or *arroti*, selected by the Signoria. As

Najemy noted, the Signoria and the Five of Mercanzia, along with the *arroti*, constituted forty-two of eighty-five, and could block any candidate. Twenty-nine votes could block a candidate, but it is not clear how likely this was to occur, insofar as "it is also certain that the members of the Signoria and their *arroti* (37) could rely on the votes of their allies among the consuls of the leading commercial guilds and the *gonfalonieri* to secure the acceptance of candidates of their choice." (Najemy 1982, 105) An overwhelming majority must have supported the candidates of the Signoria.

Although the precise origins of the two-thirds rule are not clear, we might note a few different and important features of its use. First, the mechanism of scrutiny, or the determination of qualification for officeholding, is significant: supermajority rule was used in cases in which the competence of candidates was the key criterion, as the moral or intellectual worth of the candidate ought to be sufficiently obvious to command widespread agreement. The second, which will be of critical importance in the modern era, is the use of supermajority rule expressly to capture consensus. The aim was to identify those candidates acceptable to the largest proportion of the elite as a means of ensuring political stability. (Note that stability is an indirect aim of supermajority rule in this context, whereas it is a direct goal of supermajority rules for institutional change in the modern era.) Finally, as in the modern era, granting a veto to a minority to block the preferences of a majority constituted a means of protecting (relatively powerful) interests.

The vote threshold required during the scrutiny dipped in periods when the pool of eligible candidates expanded, perhaps both as cause and effect of this expansion. In 1339, the nominating committees were made more complex to prevent factional dominance (Najemy 1982, 122). Further, each nominating committee was required to put each nominee sequentially to a vote by majority rule. "The intended effect of all of this was to open up the nominating process so that the electoral system could more genuinely reflect a broad consensus within the community of the major guilds" (Najemy

1982, 122). The popular reforms of 1343 were ushered in by a change to a 53 percent threshold (110 of 206 affirmative votes in the scrutiny), and only 90 affirmative votes were required to be approved for candidacy to the 16 *gonfalonieri*. Finally, the compromise solution between the oligarchic and popular reforms developed in 1352 split the difference vis-à-vis the threshold requirements. The scrutiny committee had 144 members, of which 99 constituted a quorum; two-thirds of those present (given the satisfaction of a quorum) were required to approve a nominee. But there were potentially 3,000 or more nominees, and each one was entitled to have an official count of his vote – the number of black and white beans he received from the scrutators. Even though in many cases, as Najemy holds, it would have been a "waste of time" to count each bean, nonetheless it was

a guarantee of what later became a cardinal principle of the republicanism of the civic humanists: namely, that even if officeholding could not be promised to all citizens on an equal basis, at least the hope of office was denied to no one, since every nominee was considered separately on his own merits. The elaborate and time-consuming scrutiny process conducted every third year was a ritual celebration and renewal of that promise. By rendering the whole process solemn, durable, and impersonal and by channeling a whole series of political choices into a lengthy ritual, the scrutiny system contributed significantly to the transformation of Florentine attitudes toward participation in politics and toward the legitimacy of the exercise of public power. (Najemy 1982, 182–183)

Thus, the counting of votes to ensure that a particular threshold had been reached constituted a hallmark of the developed Florentine republic, as vote-counting did in the democracy of Athens.

Finally, ensuring the equal and independent votes of members of the scrutiny committee constituted a key dimension of the "revolutions" of 1378. In July of that year, the rise of the *popolo minuto* into politics manifested itself immediately in a two-thirds majority on the scrutiny committee, with "near total control" over the nomination and scrutiny of the *popolo minuto*'s candidates. The committee, as outlined by the ordinances of August 4, 1378, granted considerable power (again, two-thirds control over the scrutiny committee) to the members of the seventeen minor guilds. This egalitarianism, however, was tempered by the effort to grant the *popolo minuto* a veto over the decisions of the three executive colleges of the Signoria, Sixteen, and Twelve (Najemy 1982, 240).

The use of supermajority thresholds to ensure, largely during periods of aristocratic dominance, that candidates for selection by lot were qualified for office endured through the Medici period and into the second republic. Under the Medici the scrutiny for magistracies required a two-thirds majority. Doing so raised the difficulty of achieving the threshold and enabled the regime to exert greater control over the selection of politically unacceptable citizens (Butters 1985, 198). Under the Great Council of the second republic, however, the supermajority rule was abolished, replaced at nomination and election stages (used in tandem with sortition) with simple or absolute majority and by relative majority rules. The two-thirds rule, then, was primarily the threshold used to determine qualification for office at the constitutional moments when the mix was more oligarchic than democratic.

The Principles of Supermajority Rule

Supermajority rule did not acquire a monopoly on elections, even in the papal context. The Fourth Lateran Council in 1215 promulgated the law *Quia propter*, which identified three alternative mechanisms for elections: acclamation or "quasi-inspiration," in which the outcome is perfectly unanimous (albeit without balloting); balloting or "scrutiny," by which an absolute majority vote in an episcopal election and a two-thirds majority in a papal election indicated the *sanior et maior pars*; and "compromise," by which the decision was delegated to another authority. Nonetheless, by that time, the scrutiny mechanism was clearly the dominant procedure.

The development of early Italian city-state mechanisms is somewhat less clear, but a similar story emerges. The evidence that Pisa made decisions via shouts of "fiat, fiat" (Waley 1988, 61; Monahan

1987, 152) suggests that at least at some stage a decision could have been made by acclamation. After council decision making replaced acclamation, however, electoral innovations expanded the scope of those eligible for officeholding while ensuring the worthiness of the candidates. Although the Florentines, in choosing lot, sought to generate impartiality through lending externality and non-manipulability to the process (Manin 1997, 56–57), the use of the scrutiny ensured that sortition chose only those with sufficient knowledge and moral standing. Supermajority rule here ensured both that the candidates possessed the desired qualities, as deemed by a wide consensus of the scrutineers, and that the outcome would not lead to further instability.

Thus supermajority rule, from its renaissance (if not true genesis) in the medieval period, helped lend epistemic dignity to aggregative procedures after the end of acclamation. It constituted a sounder (in terms of *sanior*) alternative to majority rule. Simultaneously, it served as an alternative to *unanimitas* in the spiritual sense and to unanimity as a decision rule, through acknowledging the moral fallibility of cardinals. Beyond that, however, supermajority rule even at this early stage began to serve some of the purposes that mark its modern use.

The first modern aim of supermajority rules anticipated in the medieval era was that of consensus. The two-thirds qualified majority rule constituted an alternative to *unanimitas*, but the goal of capturing a view widely shared by the voters remained central. Consensus in this context was valuable insofar as it conferred validity on the election: it provided confidence that the true pope had been identified, regardless of the apparently weaker authority or the potentially imperfect intentions of the overwhelming majority in his support. But a supermajority also served as a marker of legitimacy in a different sense: It demonstrated that the overwhelming majority of voters preferred a particular outcome, indicating that a minority challenge would likely be unsuccessful, and that dissent would be overwhelmed and likely suppressed. As such, a supermajority rule helped ensure the stability of the outcome.

To enhance stability in the institutional (rather than electoral) context is the second primary aim of supermajority rules in the modern era. Institutional inflexibility arises as a consequence of the difficulty of achieving a high proportion of votes in favor of change. The use of supermajority rules to stabilize either political dynamics or institutional rules is, by definition, a conservative effort. Although there is no reason why the substance of the political commitments secured by supermajority rules must preserve the privileges of an elite – they could in principle protect popular policies – it seems that such rules were primarily aristocratic in application. The high threshold requirement for candidate scrutiny meant that only those acceptable to a wide swath of the privileged members of the scrutiny committee could be approved. Efforts at expanding the candidate pool required the lowering of such a threshold: inclusion required democratization of the traits signifying competence. The second Florentine republic's rejection of supermajority rule affirms this. In Guicciardini's *Dialogue on the Government of Florence*, Bernardo del Nero holds that the consequences of popular rule will be to abolish the requirement of two-thirds majority voting in the Great Council: merely doing so "will be enough to apply sufficient pressure to prevent [the best citizens] winning" (Guicciardini 2002, 45).

Did supermajority rules aim to protect institutional and not just political stability in the medieval era? This is a harder question. Parma, for instance, had four different categories of decision making; the most important issues required the highest threshold levels for both quorum and decisions. A two-thirds majority was frequently used for critical matters. On Waley's account, "it was quite common to safeguard against rashness by demanding a larger quorum and a larger majority for certain types of decision, extending not only to a favorable vote of 3/4 or 4/5 of those present, but even to 10/11 or 16/17" (Waley 1988, 64). If the higher thresholds were used primarily in the institutional and not ordinary political contexts, we might think that this constituted evidence of some sort of commitment to the hierarchy of norms, and potentially to a form of constitutionalism. But we should be careful not to infer that supermajority rules were used in particular for institutional matters. For instance, in fifteenth-century Genoa, a two-thirds majority of a specific number of councillors was required for such decisions as the payment from public funds out of the treasury (Shaw 2001, 855–856). In the absence of more information about the substantive matters subject to high thresholds, we cannot infer that these rules were used to induce not merely political but institutional stability.

However, we might note that the almost ubiquitous use of supermajorities for quorum requirements in the Italian city-republics might have led to stability of just this sort. In the second Florentine republic, the quorum rule, per Rubinstein, was in accordance with one of the basic concepts of the new republican constitution: "that of a large council which could truly be considered *signore della città*" (Rubinstein 1997, 178, citing Savonarola, Tratto, iii, I, 40). As such, by enhancing the authority of the council, quorum rules may have served both the aims of stability and the goal of consensus. However, they may also have had another, perhaps unintended, effect, prefiguring the third use of supermajority rules in the modern era: to enable a minority to wield veto power over a majority's decisions. As Adrian Vermeule has noted, quorum rules may enable a minority bloc to thwart the preferences of even an overwhelming majority simply by walking out. As such, even if supermajority rules in the medieval era were not intended to shift power to minorities, supermajoritarian quorum rules may have had this effect, even when decision thresholds were lower (as when absolute majorities were required).

It is true, then, that even in the medieval world supermajority rules seem to have achieved some of the goals that mark their modern and contemporary use. But we ought not to lose sight of their primary purposes – to serve as a substitute for unanimity when the moral fallibility of electors rendered it unachievable, and to grant epistemic dignity to a numerical majority once the criteria for seniority became contentious. These justifications of supermajority rule, we shall see, continued to predominate into the modern era, at least until Condorcet's discoveries of the eighteenth century.

4

Unanimity and Supermajority Rule in Eighteenth-Century France

Although today we tend to invoke supermajority rules as an alternative to majority rule, the classical medieval justification for supermajority rules emerged as a substitute for unanimity. As the preceding chapter suggested, the unanimity requirement for the election of the pope broke down early in the second millennium, and was replaced with the doctrine of the *sanior et maior pars*, by which those electors possessing sounder judgment prevailed. But conflict over the criteria for sound judgment led again to breakdown. Further, following innovations designed to improve the learning and moral quality of the cardinals who served as electors, a strictly aggregative procedure could be introduced: each elector had a judgment worthy of being counted. In choosing a decision rule, the aim was to reflect the epistemic dignity of the electors through a strictly aggregative mechanism.

Supermajority rule from the twelfth century reflected commitments that made it in many ways more attractive than the unanimity it replaced. The most important of these commitments was the acceptance of fallibility, both moral and epistemic. Because people can err both in conduct and judgment, a unanimity rule came to be seen as excessively demanding. A unanimous election required perfect concord: no member could veto a candidate for his own private purposes, or fail to correctly identify the pope. In contrast, a supermajority rule accommodated the possibility that members of an assembly would fail to recognize the truth or would not agree, but wide support of the electors signified both that the outcome reflected the divine will and would command the cardinals' allegiance.

The problem of designing voting rules to elicit correct judgments reemerged in eighteenth-century France, although the rise of probability theory generated fundamental changes in the conceptual logic and language used to capture the problem and its solutions. Unanimity, of course, had a distinctive and secularized moral valence in the eighteenth century: no longer the *unanimitas* of the cardinals, unanimity represented the consensus of the enlightened. But in two key institutional contexts – in criminal proceedings and in legislative assemblies – unanimity was challenged on both epistemic and moral grounds, and for reasons that bear a striking resemblance to those advanced in the medieval period, prior to the advent of classical probability. Supermajority rule was advocated in both of these domains as an alternative to unanimity. Unlike in the context of papal elections, because majority rule was now a viable alternative, supermajority rule now required a defense from both directions: both against unanimity and against majority. As the second half of this book emphasizes, contemporary defenders of supermajority rule typically justify their institutional preferences as a remedy for the deficiencies of majority rule. Yet this logic is problematic for reasons revealed by the theoretical treatments that we explore in this chapter. Supermajority rule is its most attractive, from both a moral and epistemic perspective, when it substitutes for unanimity.

The normative valence of unanimity in eighteenth-century France is distinguishable from, if at moments evocative of, its theological origins. Scholars often assume the rejection of unanimity by thinkers in the social contract tradition, including Pufendorf and Rousseau, to have been strictly pragmatic. Although we would optimally prefer to make decisions unanimously, both because unanimity reflects reasoned consensus and preserves autonomy, it is unachievable. As such, we must adopt a weaker but more realistic standard. My aim here is to demonstrate that unanimity was rejected on normative grounds for two central reasons: (1) it was not necessary on epistemic grounds and could actually subvert the effort to reach moral certainty, and (2) it did not ensure freedom but encouraged coercion. Both grounds on which unanimity failed are linked through a conception of majority not only as sufficient from an epistemic perspective, but as optimal in terms of its ability to reflect individuals' willingness to accept the correctness of others' choices, and as such their own fallibility. The move to a lower threshold was essential for both social and political life.

Such an account both captures the true value of the Condorcet Jury Theorem and helps place it in intellectual context, notably with respect to the question of the connection between Rousseau and Condorcet. The jury theorem holds that in a body in which the individuals have a greater than 50 percent probability of identifying the right answer, a majority vote is very likely to be correct, and approaches certainty as the group increases in size. Although Grofman and Feld suggested that Rousseau might have learned of Condorcet's work from Diderot, who in turn might have been introduced to it by d'Alembert, Estlund demonstrated that the causal arrow more plausibly points in the opposite direction. Following Baker, Estlund noted that, whereas Condorcet would certainly have known of Rousseau's work by the time he wrote the *Essai sur l'application de l'analyse à la probabilité des decisions rendues à la pluralité des voix* (1989, 1335–1336), Condorcet and d'Alembert did not become acquainted until after the publication of the *Social Contract*. As Baker noted, the earliest possible date of an initial (and likely unfavorable) encounter would have been 1761, but their relationship probably did not develop prior to 1763; by 1765, d'Alembert had become Condorcet's patron (1975, 9). Grofman and Feld held that these ideas were "in the wind" (1988, 570). Alternatively, Paul Weirich suggested, "An early, intuitive appreciation of the theorem led him to advance majority rule as a method of estimating the general will in cases where voters express opinions of the general will" (1986, 119). We need not take a firm stand on the causality between Rousseau and Condorcet on the jury theorem. Yet once

we examine Rousseau's response to Grotius and to the influence
of Pufendorf rather than Condorcet on Rousseau's discussion
of voting rules, the true link between Rousseau and Condorcet
emerges in the substitution for majority or supermajority rule for
unanimity rule.

If unanimity is undesirable, what ought to replace it? Majority
rule was deemed adequate to the epistemic challenge by these
figures, so on what grounds did they defend supermajority rule?
The now standard reading of Rousseau and of Condorcet holds
that such a move was epistemic, designed to ensure the correctness of the most important decisions. But this view is not
coherent within Rousseau's thought, and Condorcet positively
disavowed it. Instead, Rousseau and Condorcet both advocated
supermajority rules on grounds familiar within constitutionalism – the desire to protect norms essential for the ongoing exercise of sovereignty and political agency. Condorcet did not defend
supermajority rules epistemically, not within the jury theorem or
elsewhere. Instead, he defended "absolute margin" rules rather
than supermajority rules; absolute margin rules prescribe a specific number of votes between the majority and minority, instead
of a proportion of the votes as a whole. The epistemic value of
supermajority rules derived from their indirect ability to slow
decision making and ensure adequate deliberation. If one wishes
to defend supermajority rules on directly epistemic grounds,
Condorcet cannot serve as a guide.

Unanimity and Certainty

One might have expected justifications of unanimity rules to
emerge in eighteenth-century France for several reasons. The
first is the obvious point that reasoned consensus was the central ideal of the Enlightenment: reason would guide men to the
same conclusion and to transcendent truth. More specifically,
the emergent doctrine of the reasonable man as a basis for
the calculation of expectations might have generated a recommendation for unanimous decision rules. As Lorraine Daston
has written, the early probabilists had hoped that reasoning

by expectation would serve as a basis for consensus – that one could calculate and quantify expectations on the basis of what a reasonable man would judge as prudent conduct. In Daston's words, the "calculus of expectations became a calculus of consensus." Once these expectations were subject to calculation, the persuasive force of numbers would generate agreement (Daston 1988, 66). Leibniz, for instance, imagined a day in which disagreement could be settled by computation: "Let us calculate, sir!" would be the gauntlet, and once proven mathematically, all would immediately concur (Leibniz 1951; Daston 1988, 15, 66).

There were important critiques of this doctrine, not least by d'Alembert, but Condorcet did indeed hope that the personal assessments of reasonable men, their expectations calculated with the guide of mortuary tables, would constitute the heuristic against which such risks as that of a false conviction might be measured. Again, one might think that such a possibility might generate a recommendation for a unanimity rule. But it did not, in part because the likelihood of a correct answer was not only not enhanced by a unanimity rule, but actually diminished by it. Why? Unanimity generated perverse incentives on the part of individual actors, both tempting individuals to veto on the grounds of particularistic interest, and encouraging the majority to coerce those who would attempt to veto.

Juries constituted a central locus of efforts to apply probability theory to the cause of legal reform, partly in response to the Calas affair. In 1762, Jean Calas was condemned to death for the murder of his son, Marc-Antoine. The Calas family was Huguenot, and Marc-Antoine's supposed imminent conversion to Catholicism was the purported motive for the murder. Simultaneously, the Huguenot Sirven family came under suspicion of murder in the drowning death of its mentally disabled child, Elizabeth, but the family fled to Switzerland before they could be arrested. In 1766 the chevalier La Barre was convicted of blasphemy and sentenced to death. These cases, *causes célèbres* in eighteenth-century France, are usually invoked as parables of intolerance, due largely to Voltaire's obsession with these cases.

His influential writings of the 1760s, most notably the *Treatise on Tolerance*, focus on persecution and bigotry.

In Voltaire's view, the problem derived not merely widespread from prejudice but from French legal procedure, followed assiduously in the Calas case. These cases thus generated substantial attention to legal reform and to the rules governing the number of votes required for conviction. The Calas and LaBarre affairs, combined with the publication of Beccaria's treatise *On Crimes and Punishments* (translated into French in 1766) and Voltaire's preoccupation with the cause, generated Condorcet's interest in the accuracy of judgments and the probability of correct verdicts (Baker 1975). Following Beccaria, who had called for the introduction of a jury, Condorcet initially wrote to Turgot supporting a nearly unanimous jury against the parlements. Turgot responded in advocating the rationality of a majority decision by a tribunal of enlightened professional judges chosen by election. Keith Baker suggests that Turgot's reservations about the jury encouraged Condorcet to begin to work on the *Essay on the Application of Analysis to the Probability of Majority Decisions*, and to the relationship between probability and judicial affairs more generally (Baker 1975). But he was also inspired by the events of Calas, LaBarre, and Sirven, and in particular Voltaire's response to them.

Voltaire defended unanimity idiosyncratically. Immediately after the execution of LaBarre in 1766, Voltaire wrote *An Account of the Death of the Chevalier de La Barre*, dedicated to Beccaria. Voltaire advocated both the use of unanimity and a strong bias toward acquittal:

> It hardly seems possible, sir, that in a civilized society a majority of five out of twenty-five should be enough to take away the life of an accused who is very likely to be innocent. In such cases the judgment ought to be unanimous, or at the very least, there should be a majority of three to one for the death penalty. Furthermore, if the latter is the case, then the quarter who judged in favor of a more lenient sentence should be allowed to prevail over the other three-quarters, made up of cruel citizens who trifle with the lives of their fellow human beings without the slightest benefit to society. (Voltaire 2000, 146)

Voltaire consistently rejected the "two-vote" requirement for conviction, savaging in his *Commentary on the* Spirit of the Laws Montesquieu's claim that such rules were divinely inspired (Montesquieu 1992; Voltaire 2009). Voltaire returned to this theme in an appeal to Louis XVI, supposedly written by LaBarre's friend Gaillard d'Etallonde, who had escaped before trial and was sentenced to death in absentia. In *The Cry of Innocent Blood*, Voltaire notes that he had been sentenced by a majority of two votes:

I shall not ask whether, in the eyes of humanity and reason, it is right that two votes should suffice to condemn innocent men to the horrible death that is normally reserved for parricides ... Parlement complained that ancient law requires it to pass sentence of death even if there is the barest majority in favour. Alas! May I point out that with the Algonquins, the Hurons, and the Chiacas there has to be a unanimous decision before a prisoner can be carved up and eaten. If unanimity is lacking, the captive is taken into one of their households and regarded as one of the family. (Voltaire 2000, 155)

Voltaire argued persuasively for the reform of the criminal justice system, but his defense of unanimity was less compelling. As Lorraine Daston has suggested, Condorcet proposed, on the basis of a technique developed by Buffon, that some risk of error in judgment was inevitable. An acceptable risk of error ("sufficient assurance") was identified by people's willingness to "voluntarily expose themselves without any preformed habit, for an interest so slight that it could not be compared to one's life, and without requiring any courage" (Daston 1988; Condorcet 1785). Condorcet conceptualized this risk as equivalent to that of sailing in the Dover-Calais packet-boat, or the difference between the probabilities of dying within a week for two different age groups. He derived $144,767/144,768$ as the probability that an innocent citizen would not be unjustly punished. (Because of the inevitability of error, one should note, Condorcet rejected the use of the death penalty on the grounds of its irreversibility.)

The probability of a correct judicial decision in the *Essai* depended on three variables: the number of judges, the required plurality, and the probability that each individual judge would decide correctly. If:

v (*verité*) = individual probability of correctness
e (erreur) = 1−v
h = size of majority
k = size of minority

then the probability that the majority is correct:

$$\frac{v^{h-k}}{v^{h-k} + e^{h-k}}$$

One could hold either v or h–k constant and achieve the level for moral certainty, again 144,767/144,768. If v = .8, the majority is 35 to 26, and this level is reached. Condorcet recommended in general a tribunal of 30 judges, with a majority of 23 required for conviction, and each of whom would have an individual probability of 9/10.

Condorcet did not speak in the proportionate language of supermajority rule: instead, he recommended an "absolute margin" of votes between the majority and the minority. Insofar as we want to ensure "moral certainty," a distinctive sort of threshold – that exemplified by h–k, not h–k/h+k – would be required. As Iain McLean and Fiona Hewitt are at pains to argue, if the jury theorem is applicable, we should talk about "a majority of eight," a "majority of 20," and so forth, not "a two-thirds majority" or a "three-quarters majority" (McLean and Hewitt 1994, 37). As we shall see in a moment, Condorcet did occasionally advocate supermajority thresholds, but not for juries, and not on the epistemic grounds provided by the jury theorem, but rather for good mathematical reasons, as Christian List has recently confirmed. Whereas an absolute margin rule tracks the truth in the limit for any value of the rule greater than 0 (that is, the probability that x is chosen given that x is true converges to 1 as the size of the group tends to infinity, as long as individuals' probability of choosing x is greater than .5), supermajority rules may fail to track the truth unless individual competence is very high (average competence is higher than the vote proportion). That is, if each individual is better than random at tracking the truth, absolute margin rules of any value track the truth in the limit, whereas proportion rules other than 1/2 may fail to track the truth unless individual competence exceeds the proportion (List 2004).

Only Voltaire held that unanimity was necessary for certainty in the context of juries; the more sophisticated probabilists rejected this assertion. In the context of political assemblies, however, unanimity met an additional set of problems. Unanimity was inimical to the capacity of collective bodies to function: such bodies required, for their capacity to command authority, a belief in the competence of their members to discern the correct decision. Anchoring this view of the competence of the majority, however, required an accompanying commitment to one's own fallibility as a member of a decision-making body. Unanimity rules, of course, provide that only if each and every member concurred could a decision be enacted. But unanimity places an extraordinary epistemic and moral burden on the members. If one is never obliged to obey a decision with which one disagrees, one is never forced to recognize her error. Because unanimity allows no room for fallibility, it does not induce the morally significant activity of acknowledging error. Further, as we shall see in a moment, unanimity may induce coercion: unanimity may signify agreement that is neither immediate nor the product of persuasion, but which derives from threats.

Unanimity and Fallibility

Pufendorf was himself a key figure in the jurisprudential origins of probability theory through his discussion of equity in aleatory contracts. However, the primary reason to turn to Pufendorf in this context is not his contribution to probability theory as such but because of the influence he had on Rousseau's account of voting rules, which may well have shaped Condorcet's own. Rousseau drew on Pufendorf's critique of Grotius as he argued that a unanimous vote was required to adopt majority rule; he may have followed Pufendorf more substantially in his broader considerations of majority rule (Schwartzberg 2008).

Although Pufendorf clearly had grave concerns that even in society people would be obstinate and quarrelsome, he viewed an appropriate decision rule as a potentially effective means of countering this tendency. An assembly, for Pufendorf, served as a forum in which the human inclination to be quarrelsome could do its worst, but decision-making bodies also could, with the proper incentives and decision rules, elicit and enforce the recognition of one's own fallibility. In *Law of Nature and of Nations*, Pufendorf found a virtue in acquiescing to the majority. Although the obstinate member of an assembly may retain the right of veto, to exercise such a right without good reason would be to violate "the obligation of a general law, which commands him to shew himself friendly and easy to others, and, as a Part, to conform himself to the Good of the whole" (VII, ii, 15). Pufendorf argued that people were obliged to accommodate the views of others, and should not stubbornly insist on their own views, lest they face exile or worse. Previously in Book VII, Pufendorf claimed that the law of nature would be insufficient to ensure peace, because "[f]ew there are of so happy and noble a temper as to have, at the same time, that piercing sagacity, which may discern what is for the lasting advantage of all men in general, and of each in particular" (VII, i, x). Human fallibility took two forms: first, "the greater number are, on account of their natural dullness, imposed upon by gross error in the likeness of reason"; second, "violence of their passions," lust, and "false appearance of advantage." He continued: "Now in so endless a diversity of opinions, what hopes can there be of peace and agreement, whilst every fool is as strongly conceited of his own way, as the wisest man is convinced of *his*, and the former will no more submit to the latter than the latter will condescend to be instructed by the former" (VII, i, x, italics in the original).

In light of these arguments, we might expect an elitist account of political rule, or perhaps a Millian plural voting rule that would maximize the votes of the wisest. Yet we have no such argument in Pufendorf. Instead, Pufendorf offered a moral defense, grounded on an epistemic conception of collective decision making, of why an individual ought to submit to the decision rather than exercise a veto: because to do otherwise would be to suggest that he "think[s] himself wiser than all his fellows."[1] Pufendorf anticipated the argument that the "weaker opinion of many" should not "outweigh the wiser opinion of the few" – and that "in determining speculative truths, opinions are not passed by number, but by weight: and the multitude of patrons is itself looked on as a mark of error" (*LNN*, VII, ii, 15). But he replied that such a claim offered a mistaken view of the "business in an assembly, the members of which have all an equal right to influence the proceedings. For who shall be the judge here where the opinion is wiser?" (VII, ii, 15). The members are divided by selfinterest and belief in their own intelligence, and take a malicious interest in rejecting others' suggestions. Appeal to an arbitrator will just lead to infinite regress. Thus, "[i]t hath been therefore thought most proper to enter upon a method as should be the least exposed either to difficulty or uncertainty: and none can be invented which should answer this character better than the counting of voices" (VII, ii, 15). Uncertainty is a loaded term here: that was the condition under which probability emerged, as a reasonable person sought to act in a prudent fashion. And in this case, the reasonable man needed to operate on the assumption that the members of the assembly will be competent. On this point, Pufendorf was careful and emphatic:

Besides, whoever is allow'd the privilege to vote in a council is presumed of sufficient ability to penetrate and comprehend all affairs that shall

---

[1] Note that we might also be able to trace to Pufendorf elements of Rousseau's insights on agenda setting; see the recent debate between Ethan Putterman and John Scott in the pages of the *American Political Science Review* (Putterman 2005; Scott 2005). In particular, we can find in Pufendorf discussions of "domain restrictions on preferences" in this context, as Scott understands them. A very brief article by Eerik Lagerspetz highlights a few dimensions of Pufendorf's contributions to the theory of collective decisions, including the pragmatic substitution of majority rule for unanimity; see Lagerspetz (1986, 180–181). Lagerspetz also identified in Pufendorf a precursor to the minimax rule, a discussion of the significance of single-peaked preferences, and an awareness of the risks associated with agenda manipulation.

fall under their deliberation. Which must be allow'd to be true of those Councils, at least, into which persons are not admitted without some kind of choice and approbation of others. Neither would it be always expedient to give any one man in the council ... the power of controlling the whole matter by his vote, and declaring which of the opinions is the better. For if the prerogative should be granted to him, he might prefer the judgment of the smaller party to that of the greater; nay he might reject both Proposals on pretence that neither was good; and thus he would, to all intents and purposes, be the sole and arbitrary governor of the state. (VII, ii, 15)

The very ability to engage in collective decision making thus presupposed competence. In the absence of the belief both that the individuals were of "sufficient ability" – despite the possibility of error – and that the assembly or council as a whole was collectively capable of acting rightly, no decision could have epistemic validity. Once the rightness of collective decisions could be called into question by a person with the ability to judge and without a healthy suspicion of his own competence, tyranny was not far off: "absolute princes," Pufendorf wrote, can take the advice of the "fewest of their counselors, or may take such measures as are contrary to the opinion of them all" (VII, ii, 15). According to Pufendorf, because no one can serve as a judge of the wisdom of the outcome, and because each person "think[s] his own parts and wisdom more considerable than his neighbors," the only option is to deem correct the outcome of a decision by a presumptively competent majority. The absence of such a belief in the ability of the assembly or council would lead both to the breakdown of society and to the end of nonarbitrary government, Pufendorf suggested. No reasonable person would arrogate to himself arbitrary decision-making power, because his reasonableness hinges in part on his recognition that he may be fallible. Prudence dictates that in such political matters the reasonable person accepts the outcome of a majority.

Pufendorf's view that unanimity cannot serve as a reliable basis for decision making, and that an individual must approach collective decision making from the perspective of humility and confidence in the judgment of others, closely resembles

Rousseau's own. In the chapter on voting at Book IV, chapter 2, of *Social Contract*, Rousseau argued that an individual's vote is necessarily wrong if it does not accord with the general will. "The tally of the votes yields the declaration of the general will," Rousseau wrote. "Therefore when the opinion contrary to mine prevails, it proves nothing more than I made a mistake and that what I took to be the general will was not" (IV, ii, 8).

Drawing on Pufendorf, Rousseau held that the ability to replace unanimity with majority rule requires us to assume that the assembly is capable of reaching a correct outcome. There is indeed no loss of autonomy in substituting majority rule for unanimity if the majority is capable of identifying the general will – which, lest all be lost, it must be able to do. As in Pufendorf's work, for Rousseau, it is not simply that majority rule constitutes a more efficient means to identify the general will. Majority rule possesses distinctive moral benefits. The process by which an outvoted minority comes to acknowledge error – the infamous "forcing to be free" requirement – encourages us to transcend our *amour propre*.[2] In language remarkably close to that of the *Social Contract*, Condorcet defended majority rule as the mechanism that best accommodated a commitment to the belief in one's own fallibility:

Thus our main task is to find the probability which, even for a law passed by the smallest majority, gives sufficient assurance that it is not unjust to subject others to that law, and that it is proper to submit oneself to it. Every man has the right to live by his own reason; but when he joins society he agrees to submit some of his action to common reason ...; his own reason prescribes this submission to him, and he acts in accordance with it even as he foregoes its use. Thus when he submits to a law contrary to his opinion, he must say to himself: *This is a question not of myself but of all; therefore I must act not by what I think reasonable, but by what all who, like me, have abstracted from their own opinion must regard as conforming to reason and truth.* (Condorcet 1785; McLean and Hewitt 1994)

---

[2] See Affeldt (1999, 310–311) for a thoughtful discussion of the way in which individuals must confront in an ongoing fashion the private will's inclination toward independence, away from the "continuous constitution of a general will."

Unanimous rule, with its emphasis on the absolute and unerring value of each individual's judgment, does not induce voters in even the slimmest of minorities to acknowledge that they might have misidentified the general will. Further, as we shall now see, whereas a unanimity rule might tempt a prideful individual to veto the choice of the overwhelming majority, majority rule properly acknowledges the likelihood of individual error, or the distorting effects of particular wills.

Temptation and Coercion under Unanimity

It is true that unanimous outcomes are desirable. But a unanimity rule has two major defects: first, it runs the risk of encouraging particularistic behavior; second, and more importantly, it generates incentives for coercion. Optimally, a vote tally would approximate unanimity, but paradoxically, the best way to attain unanimity is not through the use of a unanimity rule but through a lower threshold. For Rousseau, it was not merely a pragmatic but a moral choice that led him to abandon unanimity: whereas unanimity that emerged freely through patriotism and concern for the general good would have been optimal, a unanimity rule likely would serve instead to tempt the selfish to thwart the public-spirited – as in the Polish use of the *liberum veto*, the unanimity principle governing decision making in the *Sejm*. Rousseau held that the real source of pathology of the *liberum veto* was individual members' motivation to exercise their veto power, which he located in their attachment to "personal privilege more than to greater and more general advantages" (*Poland*, IX, 4). Indeed, he thought that one who used the veto should "be answerable for his opposition with his head, not only to his constituents in the post-session Dietine, but also subsequently to the entire nation whose misfortune he brought on" (*Poland*, IX, 12). Six months after the vote, if one had indeed exercised a veto, a special court comprised of the "wisest, most illustrious, and most respected persons" would have to vote not only on his guilt or innocence but "would either have to condemn him to death without possible pardon, or bestow upon him a reward and public honors for life" (*Poland*, IX, 12).

A unanimity rule thus runs the risk of being corrosive to the moral freedom both of individuals and of society as a whole. Even worse, perhaps, it might generate distortion and coercion in assemblies. As Rousseau noted in *Social Contract*, unanimity also reigns "when the citizens, fallen into servitude, no longer have freedom or will" (IV, ii, 3). A unanimity rule, as in Poland, may induce people to alter their votes because of impermissible persuasion or coercion, though we shall see in a moment the grounds on which Rousseau was prepared to defend it. Again, a citizen is obliged to take into account other perspectives and even, perhaps, calculate the probability that he will be the sole veto in rendering his decision. If he knows that he faces overwhelming opposition – and here Rousseau followed Pufendorf – the citizen is obliged to consider very carefully, and from a perspective of humility and awareness of fallibility, the rightness of his decision. He must be specially concerned to ensure that *amour propre* has not blinded himself to the general will; in the face of almost universal opposition, except in the most extreme of circumstances (in which case the society is at the brink of collapse), the prospective voter ought to recognize that he is very likely to be mistaken, and reverse his vote rather than exercise a veto.

By weakening the vote threshold, we reduce the incentive for individuals to vote on the basis of their particular interest – the single vote of an individual cannot derail an outcome – and encourage voting in accord with the common interest. Further, should the individual be outvoted, such a voting scheme encourages her to acknowledge that probably she has erred. Nonunanimous voting thresholds enhance the moral motivation of a voter, both *ex ante* – by reducing the incentive to derail an outcome – and *ex post*, by inducing the voter to accept that her judgment of the general will is fallible. As such, either majority or qualified majority rule may induce unanimous outcomes *for the right reasons*.

We might note, however, that a voter could not possibly know whether he was actually vetoing a decision prior to the tallying of the vote – whether his view was idiosyncratic or in keeping with the other voters – if he did not possess any knowledge of others' likely votes. Rousseau suggested "There is no need for intrigues or eloquence to secure passage of law of what each has already resolved to do *as soon as he is sure that the others will do likewise*" (IV, I, 2; italics mine). Rousseau did reject any discussion at the point of decision (*délibére*) in a passage rejecting communication among the citizens (II, iii, 3). As Manin has argued, we cannot take Rousseau's use of the term *délibération* to mean discursive reason-giving, as political theorists conventionally mean by this term; here, as in virtually all cases, he means decision (Manin 1997, 345). Yet in *Social Contract*, Rousseau offered a temporal justification for the choice of decision rule: "The more rapidly the business at hand has to be resolved, the narrower should be the prescribed difference in weighting opinions; in deliberations [decisions] which have to be concluded straightaway a majority of one should suffice" (IV, ii, 11). This complicates the issue of the permissibility of deliberation. In the absence of discussion, at least outside of the assembly, the relative urgency of the matter could not drive the selection of a vote threshold.[3] Except perhaps in the trivial amount of additional time involved in vote counting, there should be no difference between the time necessary to conduct a vote requiring a supermajority for adoption and that requiring a simple majority. So *something* must occur to cause the difference in the time between that needed to attain a majority of voters and that needed for a supermajority or for unanimity. Even if active persuasion is formally excluded, nevertheless there must be some means by which people can come over time to recognize the common good on a particularly important matter. Discussion must be that means.

Note that the very sentence rejecting communication also indicates that the rightness of the decision hinges upon a people "*suffisamment informé*." Citizens cannot come to know others' perspective through rhetorical appeals or vigorous debates, and

---

[3] The discussion of temporality here is also surprising in light of Rousseau's general wish to reduce the time between proposal and decision, which Nadia Urbinati has argued stands in contrast to Condorcet's embrace of time delays (Urbinati 2004, 62–69).

certainly not bargaining. However, the process of identifying the common good must be at least partially discursive; though the general will must be clear, no individual can have complete confidence in his judgment of it *ex ante* without ensuring that others share that view. Though communication poses a great risk – and should thus be completely forbidden – at the moment of voting, this does not require silence prior to this point. One might note here that Condorcet, as Nadia Urbinati recently argued, distinguished between informal deliberation in civil society, and formal deliberation, which he suggested should be excluded in some primary assemblies (Urbinati 2006, 203). It is possible that Rousseau had something like this distinction in mind.

A unanimity rule may serve to generate coercion and persuasion, especially given deliberation prior to voting. On this basis, Condorcet and Laplace both rejected unanimity rules on juries, despite Voltaire's crusade. In the preliminary discourse to the *Essai*, Condorcet held that the unanimity rule in England obliged jurors to "stay in the same assembled place until they are in agreement, and their union is obliged by this form of torture: for not only does hunger become a real torment, but the boredom, the disagreement, the malaise brings them to a certain point, and becomes itself a veritable torture-device" (Condorcet 1785). The unanimity rule was ill-suited to careful decision; instead, it generated only coercion, and privileged a "strong and mischievous juror over an honest but weak one" (Condorcet 1785). Similarly, Laplace held that the verdicts of unanimous juries depended on "the temperament, character, and habits of the jurors, and are often contrary to those which the majority of the jury would have arrived at if it had only heard the evidence, which strikes me as a great flaw in the manner of judging" (Laplace 1814; Daston 1988). That unanimity rules run the risk of generating distortion is a remarkable insight, from our perspective today. Because unanimity induces the minority to capitulate, it can easily serve as a cloak: a unanimous outcome might be the product of reasoned agreement, but just as easily might mask genuine disagreement and uncertainty. Better, in Condorcet's view, to relinquish the pretense of agreement: it is unnecessary for moral certainty, and only generates hypocrisy. On this point, Condorcet could not have been more prescient: the effort to generate unanimity had profound and disturbing consequences in the following years.[4]

Simple and Qualified Majority Rules

If unanimity was off the table, what rule could substitute?[5] For both Rousseau and Condorcet, the default was majority rule. Both emphasized the need to acknowledge one's own fallibility as a precondition for society. Again, for Rousseau, "when the opinion contrary to my own prevails, it proves nothing more than that I made a mistake and what I took to be the general will was not." And for Condorcet, "*This is a question not of myself but of all; therefore I must act not by what I think reasonable, but by what all who, like me, have abstracted from their own opinion must regard as conforming to reason and truth.*"

We have seen that majority rule is an inadequate substitute for unanimity rule on juries, although, as we have also noted, Condorcet did not recommend supermajority rules in their ordinary sense to increase moral certainty. Rousseau and Condorcet largely agreed that there were, however, other contexts in which majority rule was inadequate. The classic contemporary explanation of Rousseau's use of supermajority rule links it to the Condorcet Jury Theorem: in Grofman and Feld's words, for particularly salient matters, or those which are especially prone to errors in judgment, "we might wish to require more than a bare majority vote, since this will reduce the error level since it can be shown that the more votes there are in favor, the more likely is the group judgment to be correct" (1988, 571). Yet this is, as we have seen, both problematic causally in terms of timing and

---

[4] However, as Hacking has suggested, for Laplace, the fact that a verdict was unanimous was, assuming that the judges had been well-selected, evidence that the case was clear-cut (Hacking 1990).

[5] In this discussion we shall not consider the application of the jury theorem to cases with more than two alternatives.

at odds with the jury theorem itself, which relies upon absolute margin rather than supermajority requirements.

What grounds does Rousseau himself offer for the move from majority to supermajority rule? In *Social Contract*, Rousseau argued that while the vote of a simple majority could suffice to discern the general will in most cases, a supermajority threshold might be necessary for more important matters, such as the creation or abrogation of fundamental law. Rousseau suggested that between simple majority and unanimity are "various uneven divisions, at any one of which this proportion can be fixed, taking the state and the needs of the body politic into account" (IV, ii, 11). The reasons for requiring a supermajority threshold for major decisions may seem obvious to contemporary readers: such a rule may ensure that the choice to enact or alter a rule has widespread support or may reduce the risk that changes will occur with destabilizing frequency. Yet the use of supermajorities in Rousseau's work is paradoxical (Schwartzberg 2003, 2008). If law is not a genuine expression of the general will, it is illegitimate; that is, it does not oblige us. However, if law is in fact a product of the general will, the number of votes in the majority should be irrelevant. Once the process of discerning the general will amounts to the counting of particular individuals' votes, the outcome appears to become simply aggregative: in Rousseau's language, the general will seems to have slipped into the will of all. Again, although voting is the means by which the general will is recognized, the will exists independently of the votes and is not constituted by them. The particular number of votes necessary to discern the will ought to be irrelevant at best. At worst, because a supermajority rule empowers a minority to veto the majority's determination, the shift in power from a majority to a minority may indicate serious societal disorder. If the majority is incapable of identifying the general will, "there no longer is any freedom."

Rousseau did suggest that for truly important matters a very large proportion of the population must support a policy change. "[T]he more important and serious the deliberations are, the more nearly unanimous should be the opinion that prevails" (IV, ii, 11). Yet to those who would challenge the adoption of a majority decision rule – "How are the opponents both free and subject to laws to which they have not consented?" – Rousseau answered, "The Citizen consents to all the laws, even to those passed in spite of him" (IV, ii, 8). The entire logic of majority rule, then, depends on the view that the outvoted citizen recognizes that if he had prevailed, he would not have been autonomous. As a consequence, a citizen's consent to law cannot depend on his *actually* having voted for it, as an argument that supermajority rule enhances consent would run. A further possible justification for supermajority rules on stability grounds – that supermajority rules attractively slow down the rate of change – is also implausible. Rousseau did not defend stability for its own sake. Indeed, his defense of "ancient law" in *Social Contract* is not on the grounds that stability is intrinsically desirable but because of its capacity to write itself on the hearts of the citizens and the goodness implicit in its durability (III, xi, 5).

If Rousseau did not defend supermajority rules for strictly epistemic, consent-based, or stability reasons, on what grounds did he recommend them? The best explanation, it would seem, is one familiar to contemporary constitutionalists: securing fundamental law against easy alteration enables the exercise of sovereignty. It does so in part through securing the norms constituting such sovereignty, notably political equality, as well as by regulating the enactment and abrogation of such law (Schwartzberg 2003). Raising the threshold reduces the frequency of change (although Rousseau carefully noted that legislating ought to occur rarely in general) and, perhaps through the delays encouraged by these thresholds, ensures that the matter has received adequate consideration, again perhaps via discussions occurring outside the assembly.[6] In fact, in his discussion of Poland, Rousseau even justified unanimous decision rules on the grounds that fundamental laws made subject to the liberum veto will "will make the constitution as firm and the laws as irrevocable as possible" (Rousseau 1986).

---

[6] Beitz (1989, 64) offers a similar account to this one.

Condorcet, like Rousseau, ought to have been reluctant to use supermajority rules for two reasons. First, Condorcet himself did not offer a so-called Condorcetian defense of supermajority rules. Such rules cannot ensure the correctness of decisions for important matters, as they would contradict the jury theorem: a presumptively incorrect minority ought not be allowed to trump a correct majority. Rejecting bicameralism in the *Survey of the Principles Underlying the Draft Constitution*, Condorcet argued:

> If the consent of the two separate assemblies is required, this form can mean that the will of a very small minority is enough to reject what a large majority in fact approved. We know that using this system would effectively be the same as requiring some sort of relative plurality in order to adopt a proposition, but that it would lead to the same result only in a bizarre and uncertain way. It is not the result of enlightened political theory. (McLean and Hewitt 1994)

Similarly, in the *Essay on Provincial Assemblies*, Condorcet argued that a system of voting that would take account of property beyond the subsistence necessary for citizenship would allow the less probable opinion of a weighted minority to defeat the more probable opinion of the majority (Baker 1975; Condorcet 1968). So it is clear that on strictly epistemic grounds, following the insights of the jury theorem, Condorcet did not wish to authorize the use of supermajority rules – or, for that matter, bicameralism. Nor did Condorcet wish to affirm the value of constitutional stability. Whereas Rousseau, as we have just seen, did at points defend the value of "firm" and "irrevocable" laws, Condorcet endorsed the mechanisms of ongoing constitutional revision, familiar to scholars of the U.S. Constitution through the writings of Jefferson and Paine. In the *Survey* he provided for regular revision of the constitution every twenty years, and preserved the right of fundamental constitutional change by enabling citizens to call for a constitutional convention (Condorcet 1968; Baker 1975; Urbinati 2006). If a majority of primary assemblies supported an effort to convene a constitution, the legislative assembly was obliged to call one.

If Condorcet preferred to speak in terms of "absolute margin" rules, he did allow for circumstances in which a supermajority could be justified. In the *Essay on Provincial Assemblies*, Condorcet wrote:

The requisite plurality to make a decision does not always need to be the same. If it is about the establishment of a rule which will result in some inequality among the citizens, some restriction placed on the exercise of their liberty or their property, then there must be a very great probability that this rule is not a real violation of the same rights. It must only be established if there is a very great majority. I would propose, for example, that then there should be a three-fourths majority of the members of the districts, and three-fourths of the districts, one would have thereby not only a very great probability that it would confirm to the common will, but at the same time one would adopt a decision which had a plurality of at least an eighth, since the proposition would be adopted at least by nine-sixteenth of the vote, and rejected only by seven sixteenths. If, in contrast, the matter was of expanding the freedom of actions by the citizens of the citizens, the exercise of their property rights, or establishing among them greater equality, then a simple majority should suffice. (Condorcet 1968)

When freedom would be constrained through the alteration of a norm governing liberty and property, or in cases concerning exceptions to general rules, something beyond majority rule might be necessary. Condorcet's exceptions were compatible with Rousseau's general logic. In cases in which the capacity to exercise sovereign power in the future might be harmed, a supermajority might be required. Note, however, how narrow a supermajority *Provincial Assemblies* specifies: a mere nine-sixteenth of the vote, and rejected only by seven-sixteenths. But in cases in which this power would be enhanced – increasing equality, in Condorcet's example – only majority rule would be required. In the *Letters from a Freeman of New Haven to a Citizen of Virginia*, Condorcet argued that because "to add a clause, on the other hand, is to regain a right," even a small minority might be necessary: "the only reason that we suggest 1/2 rather than 1/3 or 1/3 rather than 1/4, is to prevent frequent changes" (McLean and Hewitt 1994).

The argument for using a small supermajority rule to bias against outcomes we believe to be unjust or erroneous tracks Condorcet's logic of jury decisions. In his *Survey of the Principles underlying the Draft Constitution*, Condorcet discussed precisely those circumstances under which he thought a qualified majority permissible. In his words, "standard objections" to supermajority apply to those cases in which it is necessary to take action, and there is no reason to prefer *ex ante* a particular outcome. Yet in certain contexts, supermajorities are permissible. The most important one, for Condorcet, "in every civilization" is the presence of more than a simple majority for conviction, because it is considered worse to condemn the innocent than to free the guilty. So one of Condorcet's central justifications for supermajority rules was to deliberately bias our judgments when we have reason to believe that the risks associated with one outcome outweigh those of another. Again, Condorcet regarded a contraction of property rights, the exercise of liberty, or the introduction of inequalities as those sorts of risky judgments.

Condorcet's second important argument for supermajority rules, also taken from *Survey of the Principles underlying the Draft Constitution*, relates to the urgency and significance of the matter under consideration. It would be fair, in Condorcet's words, to "require an increased plurality in important matters, where obtaining a bad decision would be more dangerous than deferring it, and in cases where the reasons for a certain decision must be clear to everyone, so that a small majority might be an indication that these reasons were not justified. And finally, it could also be required for cases which concern an exception to a general law which is regarded as fair" (McLean and Hewitt 1994). The last – on the exception – relates to the question of the circumstances under which we might reasonably bias our judgment. But the first two are different because they pertain to the way in which decision making should occur. Circumstances in which "obtaining a bad decision would be more dangerous than deferring it" speak to the question of risk in a slightly different way. There are reasons why we would want to bias our judgments systematically against predictable forms of injustice. But there are also questions that we think might, if answered hastily, lead to erroneous judgments. In those cases, what matters is that we improve our judgment through deliberation or delay. Doing so ensures that the outcome has been sufficiently debated, and reduces the risk of "enthusiasm" generated by haste, especially for important decisions. This argument might be compatible with Rousseau's, especially if we think that deliberation outside of the assembly might have generated time delays. The argument is also epistemic insofar as it bolsters reason giving: we have the opportunity to justify the outcome, both at the moment of decision and for the outvoted minority after the decision has been made. For Rousseau, such a view would be incoherent and unnecessary. Reason giving may be undesirable altogether, given Rousseau's general resistance to deliberation, but it is certain that an outvoted minority deserves no special justification, as the responsibility for its loss lies strictly with its failure to correctly apprehend the general will. These problems, however, do not arise for Condorcet, who argues without any logical contradiction that more votes constitute evidence of better argumentation.

So the Condorcetian doctrine of supermajority rules is not *strongly* epistemic, at least not along the lines of the Condorcet Jury Theorem: there is no reason to empower a presumptively erroneous minority to trump that of a majority. But the doctrine may be *weakly* epistemic, insofar as it promotes the quality of citizens' judgments through ensuring adequate deliberation. As we will see in the second half of the book, Condorcet's logic provides a powerful argument for the benefits of reason giving and time delays, but is ultimately compatible with majority rule as well. The strongest justification for supermajority rules, however, is that they bias our judgment against outcomes when the consequences of one choice are potentially much graver than the other. But the domains in which we can assess the relative weight of these consequences in advance are much more restrictive than one might think, as the second half of this book discusses.

The Contemporary Logic of Supermajority Rules against Unanimity

The analysis of voting rules in eighteenth-century France generates a set of powerful insights for institutional design today. We can characterize them, broadly, as the following: (1) the rejection of unanimity both for its epistemic and moral liabilities; (2) the defense of majority and supermajority rule as an alternative to unanimity rule for a set of decisions that would optimally receive the support of each member, both to avoid coercion and to accommodate fallibility; and (3) an emergent logic of supermajority rule as an alternative to majority rule under a set of restrictive conditions, notably those in which one decision carries substantially greater costs than another. This latter claim, however, is not the standard defense of supermajority rule's ostensible superiority to majority rule. But it does characterize, as I shall suggest, its best justification.

To see how these three claims might come together in a contemporary institutional context, let us turn to one of the most familiar uses of unanimity rules today: the criminal jury. Unanimity on the jury has since the medieval era entailed coercion, as James Q. Whitman recently demonstrated. Through *Glanvill*, a late-twelfth-century legal treatise, Whitman shows that jurors were essentially witnesses, who were summoned to render a judgment in accordance with what was publicly known in a particular area (Whitman 2008). In 1202, in a case of "novel disseisin" (recent dispossession), a dissenting juror was prosecuted for perjury. As Whitman holds, the law assumed that the vote of the eleven other jurors indicated the existence of a truth known to all; the dissenter must be perjuring himself (perhaps to avoid the moral peril associated with judgment). Unanimity was also enforced through coercion, as the jurors were locked up without food or drink until they reached agreement.

Contemporary empirical research suggests that unanimity rules on juries may indeed coerce lone holdouts. Yet one might immediately object that a single dissenter might be pressured at the point of any threshold rule. For instance, imagine that nine of twelve jurors are necessary for conviction; after initial deliberations, eight are in favor of conviction and three opposed. Would not the pivotal voter be subject to high levels of persuasion – and perhaps browbeating? Empirical studies of juries, drawing from classic work on social conformity, suggest would-be holdouts gain sufficient strength from the social support of additional dissenters to sustain deliberations, and ultimately may hang the jury. However, in cases in which there is a sole dissenter, the juror adjusts his or her vote so as not to hang the jury (Waters and Hans 2009, 523–524, 537).

Remarkably, much of the literature on the jury unanimity requirement seems to regard this coercive potential as a benefit. Because it takes time to try to persuade the recalcitrant voter to change her mind, deliberations are protracted; this ostensibly encourages all the jurors, even the non-talkative ones, to participate, and the quantity of speech in lengthy deliberations gives the evidence and the law a fuller hearing.[7] Condorcet, as we have seen, makes a similar argument on behalf of supermajority rules when which having a substantial set of justifications for decisions is desirable. Work by Kalven and Zeisel (1966) demonstrates that the major function of deliberation, however, is to persuade recalcitrant members of the minority to bring their votes in line with the majority. Psychological studies indicate that rarely does a lone holdout derail the final verdict: instead, because of peer pressure, she finally alters her vote to accord with the majority (Guinther 1988).

Further, regardless of the distribution of views prior to final voting, the unanimity rule seems to induce the jurors to feel more confident in the correctness of the verdict than does majority rule. Thus, even if agreement was generated by coercion, the presence of dissenters seems to threaten the legitimacy of the verdict; as such, many scholars regard the capacity to generate *apparent* – that is,

---

[7] Hastie, Reid, Steven D. Penrod, and Nancy Pennington, *Inside the Jury* (Cambridge, MA: Harvard University Press, 1983), pp. 76–78. See, however, Jonakait (2003, 98) arguing that nonunanimous juries have not been shown to lead to shorter trials (98).

false – consensus as an attractive feature of the rule (Saks 1998, 41).[8] In the language of Michael J. Saks, "Perhaps most troubling, when convicting, quorum rule juries did so with less confidence that they were correct than was true of juries deciding under a unanimous rule. Apparently, at the end of the day, the existence of dissenters left even the majority with some lingering doubts that it had reached the right verdict" (Saks 1998, 41).

The desire to signal perfect concord on the verdict is perhaps understandable – even Supreme Court justices may seek unanimity for major decisions[9] – but is regrettable. Again, this desire actively encourages coercion of jurors. As we saw in the discussion of Rousseau, a juror should consider very carefully, in the face of widespread opposition, whether she is misperceiving a given issue or whether she is harboring some bias. She may have good epistemic reasons to alter her vote, and if we regard a personal belief in one's fallibility as a virtue, she may even have moral reasons to do so except in circumstances in which she is positively certain. Allowing a juror to dissent under those circumstances honors her individual dignity as a distinct member of a collective body without forcing her into the difficult moral position of hanging the jury or casting a dishonest vote. Although Saks deems this finding troubling, it is normative appealing that a jury should recognize its verdict as potentially fallible. Recall, for instance, the logic of the enumerated minority in Athenian juries: a defendant could take at least cold comfort in knowing that he had supporters. A verdict in which one dissenter remained might signal an appellate court that the jurors felt some lingering doubt as to the defendant's guilt. Though it need not automatically generate grounds for an appeal, the presence of a dissenter could, for instance, trigger a review of the case.[10]

---

[8] Jonakait (2003); Hastie, Pernod, and Pennington (1983, 29).

[9] See Abraham (1992); Schwartz (1983), cited in Lax (2001).

[10] Recent scholarship also highlights the potential dangers of unanimity rule under strategic voting: for instance, Feddersen and Pesendorfer (1998) find that when jurors vote strategically, unanimity rule results in a high probability of acquitting the guilty and convicting the innocent.

Second, if it is true that jurors have less confidence in the verdict in the presence of dissent, weakening the legitimacy of the system overall, this ought not to constitute a basis for mandating unanimity. It is far from clear why a jury should take a verdict generated by browbeating the recalcitrant minority into altering its votes to be epistemically superior – and therefore more legitimate – to a verdict in which jurors dissented. Indeed, one might regard the presence of dissent as evidence of the *absence* of coercion within the jury deliberations, and therefore have *greater* confidence in the verdict. Moreover, if true, the argument that the legitimacy of the legal system rests on false beliefs about the level of agreement in jury decisions should leave us with grave concerns.

So if unanimity rule is today vulnerable on epistemic and moral grounds, should supermajority rule replace it? Drawing on Condorcet's arguments from the jury theorem, a majority vote ought to be sufficient, especially in a larger jury. Yet taking seriously Condorcet's more substantial reflections about juries seriously, we might reasonably bias our judgment against guilty verdicts. "One-way" rules, in which only convictions require (typically supermajoritarian) agreement, are the norm in all jurisdictions in Europe (Schwartz and Schwartz 2000, 445–447). The aim is to minimize the risk of false positives while accepting a slightly higher probability of a false negative. Such a view might attractively affirm and preserve the assumption of innocence, without the risks of coercion associated with unanimity rule.

There is another major contemporary context in which supermajority rules (typically referred to as "qualified majority rules" in this context) substitute for unanimity: federations, multinational associations, and international organizations. The core reason for unanimity in this arena is to preserve the sovereignty of states. As such, important decisions of such bodies – especially (but not exclusively) modification of the terms of federation – often require unanimous consent. Yet such requirements also frequently generate deadlock even in the domestic context; it is for this reason that the framers of the U.S. Constitution replaced the unanimity requirement of the Articles of Confederation with a supermajority rule. In the international realm, where conflicts of interest are endemic, the use of supermajority rule serves primarily to enable powerful actors to veto outcomes, or to generate apparent consensus in the presence of disagreement.

The allocation of veto power, once the threshold drops, tends to reflect the distribution of political power. An appeal of unanimity is that it equalizes veto power; both weak and powerful states have equal capacity to block the decisions of the body. Even under unanimity, power distributions are not nullified: stronger states retain their greater capacity to threaten weaker ones, and as such coercion remains a substantial possibility. In institutions such as the International Monetary Fund (IMF) (and the Council of the European Union prior to the implementation of the Treaty of Lisbon), qualified majority rule combines supermajority threshold with unequal voting weights, ensuring that powerful actors preserve a capacity to veto decisions. In the IMF, for instance, most important decisions require an 85 percent majority. A member's voting power derives from its quota; each member state has 250 "basic votes" and an additional vote for every 100,000 Special Drawing Rights (SDRs) contributed – an "artificial currency unit defined as a basket of national currencies" (Momani 2004, 881, 900). As of March 2, 2011, the United States possessed 17,071 voting shares, making it the sole nation with an effective veto over decisions; the next greatest shares are those of Japan at 6,118 and Germany at 5,978.

The use of qualified majority voting in both the IMF and the Council of the European Union operates in tandem with the expressed aim of consensus decision making. The executive board of the IMF does not hold formal votes on the decision to approve loans; instead, the managing director "takes the sense of the meeting." This sense must reflect the balance of power in the executive board; as Bessma Momani suggested in an examination of loan conditionality in two Egyptian cases, "[d]ecision-making in the Fund did not follow the principle of consensus building, but rather reaffirmed that US power in the Fund is enforced at all levels within the process of determining conditionality" (Momani 2004, 885).

Explicit voting occurs in only 20 percent of cases on the Council of the European Union. Unanimity remains the rule on the Council of the European Union for issues of special "sensitivity," although qualified majority voting has increasingly replaced it: 30 percent of Council decisions address topics subject to unanimity, and 70 percent are subject to supermajority (a very few are decided by simple majority) (Wallace, Pollack, and Young 2010, 78). Because of the risk of deadlock, however, under the Treaty of Lisbon instances of unanimity are subject to challenge under a "passerelle clause." The European Council with the consent of the European Parliament can unanimously authorize the Council of the European Union to replace unanimity with qualified majority rule in a specified domain without modifying the treaty.

In the Council, qualified majority rule serves explicitly but indirectly as a means of fostering consensus. The fundamental aim – "perhaps the most powerful of any in EU decision-making" – is "to preserve at least the appearance of consensus" (Peterson and Bomberg 1999, 58, cited in Novak 2010, 89). Technically the threshold is approximately 72 percent, allocated both by demography and "as a function of the blocking power" such votes would confer, but the aim of consensus is supported through the strenuous avoidance of voting (Novak 2010, 89). The qualified majority rule is instead accomplished through other means, particularly through negotiation, in which the Council members seek to avoid being in the minority (Novak 2010, 88). Ultimately, the Presidency announces that the qualified majority has been reached; whereas unanimity could be challenged by any actor raising an objection, a minority bloc does not usually emerge at that point, in part because the minority is uncertain about the number of other opponents, and often because representatives usually do not want their loss to be publicized. In one diplomat's words, "'consensus … can be used for those items to which a minority of representatives object, but would rather not be seen to object through the publicity of a vote'" (Novak 2010, 90). Registering a negative vote is thought to be costly inside the Council, so representatives almost always join the majority lest they face marginalization (Novak 2010, 92–94). In interviews, a representative of a small state expressed concern that "[i]f we vote against, nobody will talk to us anymore," and another held that "[w]e're too small to take the liberty of being isolated at the EU level" (Novak 2010, 94).

The combination of the formal mechanism of supermajority rule and the informal mechanism of consensus has a high likelihood of generating coercion. In fact, the use of a qualified majority rule in these circumstances may be worse than unanimity. Because states are uncertain as to the precise distribution of votes, they cannot know whether other states will join them in blocking if they raise an objection. This uncertainty can surely have salutary consequences; in the Council, governments in the minority tend to seek amendments rather than block progress, and register formal "no" votes and abstentions only where a signal to a domestic constituency is important (Wallace, Pollack, and Young 2010, 80).

It might be the case that the only way to secure the participation of hegemonic powers in international institutions is to grant them a veto. It might also be the case that a qualified majority rule under weighted voting could enable a combination of weaker countries to veto, instead of permitting only a few especially powerful states to veto. These are reasons why designers of international institutions might prefer a supermajority rule to any alternative. But these reasons ought to be weighed against the normative costs associated with qualified majority rule. As we shall see in Part II of the book, these costs might include the violation of the principle of equal respect: members' judgments are treated unequally in the decision of whether to loan, for instance. Further, the absence of an enumerated minority under a consensus rule may enable the fiction of agreement necessary for collective action. But it is precisely in the international context – where conflicts of interest are endemic – in which the search for consensus is most likely to generate coercion.

Diminishing the coercive potential of unanimity rules remains a strong justification for supermajoritarianism and majoritarianism alike. But introducing a deliberate bias into the judgment of the assembly or community in political contexts is problematic. As we will see in Part II of the book, constitutionalism is often thought to require us to bias our judgments in favor of those supporting the status quo and against those proposing changes. Yet Condorcet helps us see that the real value of supermajority rules for constitutionalism lies in their capacity to encourage serious, prolonged deliberation over fundamental changes. Once we establish the circumstances of sustained deliberation, and there is ample opportunity for arguments on either side, there is no longer any reason to privilege one set of claims over another *ex ante*. And surely there is no reason to permit the arguments receiving minority support to prevail. These claims will be developed in Chapters 6 and 7. Today, we typically consider supermajority rule as a remedy for the deficiencies of majority rule, a means of reducing the risks of instability, of narrow partisanship, and of tyranny over minorities. Throughout Part II, however, we should recall the lessons from Part I: supermajority rule, in contrast to unanimity, constitutes a means of accommodating our own fallibility, but it does not directly reduce the probability that we will err either individually or collectively. The primary mechanism by which we can improve individual judgments prior to aggregation is through deliberation. As we will see, supermajority rule is not, and cannot be, a substitute for the opportunity to learn from each other.

PART II

A REMEDY FOR THE PROBLEMS OF
MAJORITY RULE

5

Equality, Majority Rule, and Supermajorities

Today supermajority rules are thought to solve the core problems of majority decision making – to mitigate the risks associated with majority rule. Yet as the first half of this book has shown, supermajority rule emerged as a means of addressing different problems and reducing the distinctive risks generated by unanimity requirements. The primary liability of unanimity rule was the possibility that one erroneous or self-interested member could derail a decision. Unanimity rule could not accommodate human fallibility and had a high likelihood of generating coercion. Problems with unanimity arose in religious and political contexts alike: unanimity might subject the community to the whims of one erroneous or ill-intentioned member; the true pope or the general will might be misidentified; dissension might elicit coercion on the part of the rest. Supermajority rule reduced these risks, but majority rule did so as well. The benefit of supermajority rule compared to majority rule, according to Rousseau and Condorcet in particular, is that supermajority rule attractively biases our judgment in certain restrictive contexts: toward innocence rather than guilt, or toward the preservation of liberty. In cases where there was a grave risk of erroneous decision – in false conviction, or in disabling sovereign power – a supermajority rule could be valuable.

This logic of supermajority rule as a means of mitigating risk endures, although we conceptualize these risks somewhat differently today. We are less concerned about the threats posed by individual dissenters or small minorities. Informed by Madison in *Federalist* 10, perhaps, we believe that the "republican principle" of majority rule will take care of those problems, because factious minorities are simply outvoted. Instead, the primary challenge for democratic stability and legitimacy is usually located in the risk tyrannical majorities pose to fundamental institutions and to minority rights, rooted in part in narrow and partisan decision making. Supermajority rules are a catchall and standard solution to these problems because they raise the cost of altering the status quo, generate the need for widespread support across various cleavages, and enable minorities to veto outcomes that might threaten their very viability. The ease with which they can be deployed – the fact that they do not require new institutional arrangements for implementation, for instance – makes them an attractive recourse when majoritarian decision making seems to be perilous. For many relatively well-off members of stable democratic societies, majority decisions may seem fraught with danger. But even progressive members of such societies may gravitate toward supermajority rules insofar as they seem to generate an attractive degree of stability without the overt countermajoritarianism of, for instance, judicial review. Yet supermajority rule poses a deeper challenge to democratic decision making than its supporters typically recognize.

As we saw in Chapter 2, the counted vote emerged in ancient Greece as a means of showing respect for individuals' distinctive faculties of judgment, as opposed to acclamatory mechanisms, which sought only to discern the view of the mass as a whole. The move to recognize the dignity of individuals' judgments simultaneously generated the requirement that these judgments be treated equally. The aristocrats in the Spartan *gerousia* and Athenian *areopagus* would not have accepted the affront if asked to weigh some members' judgments over their own, nor would the citizens of Athens have tolerated such distinctions in the decisions for which individual judgments were pivotal (notably the jury courts). Similarly, the development of the aggregative rule for papal elections had as a precondition the recognition that the cardinals were of equal weight in decision making, even if a supermajority rule was chosen in order to reflect the concord once signified by *unanimitas*.

Majority decision making, in its aggregative rather than acclamatory mode, derived from the veneration of independent and individual judgments and the importance of granting them equal weight. As in ancient Athens, the majority vote arose in England only after the collapse of an acclamatory mechanism. In sixteenth- and seventeenth-century England, the acclamatory system of selecting members of Parliament broke down, as Mark Kishlansky detailed. Community members of high standing and distinction were identified through social mechanisms, typically without conflict, and acclaimed by the men of the community through celebratory shouts (Kishlansky 1986, 62). In logic closely tracking that of the Athenians, Kishlansky argued that in early modern England, acclamation was a means of affirming the community's choice. It was "neither a primitive method of determining majorities nor an indication of the superior aural abilities of an oral culture. An age whose members could compute the Year of the Beast, the movement of the stars across the heavens, and logarithmic values could certainly count a few thousand freeholders if it had any mind to" (Kishlansky 1986, 62). Once dissension among the elites generated competitions, and the means of quelling would-be aspirants ceased to operate, majority voting emerged. But from the start, the egalitarian implications of the majority vote were clear, at least to the elites.

When conflicts arose in the sixteenth and early seventeenth centuries, the community leaders sought to ameliorate them and avoid a vote, not merely because of the costs associated with conflict among the elites. Instead, "[b]y counting each man as one, the meanest freeholder equal to the worthiest gentleman, the community violated every other social norm by which it operated" (Kishlansky 1986, 61). In the words of Lord Maynard, he would not attend elections "where fellows without shirts challenge as good a voice as mine" (Kishlansky 1986, 61). The counted vote, and majority rule in particular, presumed the judgment of the freeholder equivalent to that of the elite. Thus, once acclamation had broken down, majority rule was justified – and resisted – in part on the grounds of the epistemic equality it presupposed and affirmed.

This equal capacity for judgment, as we saw in Chapters 3 and 4, was linked to the importance of accommodating human fallibility in decision making. In Chapter 3, we saw that the risk of enemies "sowing tares" gave rise to the substitution of supermajority rule for unanimity in papal elections. As we saw in Chapter 4, Pufendorf, Rousseau, and Condorcet each affirmed the significance of individuals' recognition of their own fallibility, and thus humility, in decision making. Because no one person could serve as a reliable judge of the outcome, and because all members of the community tend to believe themselves at least as wise as all the others, majority rule enabled each member to have his judgment weighed equally with the others. Thus the reasonable person would accept the outcome of a majority vote. However, the equal capacity for judgment also constituted a feature of earlier social contract theorists' claims, preceding the arguments on behalf of supermajority rule of the eighteenth century.

Hobbes, who influenced Pufendorf, held that the institution of a commonwealth depended on each man covenanting with every other man to authorize the actions and judgments of "whatsoever Man, or Assembly of Men, shall be given by the major part, the *Right* to *Present* the Person of them all, (that is to say, to be their *Representative*)" (1985, II.18, 228–229). Once the "major part hath by consenting voices declared a Soveraigne," the subject must consent or "justly be destroyed by the rest" (II.18, 231). Even though Hobbes was not explicit on this point, one might infer that the requirement of unanimity over the specific selection of the sovereign would reproduce the violent disagreements that led to the war of all against all in the state of nature. Thus majority rule was a mechanism of quelling such conflict. But a more important foundation may underlie the choice of majority rule.

Men, Hobbes famously argued, are roughly equal in their strength and, more importantly, in their "faculties of mind," thus leading to equal hope of attaining their ends (and thus the probability of violent conflict). In clarifying what he means by the equality of such faculties, Hobbes acknowledges that men are not equal in the "arts grounded upon words" and in "science," but otherwise holds that in mental capacities there is a "greater equality amongst men, than that of strength." "Prudence" is learned through life experience: "equall time, equally bestowes on all men, in those things they equally apply themselves unto." Further, all men believe themselves to be exceptionally wise, but this merely proves their equality: "For there is not ordinarily a greater signe of the equall distribution of anything, than that every man is contented with his share" (I.13, 183). Such argumentation is quite close to Pufendorf's – the universal belief in one's superior judgment helps undergird the choice of decision rule. Thus the establishment of political authority must rest on equal – majoritarian – terms.[1] To command obedience, the choice of a sovereign must be rooted in individuals' equal capacity for judgment and, if necessary, for violent action.

Likewise, it is often thought that Locke argued on pragmatic grounds for majority rule, beyond the unanimous agreement necessary to form political society. Securing the consent of every individual is difficult, because not every member will be able to attend the public assembly, and because the "variety of opinions, and contrariety of Interests, which unavoidably happen in all Collections of Men" (Locke 1988, 98, 332–333). By the "law of Nature and Reason," the act of the majority should pass for that of the whole, "unless they expressly agreed in any number greater than the majority." We might note, however, that while majority rule is the natural default, Locke there deemed it possible to derogate from majority rule through convention: to establish supermajoritarian decision making by express decision.

---

[1] Even the utilitarian defense of majority rule, at least on Bentham's account, rests not strictly on aggregative utility, as one might expect, but on the inability of unanimous bodies to concur and the closer proximity of the majority decision to the "universal will." In his words, because of this, we must be "contented with the will of the simple majority; since, how far soever this may be from the really universal will, it is nearer to it than the contrary will" (Bentham 1999).

Nonetheless, in Willmoore Kendall's words, for Locke, "The majority-principle is, in a word, implicit in the logic of community life" (Kendall 1965, 112).

Locke's so-called "physics of consent" has occasioned considerable discussion in recent years, namely his claim that the Body – the community as a whole – ought to move the way the "greater force," the majority, carries it (Waldron 1999; Risse 2004). But this requirement is not merely a function of the power and necessity of obeying the majority; moral significance underlies Locke's argument. Jeremy Waldron has emphasized that Locke took seriously the importance of our natural equality in establishing political authority. Because each of us, by nature, has the "same advantages of Nature, and the use of the same faculties," and each is capable through reason of discerning the contours of the law of nature (and the existence of God, Waldron emphasizes), our decision rules must reflect this equality. Majority rule, also by nature, is the mechanism through which a community (once constituted) ought to render collective decisions, because only majority rule reflects the equal weight – indeed, the equal *epistemic* weight – of each member (Waldron 2002, 130–131).

Is there a reason, however, to believe that this logic persists, or ought to persist, as a basis for the normative justification of majority decision making? If we are skeptical about citizens' knowledge in contemporary democracies, do we rule out the possibility of justifying any democratic institution on epistemic or cognitive grounds? We do not, because the proper route lies not through Condorcet's jury theorem or through the potential to discern right answers as such. Instead, it is through the deeper logic of the aggregative and majority vote – epistemic or cognitive equality – that underlies much of classic social-contract theory and of the broader history of democratic thought, dating back to ancient Athens.

The historical defense of majority rule has important normative implications for contemporary institutional design. Once this logic is developed, I suggest that the risks associated with majority decision making are both overstated and misconstrued. However, certain liabilities come with majority decision-making, and as such the requirement of strict egalitarianism via majority rule might be defeasible, if only for very good reasons (as we have seen, the desire to bias judgments in the context of the jury constitutes one such justification). Yet supermajority rules remain in most contexts an inapt means of remedying the defects of majority rule, and alternative mechanisms – developed more fully in the following two chapters – constitute more coherent and, likely, more effective solutions.

Equality and Independence of Judgments

Historically, as we have seen, majority rule was defended as a decision procedure in cases where individuals possessed independent judgments worthy of "counting" and where their judgments were considered to have roughly equal value. From the ancient and medieval world to early modern England, the value of individual judgments was affirmed by replacing acclamatory systems in key contexts with a counted vote. The counted vote could be compatible with inequality, and technically a majority vote does not *necessarily* entail any commitment to epistemic or cognitive equality among the citizens, or for that matter to any other form of political equality. Both a counted vote and even a majority decision could be used in conjunction with a weighted or plural voting scheme: following John Stuart Mill, educated members of society could receive additional votes (Mill 1998, 334–341), but a majority of the votes would give the decision. So majority rule in the strictest sense does not entail a commitment even to formal or pure procedural equality among voters, let alone the presumption of equal epistemic worth. And, of course, the domain of majority rule matters greatly: a majority decision rule among aristocrats does not entail broader democratic equality, even if it does entail equality of judgment among elite members. But in cases of unequally distributed knowledge, democracies – notably Athens – had alternative solutions, notably acclamation and the public, estimated vote by show of hands, in which the wiser could influence the outcome of the vote without excluding the less knowledgeable from participating.

Yet, in conjunction with the principle of "one person, one vote," the aggregative mechanism of majority rule does affirm the principle of *presumptive epistemic equality* among voters in a particular domain. Barring very compelling evidence to the contrary, participants in a collective decision are presumed equally competent to judge whatever matters are put before them. Can a presumption of equal capacity for judgment be warranted, especially when it pertains to decision making by the entire body of citizens? Many will believe that it cannot (although there is reason to suspect that this is an academic vanity in particular); surely, on any given matter, some will be better able to judge than others. If political judgments were necessarily beliefs about the state of the world in general, or about the right answer to technical questions, such inequality might be a reasonable presumption. However, if we were to doubt that the sorts of political judgments citizens are typically called upon to render were of this character, the presumption of equality might seem less outlandish. Imagine, for instance, that we believed politics was essentially about resolving distributive conflicts. In this case, we might be suspicious of the language of judgment altogether. We might prefer the language of *interests*: majority rule would, on this account, be a procedure designed to treat each person's interests equally. Equal consideration of interests is, of course, an important and influential defense of majority rule and of democratic decision making more generally.

But even if we believe that politics is about conflicts over interests, the language of judgment still matters crucially for democratic decision making – and with this, the claim that we can presume equal capacity for judgment should become more plausible. Without the presumption that each person is the best *judge* of her own interests, one might believe that equal consideration of interests ought to be accomplished through nondemocratic means – by a benevolent despot, or a group of experts, hired to assess what is in each person's interests. In the absence of the view that citizens are capable of identifying their own interests, there would be little reason to support democratic decision making in general, let alone majority rule. Indeed, the claim that ordinary people are incapable of knowing what is best for them has justified antidemocratic positions since Plato. Responses to these assertions, however, are equally famous, beginning with Aristotle's assertion in III.11 of *Politics* that the producer of a good, however knowledgeable, is a weaker judge of its quality than the one who uses it. Perhaps the most attractive contribution of the democratic turn in utilitarian thought was the view that individuals themselves, rather than an authoritarian legislator, can best judge their own interests.[2]

As Thomas Christiano has noted, "Citizens do not advance their interests directly; they advance what they believe to be their interests. So where there are conflicts of interests, they are conflicts between what citizens judge to be their interests" (Christiano 1996, 74).[3] The language of judgment is thus fully compatible with a conception of politics rooted in interest, but also is flexible enough to permit the "epistemic" move to identifying what is best for the community as a whole. We can hold that individuals, in voting, are making *judgments* about what they *believe* to be the best course of action, or about who would best represent them. They may restrict themselves to judgments of their own interests, or judge what constitutes their interests "properly understood," in the Tocquevillean sense of promoting cooperation within a political community (Tocqueville 2000, 502; Elster 2009, 50). Defended in this way, the presumption of citizens' equal capacity render judgments is not without warrant.

Robert Dahl, most notably, has argued similarly in defense of what he terms the "Strong Principle of Equality":

If the good or interests of everyone should be weighed equally, and if each adult person is in general the best judge of his or her good or interest, then *every adult member* of an association is sufficiently well

---

[2] As in Bentham's posthumous *Deontology Together with a Table of the Springs of Action and the Article on Utilitarianism*: "Every man is a better judge of what is conducive to his own well-being than any other man can be" (131). For an assessment of the "authoritarian" versus the "individualistic" Bentham, see Crimmins (1996).

[3] Note that Christiano nonetheless retains the language of "equal consideration of interests."

qualified, taken all around, to participate in making binding collective decisions that affect his or her good or interests, that is, to be a *full citizen* of the demos. More specifically, when binding decisions are made, the claims of each citizen as to the laws, rules, policies, etc., to be adopted must be counted as valid and equally valid. Moreover, no adult members are so definitely better qualified than the others that they should be entrusted with making binding collective decisions. More specifically, when binding decisions are made, no citizen's claims as to the laws, rules, and policies to be adopted are to be counted as superior to the claims of any other citizen. (Dahl 1989, 105)

Once we accept that such presumption is indeed justified, we must also support majority rule, for reasons that we will see in a moment.

This egalitarian presupposition has in fact led many scholars to reject the claim that majority rule constitutes a fair procedure. Contemporary democratic theorists – from Charles Beitz to Ronald Dworkin – often cite Mill's argument that "[n]o one but a fool ... feels offended by the acknowledgement that there are others whose opinions, and even whose wish, is entitled to a greater amount of consideration than his" (Mill 1998, 335). Dworkin dismisses out of hand the idea that we might want equality of influence – "we want those with better views or who can argue more cogently to have more influence" – and has rejected the majoritarian premise on these grounds (Dworkin 1996, 27). Richard Arneson (1993), also citing Mill, has held that the fact that citizens possess unequal capacity for practical and moral reasoning means that there is no right to any share – let alone an equal share – of political power, and thus democracy cannot be justified on intrinsic grounds.

Even those sympathetic to the use of majority rule have often ceded this claim, arguing that the inability to determine who possesses such a capacity is the problem, not the criterion of superior wisdom as such. Jeremy Waldron, for instance, writes, "If the mark of wisdom is having come up with just decisions in the past, and people disagree about what counts as a just decision, then it is not clear how we can determine who is wise and who is not without failing in respect for persons [in the sense of recognizing the 'burdens of judgment']" (Waldron 1999, 114). In

The Constitution of Equality, Thomas Christiano has similarly argued that generating a test of competence would necessarily generate disagreement over the appropriate criteria. By accepting some members' criteria over others, Christian suggests, we necessarily presuppose the merits of our judgment or of one set of citizens' judgments over what constitutes the appropriate dimension on which competence should be assessed – and thus the interests of one group over another. But the problem is not that the relevant criteria would be controversial. Nor is the primary issue that to determine who possesses superior capacities would entail "invidious comparisons," in David Estlund's (2008, 36) words. Amy Gutmann suggests, similarly, that because inequalities in the capacity for "rational planning and judicious behavior" are not associated with "easily discernible traits, with any class, ethnic, racial, or sexual characteristics of persons ... you cannot justly design political institutions that favor some groups over others."[4]

We probably could design an adequate or generally acceptable test for the talents on the basis of which we could assign votes unequal weight. We could develop a scheme for predicting the probable quality of judgments over different sorts of questions; neither the technical difficulties nor the normative liabilities might constitute an impermeable barrier. We are surely capable of ascribing different types of judgments to different bodies on the grounds that some are more competent to render decisions than others. On that basis, we could, it is true, weigh votes unequally. We could, as Mill suggested, give additional votes to some citizens. Or we could use a supermajority rule to privilege one set of citizens' judgments over another.

---

[4] Gutmann (1980, 45). Gutmann's additional direct response to those who are critics of egalitarianism is more compelling – the key capacities for a well-functioning polity are those to abide by laws and to choose a "reasonable plan of life," as well as the capacities for "self-respect and human dignity," can plausibly be taken to be equally distributed. But the contention here is that the relevant consideration is indeed capacity for judgment, and that to treat members of a decision-making body as if these capacities in general were of unequal weight is indeed an affront to their dignity.

But insofar as we are democrats, *we should not want to do so.* The reason why we ought to want democratic decision making in the first place is because we properly believe each member's views and opinions ought equally to affect the outcome of group decision making.

Treating some members as if their judgments were of less value than others' would constitute an infringement upon citizens' social basis of self-respect, precisely the sort of primary good that scholars working in the Rawlsian tradition (including some discussed earlier) might, ironically, advocate using supermajority rules to protect. Elizabeth Anderson, in responding to the luck-egalitarian claim that the state should compensate the disabled, unintelligent, untalented, and the ugly for their misfortune, argues similarly. Having sketched a hypothetical letter from the "State Equality Board" outlining to recipients the justification for sending them a check, she responds: "Could a self-respecting citizen fail to be insulted by such messages? How dare the state pass judgments on its citizens' worth as workers and lovers!" (Anderson 1999, 305). Although granting unequal weight to voters constitutes judgment about their public and political, rather than private, activities, Anderson's objection holds: the state should not habitually pass judgments on people's native endowments.

Thus citizens' judgments must be regarded as possessing presumptively equal value in decision making. To treat them differently is an affront to their epistemic dignity as decision makers. In Christiano's language, to "treat a person as incompetent in discerning her interests is to undermine a fundamental support for her self-respect. It amounts to treating her as an inferior" (Christiano 1996, 74). Citizens are not merely entitled to "equal concern," which may be compatible with their total passivity. It is also not sufficient for them to be accorded equal dignity *qua* human beings or as moral members of a community, neither of which emphasizes their political judgment. According citizens equal dignity in a democracy must entail treating them as having equal capacity to judge political matters. It does so through weighing their votes equally via majority rule.

Of course in some cases knowledge or judgment in a particular domain will be unequally distributed. In Chapter 2, we discussed public hand-waving (*cheirotonia*) as the Athenian response to the unequal distribution of information; up to the moment of decision, members could to turn to those they deemed more knowledgeable. There surely might be great differences in general education, in substantive knowledge, and even in moral reasoning, especially within large groups. This distinctiveness with respect to political judgment constitutes an important justification for political representation, as Bernard Manin has argued. If there are obvious and relevant differences in the technical capacity to judge a particular matter within a body, there are good reasons to assign that decision to the competent part rather than to the whole. Indeed, citizens should be willing to recognize that there are specific decisions for which an expert deliberative body would be valuable, and designate members of society believed to possess the requisite abilities – including technical knowledge and interpersonal skills – to serve well in such a body. (Were this not the case, we ought to choose an assembly at random.) But insofar as representation entails the selection of elites possessing superior judgment via election, the mechanism is aristocratic rather than democratic.

The move to representative government does not constitute an affront to the epistemic dignity of democratic citizens, assuming that it grants citizens themselves an equal vote in deciding who will best protect their interests, or who possesses relevant skills. Again, citizens must be presumed to be equally capable of choosing their agents and granted an equal vote, lest their capacities and interests be treated as inferior to others. In Manin's words, "Election inevitably selects elites, but it is for ordinary citizens to define what constitutes an elite and who belongs to it." The democratic feature of representation is that "all citizens [have] an equal power to designate and dismiss their ruler" (Manin 1997, 238). These special qualifications ought to count at the stage of assigning responsibility for decisions, but not once the decision has already been ascribed to a particular body. Within a representative assembly, the presumptive equality of representatives' capacity to judge the relevant matter ought also to be affirmed – whether from the perspective of the general good of the society, or of their constituents' interests. The use of supermajority rules in a representative assembly similarly constitutes an affront to the political judgment of some members. A deliberative legislative assembly should not be biased in favor of some members' judgments of the interests of society as a whole or of their own constituents.

Let me now return to the relationship between the presumption of epistemic equality and the Condorcet Jury Theorem. Strictly speaking, the presumption of epistemic equality that underwrites majority rule requires no assumption of competence whatsoever; each voter could be presumed equally myopic or stupid. (Again, insofar as we wish to affirm the value of democratic decision making, even on the narrowest of instrumental grounds, we must assume that voters are at a minimum competent to judge their own interests.) The Condorcet Jury Theorem is more demanding. The key insight of the jury theorem, as discussed in Chapter 4, is that the majority vote of a body where each individual has a greater than 50 percent chance of getting the "right answer" is very likely to be correct, approaching certainty as the group increases in size. We might well doubt that either citizens or their representatives possess this degree of competence; indeed, as already suggested, it is not obvious that these sorts of *strongly* epistemic questions of correctness or incorrectness, guilt or innocence, are the standard provenance of political decision making.[5]

Under certain restrictive conditions, we might turn to the Condorcet Jury Theorem as a basis for confidence in the power of the majority to make good decisions. For instance, if there was important but unevenly distributed knowledge within the citizen population which might be disseminated through deliberation, improving average competence, the jury theorem might

---

[5] There is also a less demanding standard available. Page and Shapiro, among others, have affirmed the possibility of Condorcetian analysis as a means of demonstrating that collective public opinion can be wiser than individual opinions (Page and Shapiro 1992, 26–27). Even if individual judgments are not well informed, as long as errors in judgment are randomly distributed, the community as a whole will capture the available information and make good decisions – that is, decisions that track the community's own preferences and values, if not "truth" as such.

well able to operate. Even if we thought that, ex ante, the level of competence of citizens might be challenged, we might believe that deliberative institutions designed to minimize the risks of polarization and cascades could improve the basic competence of citizens. As discussed in Chapter 4, the theorem itself does not incorporate deliberation, but it does not need to forbid deliberation for majority judgments to be reliable; deliberation does not necessarily generate pathological dependence. Independence in the Condorcetian sense requires only that the probability of A's voting correctly, given that B does so, equals the probability of A voting correctly considered alone, as Estlund has emphasized elsewhere in arguing that deference to (nonvoting) opinion leaders does not necessarily lead to dependence.[6] But it is also true that the presence of powerful opinion leaders in the public sphere, who do vote, might well generate deference in precisely this way: we could imagine this tendency being exacerbated by the presence of partisan figures given pulpits on cable news. Only if there were a true diversity of voices in the public sphere (so that deference to opinion leaders did not introduce distortions), and if deference (reducing the effective numbers of votes) did not reduce the effective number of competent voters below the Condorcetian minimum, would we have reason to believe that the conditions of independence necessary for the jury theorem to apply were attained.[7]

In general, the Condorcet Jury Theorem cannot constitute a justification for majority decision making in normal political life.

---

[6] Estlund, David, "Opinion Leaders, Independence, and Condorcet's Jury Theorem," *Theory and Decision*, 36 (1994): 131–162. For discussions of the effects of deference and correlated votes on Condorcetian outcomes, see also Ladha, Krishna, "The Condorcet Jury Theorem, Free Speech, and Correlated Votes," *American Journal of Political Science* 36: 617–634 (1992); Mueller, Dennis, *Public Choice III* (Cambridge: Cambridge University Press, 2003), p. 130; Dietrich, Franz, and Christian List, "A Model of Jury Decisions Where All Jurors Have the Same Evidence," *Synthese* 142: 175–202.

[7] Even then, as Austen-Smith and Banks, among others, have argued, where strategic voting is rational on the basis of private and public signals, the majority vote can be less reliable than any particular individual acting alone (Austen-Smith and Banks 1996).

Even if we held that, because of its demanding level of competence, the theorem operates only in to representative assemblies
rather than among the citizens as a whole, we might still be suspicious of its relevance, both for domain reasons (the nature of
the questions posed to political assemblies) and because of the
mechanics of ordinary assemblies. Were representatives more
than 50 percent likely to reach the correct decision, if their votes
were technically independent from each other, and were the legislature sufficiently large, then we might have confidence in the
strongly epistemic value of majority rule for a restrictive set of
issues. Yet many legislatures are set up to produce precisely this
sort of Condorcet-busting dependence. Strong party discipline
will surely alter the probability of individual members voting
correctly, as they alter their votes to align with those of other,
more powerful members or to engage in log-rolling. Once strategic considerations are brought to bear, the problems may be
further exacerbated.

The strict applicability of the Condorcet Jury Theorem, then,
may be questionable in a contemporary representative democracy, and as such defending a "strongly" epistemic claim for
majority rule – one that holds that the outcome of a vote will
track the truth – may be impossible. But majority rule may still
be justified through a "weakly" epistemic account of political
judgments, one different from "competence" in the Condorcetian
sense. The focus of this account remains the quality of citizens'
judgments, including judgments of interest (characterized as such
rather than as "brute" preferences). These judgments should be
treated as if they possessed epistemic merit, and equal merit
at that. Institutional design on the "weakly epistemic" model,
rather than the strongly Condorcetian account, aims at eliciting
high-quality judgments from citizens and then weighing these
judgments equally via majority rule. In this way, the "complex
majoritarian" model sketched in Chapter 7 aims to treat citizens
in a way that respects their capacity for judgment, and in so doing
also promotes just political outcomes. But first it is important to
understand why majority rule tends to outperform supermajority rule on these scores.

Formal Equality, Epistemic Equality, and Risk

The key starting point for most contemporary work on behalf of majority rule, May's theorem, demonstrates that majority rule is decisive, anonymous, neutral, and positively responsive. (We can set aside the decisiveness requirement, which simply entails that the rule produces a definite result, and can be satisfied by many different thresholds and both democratic and nondemocratic mechanisms.) First, let us take together anonymity and neutrality. Majority rule, in a sense, treats votes and alternatives equally: there is no bias in favor of a particular voter (anonymity), and no bias in favor of a particular alternative (neutrality). From a formal perspective, systems that enable weighted votes, or identify groups or individuals to assign vetoes, are ruled out under anonymity. Supermajority rules are excluded under neutrality, which is "nonneutral," or biased, in favor of one alternative, typically the status quo. As Rae (1975) and McGann (2006) suggest, however, to privilege the status quo may also entail a violation of anonymity. Although anonymity in the strict sense means only that the decision rule is insensitive to the identity of the voter, the fact that some voters systematically benefit from the existing policy may mean that in effect anonymity may be threatened by supermajority rules.

As Charles Beitz writes, these two conditions – neutrality and anonymity – together embody a conception of political fairness that holds "any fair method for aggregating individual preferences should treat each person's preference equally" (though this is not his own theory) (Beitz 1989, 59). The responsiveness of majority rule to preferences suggests other egalitarian dimensions. Positive responsiveness entails, in McGann's words, a "knife-edge" result: a shift of one vote from one alternative to another, or the addition of a vote that was previously an abstention, can change the outcome of the decision (McGann 2006, 18). Combined with anonymity, this entails the equal potential capacity of each voter to be decisive. More generally, majority rule gives to each voter *ex ante* an equal probability of being decisive (Rae 1969).

The value of anonymity is akin to that of the notion of epistemic equality sketched above. The identity of the voter is immaterial in deriving the social preference (Austin-Smith and Banks 1999, 78). The merits of the voter are presumed irrelevant, and, as such, the judgment contained within the vote is treated as equal to any other. Although citizens certainly differ greatly in their political knowledge and perhaps even their "prudence" more generally, *pace* Hobbes, the use of majority rule obviates these distinctions for the purposes of political decision making. Likewise, even if a representative system affirms certain community members' distinctive capacity to make important decisions, majority rule equalizes them within the body. Epistemic equality also captures the normative appeal of positive responsiveness, which is often treated as elusive. The attractiveness of positive responsiveness is that when the society is otherwise divided, any member can be decisive, and the outcome will reflect the fact that her individual, independent judgment was sufficient to tip the balance. Such logic affirms the view that an aggregative system is one that privileges individual judgment, and what appeals about majority rule is that it weighs these judgments equally.

The neutrality condition, which prescribes equality in the number of votes necessary to choose each alternative, directly challenges the use of supermajority rules, and thus is the most important condition for our investigation. By requiring more votes to adopt one alternative rather than another (typically but not necessarily the status quo), supermajority rules treat policy alternatives unequally. Especially in the constitutional context, however, there likely exists a very tight connection between anonymity and neutrality. If a constitution reflects distributive inequalities at the time of its framing, and if, as a consequence, at least some of its provisions promote the interests of some citizens over others, a supermajority rule may systematically generate a bias in favor of those citizens' preferences or judgments. Even beyond constitutionalism, a status quo bias – the typical if not inevitable effect of supermajority rules – does not merely promote one "alternative" over another. Supermajority rules presuppose that one alternative – supported by one set of individual judgments – is *prima facie* superior to another, and that only if a sufficiently great number of these judgments translate into votes ought it to be adopted. If voters are presumed to have equal capacity to judge, then to systematically bias decision making in favor of some voters' preferences is to treat them unequally. One might hold that insofar as citizens are likely to support the status quo in some cases, and oppose it in others, supermajority rule is in a sense anonymous; one might argue, then, that although the rules are partial with respect to the treatment of judgments, they are impartial with respect to the agents make them. But insofar as policies, and the institutions that produce them, are not causally independent from each other, and insofar as (bundles of) policies reflect the distribution of political power at the time of their enactment, supermajority rules will tend to systematically privilege the judgments of one group of citizens. Even if the group benefiting from supermajority rules is likely to change over time, the stickiness induced by supermajority rules will weaken many citizens' prospects of seeing their judgments translate into policy change even in the relatively long term.

Political theorists often challenge the normative implications of the neutrality condition. Charles Beitz offers one especially thoughtful critique. Supermajority rules help ensure that "results that could be severely damaging to some people's interests and rights will be less likely to occur" (Beitz 1989, 65), and that without such a "constraint" on majority rule "there would be less reason for the minority (and perhaps for others as well) to accept the outcomes the political system produces" (Beitz 1989, 65). More generally, it "enables citizens to reach political decisions on the basis of adequately informed deliberation and in a way that avoids predictable forms of injustice" (Beitz 1989, 66).[8] By violating the neutrality condition, we may *rightly* bias

---

[8] Beitz defends this insight through a reading of Rousseau, whom he takes to have believed that "sustained, and perhaps repeated, examination to ensure that decisions are adequately informed and responsive to enduring changes in the environment and that a supermajority requirement would encourage this" (Beitz 1989, 64). For reasons that were explored in Chapter 4 – including Rousseau's general rejection of deliberation – and that supermajority rules will likely decrease rather than increase responsiveness inasmuch as the threshold is more difficult to achieve, this interpretation of Rousseau is not quite correct, but that is a separate issue.

our judgments. Questioning the reasons why we might want to violate neutrality, and perhaps anonymity as well, will occupy the rest of the chapter and much of the remainder of the book.

Yet before we turn to these issues, it is important first to consider the ways the key risks of majority rule are conceptualized, and how these connect to the fundamental commitment to equal and independent judgment as presupposed and affirmed by majority rule. We will take up these risks at greater length in a moment, but we might characterize them broadly as the failure to take seriously the rights and interests of all members of society, especially the most vulnerable. By choosing supermajority rule, we hold that by requiring more votes to reach one outcome rather than another (typically the status quo), we attractively bias our judgments in favor of the minority's rights. This claim, however, is problematic for several reasons. First, it presupposes that status quo institutions protect minority interests, and that decisions enacted today will more likely run contrary to vulnerable interests than those rendered in the past. In this way, supermajority rule weighs the judgment of past generations of decision makers over that of the present, on the ground that the judgments of the former are likely to be superior to those of the latter. This may in certain instances be justifiable, but it requires serious investigation. Second, the call for supermajority rules to mitigate the risk of majority rule suggests that we reduce the likelihood of rendering a tyrannical decision by requiring greater numbers than a mere simple majority. To be sure, when a body is judging the question of whether a particular decision will benefit a minority, the minority itself may be more reliable than the majority. But if we believe this to be the case, then there is little reason for consulting the majority at all. Why not simply grant the affected minority the power to decide, instead of implementing a voting rule that enables any minority, whether vulnerable or powerful, to exercise a veto? Insofar as we are skeptical about the possibility or even the merits of consensual decision making, perhaps because we believe that distributive conflict is a pervasive feature of political life, a supermajority ought to be unnecessary. Recall that the move toward a counted vote constituted a repudiation of consensual, acclamatory decision making; it deliberately acknowledges disagreement. If the putative risk of majority rule is that of individual judgments motivated by narrow self-interest or partisanship, then the presence of a supermajority – of a very large number of self-interested or partisan verdicts – ought to be immaterial. If the goal is societal consensus in the sense of communal support, there is at minimum tension inherent in using an aggregative voting rule that prescribes a precise number of individual votes over a simple majority to identify it.

In the next section we will evaluate three strong arguments for supermajority rules: to stabilize institutions, to secure broad-based consensus for important changes, and to protect vulnerable minorities. As we shall see, the appeal to institutional stability emphasizes the epistemic weight of the framers and of past generations. The logic of broad-based consensus reflects democracy's persistent attraction, I shall suggest, to acclamatory mechanisms rather than strictly aggregative ones for fundamental decisions. Finally, the protection of the rights and interests of vulnerable minorities may indeed give us reason to bias our judgments, diverging from the formally egalitarian features of majoritarian decision making. We may reasonably permit violations of both anonymity and neutrality in circumstances when there are good reasons to think that certain decisions would be especially harmful to the interests of the least well-off. However, it is also the case that supermajority rules are a less secure route than another institutions to the protection of vulnerable minorities, and may have the unintended consequence of benefiting powerful groups. In sum, the risks associated with majority rule and its egalitarian features, while severe in certain contexts, are not appropriately mitigated through the use of supermajority rule.

Institutional Stability

One primary concern associated with the egalitarian features of majority rule is that outcomes of votes may be unstable. There are several reasons for this. First, majority rule readily permits cycling, that is, the circumstance in which a majority of voters prefer x to y, a majority prefers y to z, but a majority also prefers z to x. This kind of instability has sometimes been defended on the grounds that it signifies the presence of multiple potential coalitions, which may be highly beneficial to minority groups. If a defeated minority can readily form a new coalition and overturn an outcome – and if the members of a majority anticipate their capacity to do so – the winning coalition has an incentive both to refrain from abuse and to offer concessions to the minority (McGann 2006, 109). Although such flexibility in coalition formation under majority rule might facilitate log-rolling in legislatures, it is usually thought that the core "rules of the game" ought to be relatively less flexible. Supermajority rules, because they are less susceptible to cycling under certain conditions, tend to stabilize outcomes.[9]

Of course, supermajority rules do not only induce stability by reducing cycling. As just shown, supermajority rules violate neutrality: they bias toward a particular outcome, notably the status quo. This bias toward the status quo for constitutional matters is widely thought necessary because of the "security of expectations" such conservatism affords, and because once the "rules of the game" are protected, constitutionalism can enable the conditions for ordinary politics (Holmes 1995). Neutrality is not necessarily normatively attractive: if we had grounds to believe that our constitution contained provisions worth protecting, we might have good reason to want to stack the deck to preserve them. As Beitz (1989) and Gutmann (1980) have both suggested, if we thought that sacrificing formal equality between alternatives would enhance our chance of attaining substantive equality among citizens, we might want to use supermajority rules to secure rules constitutive of such equality.[10] There might also be

---

[9] Within a large literature, see Greenberg (1979); Caplin and Nalebuff (1988); Balasko and Crès (1997).

[10] I take this claim to be implicit in Amy Gutmann's argument that fair democratic procedures presuppose civil and political rights, basic welfare rights, and the difference principle (or some other egalitarian distributive principle), and that therefore, "If any procedure is permitted to alter just rights policies it would be akin to the amendment procedure in the United States Constitution, a procedure that protects rights against all but the *most* determined and widespread public disapproval" (Gutmann 1980, 177, italics in the original).

epistemic reasons in support of biasing in favor of fundamental norms by supermajority rule, as we shall discuss.

Before we take up these normative claims in depth, let us first briefly sketch the general circumstances under which we should expect supermajority rules to effectively stabilize institutions. The goal must be to raise the costs of altering the constitution, and so the veto threshold would have to be relatively difficult to attain given the distribution of preferences and interests in a society. Given a pluralistic society, placing the threshold high enough to inhibit change is easily – perhaps too easily – achievable. But choosing the threshold does entail a problem of *phronesis*, which we shall discuss in the next chapter. It is not a trivial task to assess where, precisely, the threshold should be set so as to make change difficult without inducing sclerosis with respect to the existing constellation of political interests; it is harder still to foresee where this threshold should be placed given fundamental changes to societal preferences. For now, however, let us bracket the problem of practical judgment over the choice of the threshold and turn to the question of how we might know that our institutions are worth stabilizing.

Note that this is a different question from the benefits associated with institutional stability more generally. Stability is attractive for many reasons, especially for constitutional laws and other fundamental rules. Stable institutions afford us the security of expectations: by regulating behavior and ensuring predictable consequences for violations, institutions can encourage investment and growth in a community, and provide the framework necessary for meaningful personal and political interactions. By protecting the institutions that "constitute" our political arrangements, we can enable ordinary political life – the creation of legislation, most fundamentally – without constantly renegotiating the "rules of the game" (Holmes 1995). Through entrenching rights against easy change, we improve the chances that membership in our society is marked by robust substantive equality of treatment. Although supermajority rules may not be required to achieve such ends (in the following chapters, I suggest alternative means by which they could be accomplished), all are laudable goals. Indeed, broadly speaking supermajority rule is an *effective* means of stabilizing institutions.

But how can we determine which norms are worth stabilizing? For any given political community, different institutional arrangements could ensure security of expectations and make ordinary political life possible – even the set of rights and their scope could vary. Each arrangement distributes the costs and benefits of political life somewhat differently, both on the first- and second-order level of institutional design. Political institutions, including rights, can mitigate or exacerbate inequalities, by determining who is a member of a political society (e.g., illegal immigrants or fetuses); by creating a particular property-rights scheme; by regulating the rights and obligations to serve in the military; by specifying who constitutes a family for medical, educational, and taxation purposes; and so forth. The second-order question – how stable do we want such a distribution to be – is the important one for us. In part, the answer should derive from our confidence in our first-order decisions. As we shall see, however, if our certainty about the normative attractiveness and distributive fairness of our first-order decisions should be circumscribed, we should wish to preserve a greater level of flexibility, regulated at the second-order level. In other words, our beliefs about the quality of our constitutional norms in particular ought to affect our judgments of the extent to which we should entrench them – whether we want a supermajority rule to protect them, and if so, where the threshold ought to be. So, again, the question remains: under what circumstances ought we to have sufficient confidence in the quality of our fundamental norms so as to want to entrench them by supermajority rules?

Consent-based arguments provide a set of answers to this question. In *Calculus of Consent*, Buchanan and Tullock famously argue that given unanimous agreement on a preexisting distribution of rights and property, only a unanimity rule governing future changes can guarantee Pareto-optimality (Buchanan and Tullock 1962, 3.7.20). However, when the decision-making costs of unanimity outweigh "those expected to exceed those that might be imposed on potentially damaged minorities, the individual confronted with constitutional choice may decide to allow collective action to proceed under some qualified majority rule" (Buchanan and Tullock 1962, 3.7.17). For Buchanan and Tullock, supermajority rules constitute a pragmatic, second-best alternative to the favored unanimity rule, the normatively ideal basis for constitutional choice.[11] Supermajority rule is superior to majority rule, in their words, because "[t]he distinction between the power of taking action and of blocking action proposed by others is an essential one; it represents the difference between the power *to impose external costs on others* and the power *to prevent external costs from being imposed*" (Buchanan and Tullock 1962, 3.17.23). Yet Buchanan and Tullock's assumption that the status quo (in which such public goods are not provided or the tax rate remains unaltered, for instance) does not itself generate substantial costs to the majority while securing benefits to the minority is unwarranted, as many have argued. As Brian Barry responded, the belief that the status quo would enjoy unanimous support is implausible, possible only where, as Wicksell noted, all concerned accepted as fair the initial distribution of income and property (Barry 1965, 313; Buchanan and Tullock 1962). The absence of action, if thwarted by unanimity rules, can affect members of a society as much as the activity of choosing. Given this "utility drift," in Douglas Rae's language, unless we assume that society is completely stagnant, *not* altering institutional arrangements may be more disruptive than deliberately engaging in change.[12]

A second set of arguments, rooted in the logic of hypothetical consent, also might justify institutional stability. If we believed that a constitution protects norms to which all could reasonably assent, there would be no reason to permit change, unless these rules could be formulated in a more felicitous way, or unless radical circumstantial change called the validity of the norms into

---

[11] See also McGann (2006).

[12] Rae (1975) offers a similar critique of the unanimity requirement in Buchanan and Tullock: there is no reason to presuppose ongoing support for the status quo, and so there is a substantial risk that unanimity will lead to disutility. See also Shapiro (2003, 16–19).

question. There are, however, two problems with securing such norms by procedural barriers such as supermajority rules. The first is that these norms ought to be stable without such impediments. Only an unreasonable society would seek to alter rules to make them incapable of commanding unanimous agreement. If hypothetical consent is a meaningful guide for actual political decision making, it ought to be self-sustaining. If consent is merely a heuristic, which actual political assemblies may or may not satisfy, the validity of such norms will be subject to challenge; the question remains alive as to whether the norms adequately approximate the ideal standard, and there is little reason to bias in their favor. The second problem is that if a norm ought to command unanimous assent, the number of votes in support of it should be irrelevant. Even if a supermajority voted to overturn it, such a change should be deemed illegitimate.

A third set of arguments takes the endurance of constitutional norms as evidence of their quality, and suggests that alteration is fraught with moral and epistemic risk. Such an argument could take different forms. One version is the seventeenth-century common lawyers' claim that the activity of being "fined and refined" through interpretation over time gave laws not merely customary force but rationality. Because our laws embody the knowledge of agents over time, their epistemic weight supersedes that of any transient majority. Only in the case of an overwhelming supermajority vote in favor of alteration should we accord the decision sufficient epistemic status to override the collective knowledge of generations. A second, related claim is that the laws' durability constitutes direct evidence of their quality: to paraphrase Rousseau, were "yesterday's laws" designed poorly, they surely would have been amended already, and so their wisdom ought to be assumed. A high procedural barrier to amendment, such as a strenuous supermajority threshold, may temper this claim, however: the more difficult it is to alter laws, the less easily we can infer their quality from citizens' failure to amend them. A final logic depends on a systematic distinction between the wisdom of the framers and that of contemporary citizens or legislators. If we believe that the framers were substantially wiser than we are, we might think that only when a supermajority of our weaker minds agree do we have epistemic warrant to warrant the decisions they rendered even by a bare majority.

More generally, the overarching logic of constitutionalism may rely on some account of epistemic disjuncture. In our society we rightly regard some norms as morally correct, and our aim in constitutionalism is to protect them: our framers or legislators got them "right" at some point, and by enshrining them we hedge against the risk that we as citizens or our legislatures will act wrongly. Even scholars generally skeptical of epistemic arguments – either on the grounds that democratic decisions emerge from distributive conflict or the interplay between power and interest, or because appeals to truth are coercive in a political context – often are not prepared to dispense with rights-based constitutionalism. Though even our most sacrosanct laws emerged from a political process, marked by arguments and bargaining as they took determinate shape, we cannot dismiss epistemic appeals simply because such norms were created like proverbial sausages. If we believe there are rights worth protecting, we must think these rights have both moral and epistemic validity; if we believe that racial discrimination is unjust, we must believe that it is true that racial discrimination is unjust.[13] However, our knowledge of the political process also means that we need not be committed to the view that a particular formulation of a constitutional provision prohibiting racial discrimination embodies truth or universal validity; we might think that the clause could be improved upon or respecified, without any necessary weakening of our commitments against racial discrimination. So constitutional revision would not necessarily entail the decision to permit racial discrimination. But it might, and this is without question the sort of moral and epistemic risk constitutionalists seek to mitigate.

Should we conclude that the epistemic weight of our commitments against racial discrimination, as embodied in a constitutional provision, means that only a supermajority should be

---

[13] See Estlund (2008) for a discussion of truth and politics along these lines.

strong enough to overturn it? Does a supermajority rule mitigate epistemic and moral risk, as compared to majority rule? It is surely the case that supermajority rules raise the cost of decision making, and correspondingly reduce the frequency of legislative and constitutional changes. Insofar as they preserve morally salutary norms, they do reduce the risk of harmful amendments. The necessary corollary, of course, is that insofar as constitutional rules, backed up by supermajoritarian amendment clauses, preserve bad norms, they also reduce the capacity to enact normatively attractive changes. They also limit the ability to revise the norms to make it clear in response to legislative or judicial decisions, for instance, that racial discrimination also entails discrimination on the basis of national origin.

Not all laws, not even all constitutional laws, have moral or epistemic value. As such, they do not carry the same degree of risk. It is true that even procedural rules that have no intrinsic validity can contour decision making in ways that are more or less responsive to high-quality information or careful deliberation. But some decisions essentially operate to coordinate us, and if we want to defend supermajority rules for these norms, we must do so either on non-epistemic grounds, or, at most, because we wish to affirm their instrumental value in structuring a political life marked by high-quality decision making. So is there a reason to ensure the stability of norms we do not regard as fundamental to a just society, that are essentially without epistemic or moral value?

We might think that the real value of constitutions is to coordinate our decision making. As Russell Hardin has argued, a coordinative account of constitution making emphasizes that the constitution is "backed by default, by the difficulty of recoordinating on an alternative arrangement": it is therefore self-enforcing (Hardin 1991, 1999, 88–89).[14] Because the relevant actors know that recoordination will be costly, however, there

---

[14] The *locus classicus* of the discussion of focal points is in Schelling (1960); see also Lewis (1969) for the analysis of the emergence and analytical significance of conventions.

is no reason to raise the costs further. By this logic, if there is a Pareto-superior alternative, it will – and should – be adopted. If there is not, then there is little risk that there will be unnecessary recoordination. However, even apparently neutral norms, norms that seem to have little epistemic or moral content, may have distributive consequences. For instance, age qualifications for office affect the generational character of members of legislatures. Insofar as the legislature makes decisions about intergenerational transfer programs or military action, such norms may generate, as Sanford Levinson has argued, a category of "second-class citizens" incapable of defending themselves directly against costs offloaded onto them (Levinson 2006, 145). The use of supermajority rule in this context biases in favor of a particular coordinative outcome, which at best merely serves to reduce future decision-making costs and at worst locks in inequalities.

From the perspective of institutional stability, the primary argument for supermajority rules is to mitigate epistemic and moral risk. Of course, as we saw in Chapter 4, Condorcet defended supermajority rules on these grounds. Further, we might note, this is why supermajority rules might be appropriate for juries, particularly to minimize the risk of a false conviction. Nonetheless, identifying those constitutional norms about which we ought to be especially concerned is not unproblematic. We shall take up this issue in the constitutional context in the next chapter. But if we believe that we citizens, or at least our constitutional framers, have a means of reliably identifying these norms, we might have good reason to mitigate the risk of their alteration.

Securing a Consensus

Another argument for supermajority rule is that majority rule enables purely partisan or bare majorities to enact sweeping changes. Neutrality between the status quo and an alternative, as majority rule prescribes, is inappropriate for important legislation. Key political decisions are thought to require support of a wide consensus of citizens or their representatives, and not merely from the dominant party or from one vote over half.

In other words, the mere product of a majority vote, rooted in the epistemic equality of the members, is inadequate. Because our constitutional norms and other important political institutions are assumed to reflect and embody the fundamental values of our community, a majority of votes is insufficient to overcome the epistemic weight of the longstanding commitments, rightly protected by the minority. Only when a change is broadly supported across the aisle can we have confidence that a proposed law adequately reflects the deep commitments of the society as a whole.

Although, as Binder and Smith (1997) have conclusively demonstrated, the filibuster has been used for narrowly partisan purposes since the nineteenth century, the desirability of broad-based consensus is a core argument offered for the preservation of the 60-vote supermajority rule for cloture in the U.S. Senate. Indeed, in 2010 Senate hearings on the filibuster, senators repeatedly invoked the importance of the rule's consensus-building function. In the words of Sen. Pat Roberts (R-KS), "The filibuster is the essence of the Senate. It is not a tool of obstructionism or dysfunction. It is meant to foster greater consultation, consensus, and cooperation between the parties."[15] In Sen. Lamar Alexander's (R-TN) words, "The whole idea of the Senate is not to have majority rule. It is to force consensus. It is to force there to be a group of senators on either side who have to respect one another's views so that they work together and produce 60 votes on important issues."[16] To be sure, defenders of the filibuster offer other justifications – the importance of protecting minority rights and of ensuring adequate opportunity for debate most salient among them – but the putative core commitment of filibuster supporters is to ensuring that key pieces of legislation and important nominees receive bipartisan support.

In a series of articles in defense of supermajority rules, legal scholars Michael Rappaport and John O. McGinnis argue in

---

[15] http://www.gpo.gov/fdsys/pkg/CHRG-111shrg62210/html/CHRG-111shrg62210.htm (accessed 12/28/12)
[16] ibid.

essence that the capacity to block narrowly supported legislation is perhaps the most important and attractive function of
supermajority rules. Rappaport and McGinnis analyze this
power through the concept of "marginal legislation" – legislation
that is capable of commanding majority, but not supermajority,
support. To quote:

The main difference between supermajority and majority voting rules
is that a majority rule will allow, but a supermajority rule will prevent, the passage of legislation that can secure only a mere majority.
We call such legislation 'marginal legislation.' A supermajority rule
will improve the quality of legislation only if the legislation prevented
by the supermajority rule – the marginal legislation – is undesirable.
Under what circumstances will the marginal legislation in an area be
undesirable? The most common situation in which marginal legislation
will be undesirable occurs when legislation that can secure a supermajority is desirable, but marginal legislation is not. (McGinnis and
Rappaport 2002)

This argument is tautological unless McGinnis and Rappaport
can offer substantive criteria for identifying "marginal legislation." But their main criterion is "capable of passage by a
supermajority," and so any piece of legislation not passed by a
supermajority, by definition, becomes marginal and undesirable.
McGinnis and Rappaport suggest that there are two "variables,"
or "key indicators," of whether legislation will be improved
under supermajority rule. The first is: "The worse the legislation
passed under majority rule, the more likely that the marginal
legislation will be undesirable." The second variable is "how
strong the filtering is" – that is "how much better are the laws
that can pass with a supermajority than the marginal legislation.
The stronger the filtering, the more likely it is that the marginal
legislation is undesirable" (McGinnis and Rappaport 2002). But
again these are not substantive criteria; they do not give us any
capacity to evaluate the quality of such legislation independent
of its passage or defeat.

The sole substantive criterion McGinnis and Rappaport do
provide is the role of special interests, which they believe wield
especially significant influence in spending bills. In logic similar

to that of Buchanan and Tullock, they hold that a supermajority rule will block federal spending supported by special interests, without blocking spending bills that serve the public interest more broadly. If we accepted this empirical claim that special interests dominate spending bills, and we believed that biasing legislators' judgment against new federal spending is thus morally warranted, we might find such an argument compelling. At a minimum, however, the claim that federal spending bills are so fraught with such risk as to warrant a systematic bias against them is likely to be contentious. Indeed, one might expect that it would generate partisan disagreement precisely of the sort that McGinnis and Rappaport believe the supermajority rule would help transcend.

If we imagine restricting supermajority rules to matters of unquestionable importance – the rights and institutional structures spelled out in the Constitution, for instance – the desire for consensus may seem more attractive. We might well want to ensure that transient majorities cannot alter the rules of the game – especially not partisan majorities, which might have an incentive to do so in a way that enables them to lock in electoral advantages. (It is worth noting that the general failure to incorporate electoral rules and boundaries in constitutions makes them subject to manipulation, and so if any element of the constitution ought to require supermajoritarian support for changes, it would be rules that partisan majorities have incentive to alter for their long-term benefit.) Regardless, there might be a good reason to think that something more than majority support should be required before the fundamental laws of society are altered.

We will speak more specifically about whether constitutionalism depends on supermajoritarian support in the next chapter. For now, let us consider more generally what consensus entails. It is important to distinguish between different uses of the word "consensus." One version of the term is aggregative, or, in Margaret Gilbert's language, "summative" (Gilbert 1987). A consensus belief of a group, in this form, is given by the beliefs or preferences of all or most of its members. To ascribe a consensus belief to the United States that "freedom of the press ought to be unlimited" would entail the claim that all or most of the citizens of the United States believe that "the freedom of the press ought to be unlimited." It might be the case that constitutional rules ought to be supported by consensus in this aggregative sense, perhaps because we would therefore have epistemic warrant for preserving them, perhaps because we think that only fundamental laws that have such support ought rightly to oblige us, or perhaps because we think that only those laws will be command sufficient agreement for them to structure ordinary political life. If we found this logic compelling, we might have good reason to use a supermajority rule. On the aggregative consensus model, if we assumed that constitutional provisions possess consensual support in the sense that most citizens believe that they are substantively just, only if all or most of the citizens changed their minds to believe that the provision should be altered would we have a reason to amend the constitution on the consensus model.

On the aggregative conception of consensus, the actual beliefs of the members of the group (in this case, the citizens of the United States) matter. If in fact many citizens did not believe in unlimited freedom of the press, we could no longer ascribe such a consensus belief to the United States. Naturally, the question of specifying "many" or "most" arises here; we would need to identify a sufficient threshold over which we can ascribe a consensus belief to the group. Even if we stipulate that the asymmetry is desirable for reasons of institutional stability discussed earlier, we might still have difficulty discerning the threshold above which we can claim to identify a consensus. A relatively high threshold carries a serious risk of type II error: a minority can veto a proposed change supported by a very wide margin of the population though not wide enough for consensus as given by the threshold. Specifying a benchmark for the attainment of consensus is one of *phronesis*, or practical judgment, and it is difficult to know *ex ante* what sort of divisions we would wish the threshold to be high enough to transcend. We shall return to these issues in the following chapters.

Further, if recent polls are accurate, only 60 percent of U.S. survey respondents believe that newspapers should freely criticize the U.S. military about its strategy and performance.[17] We might reasonably suggest that this is below what would constitute a "consensus view." So the aggregative version of consensus raises a set of issues for constitutionalism in particular, including the need to ensure that members over time continue believe in the merits of the laws, and the problem of determining what constitutes a sufficiently high proportion of members to ascribe the belief to the group as a whole.

Although we cannot presume that the constitutional status quo commands consensus in the aggregative sense, we might have reason to believe it reflects consensus in a different sense. On what I wish to term the "acclamatory" conception of consensus,[18] so as to emphasize the continuity with earlier such conceptions, to ascribe a belief or commitment to the group does not require that all or most members in fact hold that belief. All that really matters is that the members of the group – in our example, the citizens of the United States – are willing to let a belief stand as the group's view.[19] To simplify, let us return to the example of the First Amendment. Many citizens believe that newspapers ought not to be able to criticize military tactics during wartime. But they are willing to accept that the view of the United States is that Congress should not restrict the ability of newspapers to publish as they fit. As citizens of the United

[17] http://www.firstamendmentcenter.org/madison/wp-content/uploads/2011/03/ SOFA2007results.pdf (accessed March 21, 2013)

[18] Gilbert calls this the "nonsummative" or "joint acceptance" account (Gilbert 1987). Dworkin drew a similar distinction between statistical and communal collective action, suggesting that the former derived from the wishes or votes "of some function – a majority or plurality – of individual citizens" (Dworkin 1996, 20) whereas the latter would constitute action on the part of the people as a whole.

[19] Gilbert's rigorous formulation of this view is that:
  (i) A group G believes that p if and only if the members of G jointly accept that p.
  (ii) Members of a group G *jointly accept* that p if and only if it is common knowledge in G that the individual members of G have openly expressed a conditional commitment jointly to accept that p with the other members of G. (Gilbert 1987, 195)

States, they recognize that they are implicated in this view, even if as private individuals they disagree with it. They therefore believe that Congress would act wrongly were it to establish a law abridging the freedom of the press.

Supermajority rule is more difficult to defend on this "acclamatory" version of consensus, because the validity of the belief or the commitment is not strictly a function of the number of members who hold it. As we have seen, supermajority rule is in tension with the logic of the general will for the same reason: it seems to elide the difference between the "will of all" – the aggregative conception of voting – and the transcendent status of the general will. But this acclamatory consensus is likely the tacit understanding of the shared agreement we expect around constitutional provisions, rather than the view that either all or nearly all members of the society individually affirm the law. We might also think back to the Athenians, who wanted fundamental decisions, especially those requiring collective action, to emerge from the whole, rather than a clear proportion of the membership with an enumerated minority.

If the acclamatory model of consensus is normatively attractive, supermajority rules are inappropriate. As I have suggested, supermajority rules valorize, perhaps preeminently among decision rules, individual judgment: there is no non-aggregative form of supermajority rule, whereas both majority and unanimity rule can take acclamatory form. But we might still believe that there should be some way to ensure that narrow, partisan majorities cannot assume the mantle of the whole. Fortunately, deliberative democratic theory provides us with ways of conceptualizing consensus that can help bridge the gap between the strictly aggregative and acclamatory conceptions of consensus.

A famous strain of deliberative theory aims at consensus: agreement on one among a set of options optimally for the same reasons, rooted in the common good.[20] However, as has frequently been noted, the goal of deliberation need not be substantive consensus; instead, deliberation can simply clarify and structure

---

[20] Habermas, perhaps most famously, defends the view that "rationally motivated consensus" cannot be supported by different parties accepting the outcome for different reasons (Habermas 1996, 166).

conflict, followed by a majority vote (Mansbridge 2010, 64–65; Knight and Johnson 1994; 2011).[21] Yet one way of recapturing the value of deliberative consensus does not require substantive agreement. John Beatty and Alfred Moore characterize this as a variation on Gilbert's conception of joint acceptance, which they term "deliberative acceptance": "A group deliberatively accepts *p* if and only if the individual members, based on the quality of their deliberation, have openly agreed to let *p* stand as the position of the group" (Beatty and Moore 2010, 209). The advantage of this model, according to Beatty and Moore, is that the alternative was tested against a competing position, the minority felt its arguments had been heard and taken seriously, and "having been heard, even the minority agreed to let the position in question stand as the group's" (Beatty and Moore 2010, 209). This concept of "deliberative acceptance," we might think, would satisfy much of the animating desire for supermajority rules as a means of consensus: the concern that majorities could impose their will on fundamental community issues. Indeed, the most important means by which supermajority rules ensure consensus is through the deliberation they effectively mandate: the obligation to gain more votes will likely require greater efforts at persuasion and argumentation.

As I suggest in the next chapter, supermajority rules only indirectly ensure the sort of consensus we ought to care about in constitutional change – that laws reflect the shared commitments of the community as a whole – through mandating sustained deliberation. But supermajority rules are both unnecessary and

---

[21] This is not, however, Mansbridge's view of the way in which constitutional matters, in which "the members of the polity have arguably generalizable interests such as basic rights," should unfold; those, they hold, ideally should be deliberated to consensus. Where that is unachievable, there should be voting, "but that vote should be conceived deliberately as a temporary conclusion that establishes a political burden for future justification. The more an issue involves basic rights and fundamental justice, the less ought it to be decided by votes conceived simply as the exercise of power in a field of competing wills" (Mansbridge 2010, 89). Whether this is the way we ought to imagine deliberation in the constitutional context is something that will be explored in the next chapter.

insufficient to ensure that such consensus has been reached. They are insufficient, as we have suggested, because a minority can veto changes to a status quo that no longer commands such consensus. And they are unnecessary, because properly structured deliberation can encourage consensual decision making of the right sort, even if ultimately the constitutional amendment is determined by an institutionally complex form of majority rule.

Vulnerable Minorities

Supermajority rule enables a minority to exercise a veto over majority decisions. If the minority were especially vulnerable to abuse at the hands of the majority, this feature of supermajoritarian decision making might be extremely important. Of course, the formally egalitarian features of majority rule may operate in the presence of economic and other forms of substantive inequality. As defenders of minority rights have long held, formal equality lead us to overlook, or to reify, persistent distributive inequalities. Worse, under simple majority rule, access to the resources necessary to ensure the survival of indigenous or other cultural minority communities may be limited or even eliminated, as Will Kymlicka and many others have argued (Kymlicka 1989, 187).

Recall that one egalitarian feature of majority rule is its anonymity: the rule remains unbiased in favor of a particular group or opinion. As scholars of multiculturalism maintain, where there is a dominant ethnic or cultural majority, formal equality constitutes a bias toward this dominant group – majority rule is in effect not anonymous. Thus the "sacrifice" of anonymity under supermajority rule is no loss at all. Where a permanent majority and a permanent minority exist, a supermajority rule can give the minority an effective veto. (In this case, the key requirement will be to place the threshold *high* enough to ensure that the minority is capable of wielding the veto – if the demography changes, and the proportion of the minority drops, they may not be able to block majority decisions.) Nonetheless, the justification for supermajority rule is clear in this case., Because of scenarios like this, normative political theorists frequently advocate supermajority rules to protect the rights and interests of vulnerable minority groups against majoritarian threats.

Lani Guinier argues that supermajority rules can justifiably grant a minority a veto "to overcome the disproportionate power presently enjoyed by white voters in certain jurisdictions. In this sense, supermajority rules provide minorities with an equal opportunity to influence the political process and, consequently, comport with one person/one vote" (Guinier 1995, 117). For now, let us sidestep Guinier's claim that such a veto protects equality of influence over outcomes, and consider the identification of supermajority rules and a vulnerable-minority veto. Guinier cites approvingly the Reagan administration's support for supermajority rules as a means of enforcing the Voting Rights Act in places like Mobile, Alabama, in particular the "five-out-of-seven rule" for municipal decision making. In Mobile today, however, supermajority rules have a mixed reputation. In the words of two local officials in Mobile:

It's probably another case of the 'law of unintended consequences.' Things just never worked out just like you thought. I recall discussing it with Michael afterward. A white minority was able to use the super majority against a black/white majority. It's really been used a lot more by white minorities than blacks because blacks had to pick up white votes to do anything. Just one [vote] wouldn't do it. It just didn't work out that way [regular 4–3 votes along racial lines]. It came to be accepted and sometimes people were able to use it to their advantage. From both races I think, but I think whites have used it more. It's faded from the scene but every now and then it crops up. Something cropped up a year or so ago [an affordable housing dispute] and we almost went back to court.[22]

Now it is almost the opposite effect. Before it was intended to guarantee a level of black involvement in the process. Now it has evolved into a protective tool of some white council members. In recent times, Steve (redacted), Connie (redacted) and Ben (redacted) have used it more to their advantage than the other way.[23]

---

[22] Ann Bedsole, quoted by Chip Drago, at http://mobilebaytimes.com/supermajoritypa.html (accessed March 20, 2013)

[23] John Peavy, quoted by Chip Drago, at http://mobilebaytimes.com/supermajoritypa.html (accessed March 20, 2013)

A veto intended for a vulnerable minority but deployed by a powerful one is not an idiosyncratic feature of Mobile politics. Instead, it is a feature of the blunt character of supermajority rule: it is relatively insensitive to the identity of the minority. Paradoxically, to the extent that a supermajority rule is anonymous, any minority, or any coalition of minorities, can veto the outcome of majoritarian decision making. Guinier herself recognizes that supermajority rules are "race-neutral," responding to her critics that "supermajority remedies give bargaining power to all numerically inferior groups, be they black, female, or Republican" and are not merely a mechanism for ensuring the representation of racial minorities (Guinier 1995, 17). Kymlicka, too, has argued, "A veto power can promote justice if it helps protect a minority from unjust policies that favour the majority; but it is an obstacle to justice if it allows a privileged group the leverage to maintain its unjust advantages" (Kymlicka 1995, 110).

There might be circumstances under which legislators and constitutional framers would be at pains to protect the rights and interests of especially vulnerable minorities, such as indigenous populations, as they design electoral and other key institutional rules. Yet we rarely expect angelic behavior from political actors. Inasmuch as we believe that institutions arise as a result of strategic interactions among framers at constituent assemblies, or among the key members of legislatures, the outcome is unlikely to be biased deliberately against their interests. Even if we do not believe political elites are primarily motivated to protect their own economic interests in designing institutions, there is little reason to think that supermajority rules will emerge to protect disadvantaged minorities, unless they are sufficiently powerful to get a seat at the bargaining table during the design of constitutional or legislative institutions. In that case, their need for a veto might be questioned..

We need to ask two important questions before we can feel secure that a supermajority rule would effectively protect the "right" minorities. First, a partly empirical question: Are there ways of composing constituent assemblies to increase the probability that supermajority rules for constitutional change will protect vulnerable and not privileged minorities? Are there any cases in which supermajority rules were implemented specifically with redistributive or "special concern" aims, and were they consistently effective – or were they reappropriated to benefit other, more powerful groups? The second question, one of comparative institutional design, is whether a targeted minority veto would not be a more reliable means protecting truly vulnerable minorities without enabling powerful minorities to appropriate this veto. Such a veto might in most cases be normatively unattractive. But if the rights of a particular minority community were threatened in a given domain (land rights of an indigenous population, for instance), a targeted veto might be more effective and attractive than a supermajority rule. In the next chapter, we will seek to answer these questions.

Conclusion

As we have seen, the three key purposes for introducing supermajority rules – institutional stability, consensus, and minority protections – seek to mitigate some of the apparent weaknesses associated with the formally egalitarian properties of majority rule. But they also press at the presumption of epistemic equality, which has constituted an uneasy commitment for even red-blooded democrats. Supermajority rules suggest that our existing institutional choices, our existing conceptions of rights, put in place by our framers and refined across the centuries by legislatures and courts, ought to have presumptive weight over a simple majority decision rendered today. The wisdom of generations should be accorded greater value than the reason of a contemporary bare majority. Only in the presence of an overwhelming consensus – given by a very high number of individual voters under an aggregative conception – can the majority outweigh the bias toward the past. Finally, because we are confident in the value of our commitments to protect disadvantaged minorities, we want our decision making over time to reflect this concern.

Because constitutionalism may be understood as a project to mitigate moral and epistemic risk – a strong case for supermajority rules, as argued in Chapter 4 – there is a *prima facie* reason for thinking supermajority rules valuable in this context. Indeed, constitutionalism has the strongest normative case for the use of supermajority rules. However, while the aims of supermajoritarian decision making are attractive, especially within constitutions, supermajority rules are neither necessary nor sufficient to attain those aims. Their sufficiency, as we shall see, is contingent on the broader political circumstances in which they are deployed, and on how the particular threshold is chosen and operates. Their necessity depends on whether other institutions could accomplish these aims while raising fewer normative concerns, perhaps because they do not severely violate the egalitarianism fundamental to democratic decision making. Further, it might be the case that alternative institutions are better than supermajority rules at mitigating epistemic and moral risk. If we can demonstrate that even in the hard case of constitutionalism, supermajoritarian decision making raises serious normative concerns that complex majoritarian institutions do not, we will have a good reason to reconsider their use in other, less challenging contexts as well.

6

Constitutionalism without Supermajorities

Although supermajority rules originally emerged as an alternative to unanimity to address the risk of human fallibility, in the modern era, supermajority rules are typically used to remedy the risks associated with unfettered majority decision making. Drawing on the work of Condorcet, we have seen that the strongest justification for supermajority rules is to bias decision making to reduce the probability of serious moral or epistemic error. Condorcet developed two key arguments on behalf of supermajority rules. First, supermajority rules bias our decisions when consequence of acting wrongly is much greater than not acting at all; when one option (acquittal) is clearly preferable to an erroneous choice (false conviction), as in Condorcet's example of the jury; or perhaps when a rule is proposed that would generate inequality among the citizens. Second, because more individuals must be persuaded, supermajority rules prevent hasty decision making and ensure full consideration of reasons.

To mitigate such risks, of course, is a central goal of constitutionalism. One key aim of constitutionalism is to introduce a strong status quo bias into democratic decision making. This is, first, because stability is intrinsically desirable, as it affords the security of expectations. Second, a status quo bias enables ordinary political life, including legislation, to operate without constant renegotiation of the terms. An unstable framework hinders political and economic development, and potentially generates interminable conflict over the core structures of politics. But constitutionalism also seeks to reduce familiar normative risks: the threat of "tyranny of the majority," of violations of the rights of minorities in particular, of a partisan majority acting to alter the terms of the political arrangement to enhance its reelection prospects, and so on.

There is a deep and natural affinity between the strongest justifications for supermajority rule and for constitutionalism in democratic decision making. Further, the vast majority of contemporary constitutions feature supermajority rules for constitutional amendments. This empirical regularity and the compatibility in justificatory logics lead many constitutional scholars, not unreasonably, to believe that in fact constitutionalism depends on supermajority rule. If we believe that the greatest risk facing a constitutional democracy is instability, a supermajority rule is a distinctly effective means of protecting the status quo. If we have good reasons to be confident in the moral and epistemic superiority of the status quo against potential alternatives, a supermajority rule can bias decision making attractively in favor of existing norms.

But supermajority rules do have certain normative liabilities, as we have already seen. If democracy entails a commitment to the presumption of epistemic equality among its citizens, manifested institutionally in formally equal voting power, supermajority rule presses against such a principle. In violating neutrality, supermajority rules may in some circumstances protect the substantive equality of citizens, but may also protect norms that in fact reflect power disparities dating to the founding. Supermajority rules may also privilege certain minorities, and generate greater inequalities rather than rectifying disparities insofar as these minorities are powerful instead of vulnerable..

A committed constitutionalist may reply that the potential benefits of constitutionalism greatly outweigh risks associated with raising the costs of amendment. The constitutionalist maintains that supermajority rules are a necessary condition for constitutionalism *per se*. That is, only if constitutional amendments require a supermajority vote (of some body or bodies, or of the population as a whole) will they protect the constitution against easy change. Without supermajority rules, higher norms could not serve their constitutive purpose to create ordinary legislation, as statutes could easily contravene them. In other words, the hierarchy of norms would be unstable. Beyond destabilizing the system of government more generally, removing barriers to constitutional amendment would leave democracy itself insecure: the norms that structure democratic decision making, including fundamental rights of freedom of expression and participation, would be vulnerable to easy change by transient majorities.

The constitutionalist is surely right in saying democracy depends on a durable commitment to a set of norms and procedures. She is right that these norms need to be secured procedurally to ensure that a simple legislative act could not invalidate or override them. But she is mistaken that supermajority rules are the only way to reinforce these commitments. As I intend to show in this chapter, supermajority rules are unnecessary for constitutionalism. They are also less attractive than various alternatives under the broad rubric of "complex majoritarianism."

The argument in Chapter 6 proceeds in stages, drawing on some of the normative claims developed in the preceding chapter. First I examine some of the costs associated with the use of supermajority rules in the constitutional setting, particularly the arbitrary selection of the supermajority amendment threshold. This arbitrariness is problematic insofar as it secures distributive inequalities down the line, and then the conditions by which these inequalities might be remedied. Nonetheless, the constitutionalist might discount the issues of arbitrary selection if the benefits of constitutionalism could be realized only through supermajority rules. Second, I examine the work done by supermajority rules in helping accomplish the three core goals – institutional stability, consensus support, and minority protections – within constitutionalism. Third, I suggest that the effort to protect vulnerable minorities via supermajority rules – to grant such groups a veto – is likely to be ineffective and will, at worst, court the dominance of powerful minorities. Granting a targeted veto to a permanent minority that has historically and consistently suffered abuse at the hands of majorities over some issues is preferable to offering less reliable protection through supermajority rules. Finally, I conclude that supermajoritarian decision making, unlike constitutionalism more generally, is at its core compatible with democratic decision making.

Distinctive Liabilities of Supermajority Rule within Constitutionalism

Two core issues are of particular importance within the constitutional context. The first is threshold selection, and the risk associated with grounding durable distributive inequalities on arbitrary decisions. The second is the question of whether biasing our judgments in favor of especially important constitutional norms, notably rights provisions, can be reasonably justified. We shall take these up in turn.

Arbitrariness and Threshold Choice

The choice of a supermajority threshold is deceptively straightforward, even if, in practice, supermajority thresholds governing constitutional amendment vary. The passage of a constitutional amendment most often requires as an initial step[1] a two-thirds vote of the legislative body (found in many countries, including Albania, Argentina, Brazil, Finland, Germany, India, Japan, and Namibia), but thresholds vary, from three-fifths, as in France and Greece; to three-quarters, as in Bulgaria. In many constitutions (e.g., Lithuania and South Africa), supermajority thresholds vary depending on which provision is subject to amendment, and in many countries, the thresholds for proposal, passage, and/or ratification differ. These thresholds typically emerge in constituent assemblies after little deliberation. They may reflect strategic

---

[1] A ratification process typically follows an initial successful vote by the legislative body.

efforts at granting or denying a particular political faction veto power, but more often they appears to have been chosen essentially at random, guided, perhaps, by reference to other salient constitutional thresholds. The dominance of the two-thirds threshold may reflect the influence of the U.S. Constitution, for instance.

The variation in threshold choice reflects not merely the contingent behavior of constituent assemblies, but an intrinsic feature of supermajority rules: there is no determinate threshold recommendation between the 50%+2, and 100%−1, once the decision to use a supermajority rule has been made. Whereas defenses of majority and unanimity rule, even when they differ, give rise to clear threshold choices, justifications of supermajority rule do not generate a recommendation for a specific decision rule. Further, because no particular supermajority threshold can be rationally justified as superior to close alternatives, their selection is vulnerable either to pure "picking," in which we select an option though we are indifferent among the alternatives (Ullmann-Margalit and Morgenbesser 1977), or to bargaining. Although bargains are endemic to the constitution-making process, there are far-reaching consequences associated with bargaining over the threshold for constitutional change. If we assume that the outcome of the bargain will reflect power asymmetries (Knight 1992) in the constitutional convention, the relatively powerful will be able not only to shape the substantive content of the constitution, but also, through choosing a supermajoritarian amendment threshold, to control the conditions under which the bargain can be renegotiated.

Neither arbitrariness nor strategic behavior is intrinsically problematic as a basis for constitutional choice. However, the intersection among (1) arbitrariness or strategic behavior; (2) the importance of the decision, including from a distributive perspective; and (3) that the potential remedy for either unforeseen or unjust outcomes is given by (1) leads to concerns about the use of supermajority rules for constitutional amendment rules. The technically unjustifiable nature of specific thresholds means that those disadvantaged by supermajoritarian constitutional amendment rules can be given no rational or reasonable explanation for their defeat other than the *de facto* power of coordination on a threshold. Although the benefits of supermajoritarian amendment procedures in mitigating risk may outweigh the consequences associated with their *ex ante* indeterminacy, the arbitrariness of supermajority rules may have long-term implications for the legitimacy of the constitution, as we shall discuss.

Like all constitutional provisions, a supermajoritarian threshold for constitutional amendment is *ex ante* indeterminate. Even if there is a rough sense of what provisions would be necessary for a "downstream authority" to ratify the constitution (Elster 2000, 113–115), constitutional norms are only vague before the process of constitution making gives them shape. So this sort of indeterminacy is unproblematic. Likewise, "legal indeterminacy," in which the generality of laws leads to interpretive quandaries – a problem notably identified by Aristotle as consisting in "equity" (Aristotle 1992, V.10, 1137b12–35) and by H. L. A. Hart (1994, ch. 7) as derivable from the "open-textured" nature of language – is not a major issue confronting supermajority rules. The threshold, once specified, is relatively easy to interpret. Supermajoritarian thresholds for amendment give rise to a different type of indeterminacy, both because of the importance of amendment clauses in general[2] and because of the potential paradoxes of collective choice they generate. This indeterminacy takes three forms: (1) individual or party preferences over the threshold are themselves indeterminate, both intrinsically and because of uncertain technical beliefs; (2) potential arguments for supermajoritarian thresholds may support a range of thresholds, and thus the reasons for supermajority rule do not generate clear threshold recommendations; and (3) the collective choice over threshold may be indeterminate because of standard aggregation problems. Supermajoritarian thresholds cannot be supported by distinctive good reasons By definition, their selection

---

[2] The salience of amendment is highlighted in the essays contained in Levinson (1995).

must be arbitrary (or strategic, and thus likely morally if not politically arbitrary).[3]

First, why are individual or factional preferences over the threshold themselves indeterminate? Imagine a person who knows he wants a supermajority amendment threshold, say, to make institutional change difficult but not excessively so. He confronts a problem of practical judgment or *phronesis*: what supermajority rule will accomplish this aim? He wants to specify a sufficiently high threshold to slow down the rate of change. But he also needs to ensure that the threshold is not too high, thereby disabling the possibility of amendment. And he cannot know *ex ante*, unless he has a very clear map of the political landscape, what that threshold will be, and he surely does not know where that cutoff might be in the future. Part of the problem, then, is informational or epistemic. Even if he assumes there is some optimal threshold, he cannot know where precisely it lies.[4] Thus, to follow Herbert Simon's logic, he may just wish to satisfice (Simon 1957): if he thinks a two-thirds threshold will do, he may just want to adopt it (after all, he has ample evidence that other constitutions have endured with such a threshold). However, imagine he thinks that relatively easy amendment is desirable, but he wants to ensure that it does not become majoritarian, perhaps because he fears that shifting electoral majorities will revise the constitution to suit their political preferences. He thinks that ease of amendment reflects certain democratic values – innovation or

[3] In discussing the filibuster, Wawro and Schickler (2006) argue that the placement of a veto point – the cloture rule – helped reduce a different sort of uncertainty: the size of the coalition necessary to secure passage for legislation, which would be especially important near the end of a congress. There are of course other sorts of uncertainty reduced by *garnering* a supermajority compared to garnering a minimum winning coalition (the risk that there will be defections because of bribery or for other reasons), but such arguments are distinctive from the uncertainty reduced by implementing supermajority rules, because under a supermajoritarian threshold rule a minimum winning coalition will already entail supermajority support (and thus would require additional votes beyond the threshold). See Baron and Ferejohn (1989); Groseclose and Snyder (1996); Banks (2000); Groseclose and Snyder (2000).

[4] My thinking here was influenced by Richard Tuck's fascinating discussion of the Sorites paradox in his recent book, *Free Riding* (2008).

fallibility, for instance (Schwartzberg 2007) – and helps ward off the entrenchment of distributive advantages. The question, then, is to find the lowest threshold that will prevent strictly partisan efforts at amendment, for instance, but still slow down the rate of change. This strictly technical problem gives rise to indeterminacy: he does not know what threshold will enable him to attain the goal. Three-fifths might be preferable, but would 59 percent be optimal? Or 58 percent? Thus even individual-level preferences may be indeterminate, because individuals may be unable to order them within a range, and because they know their technical beliefs are imperfect. These questions become even thornier once the matter becomes one of collective rather than individual choice.

The second sort of indeterminacy derives from the inability to give theoretical support for particular thresholds. The lack of shared justifications for the adoption of constitutional provisions is not necessarily problematic. Cass Sunstein recently defended the utility of "incompletely theorized agreements," in which people "agree that a certain practice is constitutional or is not constitutional, even when the theories that underlie their judgment sharply diverge" (Sunstein 2001, 50). Yet whereas majority rule or unanimity rule may emerge as a "'focal point' around which diverse people can bracket their debates" (Sunstein 2001, 53), without theoretical support, supermajority rule cannot do so. Majority rule can easily emerge as a consensus threshold without shared theoretical foundations. One group may support majority rule on the grounds that it makes constitutional change relatively easy, enabling the constitution to keep pace with circumstantial change. Another group supports majority rule because, as a minority, it hopes to be able to gain power in the future and alter the terms of social cooperation for its own benefit. A third supports majority rule because it believes that this is the one rule that ensures that each vote counts equally. That all members have different reasons – good or bad, self-interested or concerned for the common good – for preferring majority rule matters not. The decision is sufficient to coordinate them regardless of their various rationales. A single decision resolves the matter: the choice of threshold is *contained* in the vote for majority rule, because in choosing majority rule they know that the threshold will be 50 percent plus 1.

The same logic governs unanimity rule. Again, the relevant groups have different reasons for preferring it. One subscribes to the medieval rule of *quod omnes tangit ab omnibus approbari debet* (what touches all ought to be approved by all) (Burns 1988, 449; Post 1964): everyone affected by a matter as consequential as constitutional change ought to have the right of consent. Another believes strongly that a high level of institutional conservatism ensures the "security of expectations" necessary for economic growth, and so forth. Again, the vote for unanimity rule implies a 100 percent vote threshold; the choice of unanimity is determinate.

In the case of both majority rule and unanimity, the absence of agreement about the theoretical basis for the threshold does not lead to difficulties. Consider now, however, the adoption of a supermajoritarian threshold. As in the case of majority rule and unanimity, each faction has a different reason for supporting supermajority rule. One group wants to ensure that constitutional change is difficult but not insurmountably so. It argues that a three-fourths threshold would be necessary to induce institutional stability, because its members believe that lower thresholds do not signal a sufficient public commitment to conservatism. A second group thinks that institutional changes ought to be supported by a broad consensus, though not necessarily everyone, given the risk of individual fallibility or self-interest. This group believes two-thirds would suffice to ensure a degree of bipartisan support for amendments, but that three-fourths constitutes insurmountable entrenchment. A third group wants to protect the interests of an indigenous population, amounting to approximately 20 percent of the population, and thus advocates an 85-percent threshold for constitutional amendments. Each justification gives rise to a different view of the optimal supermajoritarian threshold. So reaching an untheorized agreement over the supermajority threshold is more problematic than it might seem.

Given preferences over different thresholds, the third form of indeterminacy is an obvious consequence. If we confront disagreement – which we surely will – about the choice of a threshold, aggregating preferences over the threshold may lead to familiar problems, including cycling, especially if these preferences are not single-peaked. Combining the epistemic indeterminacy of the appropriate threshold with the Condorcet paradox may mean that, as a practical matter, it may be impossible to generate rational agreement on a threshold. In that case, the threshold would be chosen essentially at random: once bargaining fatigue sets in, the group would accept whatever constituted the last proposal, facing no apparent opposition.

Indeed, this was the mechanism by which the supermajority threshold in the U.S. Constitution was chosen. The lack of reasons supporting the supermajoritarian amendment threshold – at least in the Federal Convention, if not in the ratification debates – highlights this point. The inclusion of an amendment procedure itself was justified on the grounds of three varieties of fallibilism – epistemological (the likelihood of human error); circumstantial (the limitations of human foresight); and progressive (the possibility of advancement in human knowledge) (Schwartzberg 2007, 117–128). But the threshold by which amendment was to occur received very little discussion. Although the framers disagreed about the relative role of the national and state legislatures, contention did not extend to the threshold, which was not even an object of discussion once proposed by the Committee of Detail. At the Convention, Elbridge Gerry raised the lone concern that two-thirds of the states would call a convention that would have a majority voting rule, and as a consequences the states received a role in the ratification of amendments (Farrand 1966, II, 557–558). James Wilson moved to revise the initial phrasing –"no amendments shall be binding until consented to by the several States" – to insert "two-thirds of" before "several States," but this was voted down five to six. Wilson then inserted "three fourths of," which was agreed to *nem. con.* (Farrand 1966, II, 558–559). Given that the framers approved nine as the ratification threshold some ten days prior, it is surprising that they voted down the two-thirds amendment threshold while approving without opposition the three-quarters threshold. Following Madison's critique of the proposed ten-state ratification threshold, this threshold would have empowered the small states to veto further changes. So it is possible that the nine-state outcome constituted a strategic concession to the small states, but there is no record of argument or bargaining.

In the case of the U.S. Constitution's supermajority rule governing constitutional amendments, we lack evidence either of reason giving or of sustained negotiations. Further, it is not clear that a supermajority rule constituted the only option. Given the failure of the Articles of Confederation, a unanimity rule would have been impossible, but – except for the concerns of the slave states, which might have been addressed through the sunset-clause entrenchment of the slave trade through 1808 (Schwartzberg 2007, 129–139) – there is no evidence that majority rule was off the table. Madison in *Federalist* 43 offered the clearest defense of the supermajority rule, and even that is equivocal and generic: "The mode preferred by the Convention ... guards equally against that extreme facility, which would render the Constitution too mutable; and that extreme difficulty, which might perpetuate its discovered faults" (Rossiter 1961, 43, 278). Indeed, in commenting upon Articles of Confederation, Hamilton provided the basis for opposition to supermajority rules:

The necessity of unanimity in public bodies, or of something approaching towards it, has been founded upon a supposition that it would contribute to security. But its real operation is to embarrass the administration, to destroy the energy of the government, and to substitute the pleasure, caprice, or artifices of an insignificant, turbulent, or corrupt junto, to the regular deliberations and decisions of a respectable majority. ... If a pertinacious minority can control the opinion of a majority, respecting the best mode of conducting it, the majority, in order that something may be done, must conform to the views of the minority; and thus the sense of the smaller number will overrule that of the greater, and give a tone to the national proceedings. (*Federalist*, 1961 #79, 22, 147–148)

One might accept that supermajority rule was not the necessary outcome of the debate, concurring that it is both undertheorized and even arbitrarily chosen. Nonetheless, given the social fact of agreement over the threshold at this point, one might reasonably ask whether arbitrariness ought to remain a serious normative concern. In cases in which the distributive implications of a choice are relatively mild, or an improvement would be risky or at best very minor, such arguments may be compelling. But when the threshold itself has generated or exacerbated distributive inequalities, or injustices, the argument that it is adequate to coordinate us is insufficient.

Again, arbitrariness in political decision making, even in the constitution-making context, is not necessarily problematic.[5] When numerical decisions need to be made – for instance, the total number of representatives or constitutional court justices, or the days that must pass between proposing a piece of legislation and a vote – the choice will almost certainly be made, in essence, at random. However, although in many cases "picking" may be inconsequential, the matter is much more serious with respect to amendment procedures, because the threshold could entrench systematic distributive inequalities, capable of being remedied only through the pathological threshold (or constitutional revolution).[6] When arbitrariness intersects with highly salient inequalities and, most critically, with the self-corrective nature of the norm – as in amendment thresholds – the problem is especially grave. The ability to revisit the decision to rectify inequalities or unforeseen consequences (the latter is especially important when decisions are made essentially at random) is itself constrained by the choice of threshold. In other words, arbitrariness in terms of the amendment threshold is problematic insofar as the amendment clause is the means of redressing

---

[5] I am grateful to Jeffrey Lenowitz for pressing this point with me.
[6] It is also possible that the apparent randomness or triviality of the matter could enable proponents to "smuggle in" strategic advantages, although evidence of this behavior is slim.

distributive inequalities *it itself generates*. The amendment clause secures the constitutional bargain and its distribution of advantages and burdens across the society. To the extent that these distributions can be revisited or inequalities remedied, such efforts require the use of the amendment clause itself, and insofar as its threshold has no rational or reasonable basis, those who lose under its strictures may rightly perceive it as unjust.

Although supermajority rule does not necessarily disadvantage particular groups, each decision it governs prescribes unequal voting power. The bias toward the minority – the lower number of votes necessary to veto the majority decision – means that each vote in the minority counts for more than each vote in the majority. The problem may be especially egregious if the existing bargain, and thus the status quo distribution of political power, is relatively unequal. Those who confront the long-term limitation of their potential to redistribute the gains of the constitutional bargain because of mandated institutional stability are perhaps especially inclined to challenge the legitimacy of the constitution. Recall that this was the plight of the ERA proponent, the first example in the Introduction.

These concerns about arbitrariness and distributive inequalities give us one reason to resist the use of supermajority rules for constitutional amendment. Avoiding the normative pitfalls associated with the choice of supermajority thresholds is nearly impossible, because they derive from intrinsic features of supermajority rules. The best that could be hoped for, it seems, is a threshold that does not *deliberately* seek to lock in distributive inequalities, and one sufficiently low to be revisable if the unintended consequences of the threshold prove unacceptable. If a weak bias, such as that prescribed by Condorcet, were introduced as a means of protecting norms that we might reasonably believe possess epistemic and moral value, we might well believe that this benefit of supermajority rules would outweigh the concerns about arbitrariness. But, as we discussed in the previous chapter, identifying those norms that deserve special protection is problematic.

Biasing Our Judgment in Favor of Constitutional Norms

Because liberal democrats typically agree on a core set of rights, it may seem implausible that we do not have warrant to bias our judgment in favor of these norms. Yet the assumption that a particular constituent assembly has framed these norms in a way that merits protection is also difficult to justify. There is no pure moment of constitutional design: constituent assemblies are as marked by moral, intellectual, and ideological disagreement as any other political body. Framers are as sensitive as any legislators to the effects of decisions on their, and their parties', status. There is no reason to build our political arrangements around the assumption that framers' behavior will be distinctly different from that of ordinary legislators, especially because, like legislators, framers typically have future political or legal careers to consider. They will be motivated by both self- and institutional interests, and even if they may well transcend such interests during the constitution-making process, there is no reason to believe they will do so systematically, or more reliably than do legislators. The absence of an electoral incentive and insulation from popular pressures, for instance, may make them more likely to shirk, rather than enabling them to act on the basis of pure reason.

If we accept these claims, then the products of constituent assemblies ought to possess no *prima facie* moral or epistemic weight that would warrant bias in their favor. There are good reasons to use constitutionalism as a means to coordinate our behavior and structure the terms of ongoing political life. And these norms ought to be somewhat more difficult to change than ordinary legislation because they help us organize our lives in common. But these capacities afforded by constitutionalism need not hinge on our view that they possess moral or epistemic superiority. Again, to make this judgment would require a different sort of evaluation; for one, we could assess from an abstract perspective whether these are norms to which all reasonable people could agree. As we discussed in the previous chapter, if reasonable acceptability is the standard, the margin by which the community in fact approves the constitution or proposed changes to such is moot; the constitution either meets or fails the standard. Indeed, in principle, a constitution could meet the acceptability standard and be rejected by a majority of its members, and from a strictly moral standpoint, it ought still to be adopted.

The second mechanism by which we could assess the merits of the constitutional norms is through popular ratification. Ratification would itself constitute a test of the quality of the constitutional norms; their legitimacy would not merely derive from the fact that a popular mechanism produced them but from selection by a procedure that is likely to select meritorious norms. If the vote followed deliberation, we might be willing to accept that the outcome had a claim to such validity; the norms adopted had the force of the better argument behind them. But only if we are prepared to accept some version of the "wisdom of crowds," such as the Condorcet Jury Theorem, should we believe that the outcome of a ratifying vote itself provides evidence of the epistemic or moral quality of the norms. Even if we believe ratification may serve as such a test of norms' value, we would have to believe that today's citizens are less reliable than past generations: hence we need to bias our decision making against contemporary citizens. Unless we believe that the arc of our political universe bends toward injustice – and the expansion of civil and political rights to racial minorities, women, and gays and lesbians, suggests this is not the case – it is hard to imagine why we would want to ascribe greater risk to citizen actions today than in the distant past.

This is not to claim that "tried and true" institutions, or those that seem to accord with our most fundamental commitments as citizens or moral agents – the equality of persons, for instance – necessarily carry same degree of risk as novel institutional choices. But presupposing the superiority of constitutional norms that reflect these institutional or moral commitments through explicitly weighting votes in their favor is difficult to defend from the standpoint of real political action. It is hard to explain why rules proposed by contemporary citizens should not be presumed equally valuable to those made by citizens at earlier times, especially given historical improvements on certain key dimensions of social justice. We should ensure that proposed constitutional changes are subject to a sustained and serious process of public argumentation and reason-giving. However, we need not presume that the existing structure of political institutions possesses special epistemic and moral value.

Fundamental constitutional rights might merit such a presumption. Insofar as basic rights – including freedom of expression and of assembly, the rights to vote and stand for office, freedom of religion and conscience, and freedom from arbitrary search and seizure – are themselves constitutive of high-quality judgments, it may be worth biasing our judgment against their alteration. It should be noted, however, that the formulation of these rights may be imperfect, and as such ought to be treated as fallible and subject to revision (Schwartzberg 2007). Moreover, once interpreted by judges, citizens may wish to reformulate constitutional rights to clarify, for instance, that the equal protection clause prohibits discrimination with respect to marriage on the basis of sexual orientation. Given the general normative deficiencies associated with supermajoritarian thresholds, the complex majoritarian mechanism sketched in Chapter 7 might be preferable even for the protection of fundamental rights.

Regardless, we may reasonably believe that there are good reasons, apart from the putative moral or epistemic value of these norms, to make constitutions more difficult to change than ordinary legislation; risks associated with constitutional instability are separable from the question of the merits of the norms themselves. The question now is whether supermajority rules are the sole or the best means of ensuring such stability.

Does Constitutional Stability Require Supermajorities?

Informed by Hans Kelsen, perhaps, the constitutionalist is committed to the importance of the hierarchy of norms for constitutionalism, and seeks evidence that the hierarchy of norms does not depend on a supermajority rule for the amendment of higher laws. Not even Kelsen regarded supermajorities as indispensible for constitutionalism. Constitutional rules require a procedure for amendment "different from and more difficult than" that for statutes, but the distinction need not be marked by supermajority rules. The key, in Kelsen's view, was the "presupposition that the ordinary statute does not have the power to abolish or amend a statute having the character of a constitution because it determines the ordinary statute's creation and content; that this statute can be abolished or amended only under more rigorous conditions, such as *qualified majority, increased quorum, and the like*" (Kelsen 1989, 224, italics mine). In other words, alternative mechanisms could perform the work of distinguishing between higher and ordinary laws; it must only be more difficult to alter the former than the latter. This condition, I hope to show, is achievable even if the vote threshold is identical, and generates fewer normative concerns.

Recall that a supermajority rule's ability to render constitutions less flexible by slowing the rate of change is contingent upon the presence of partisan or ideological divisions among the relevant political actors or the populace. If the size of the partisan majority mirrors the vote threshold in the relevant institutions, supermajority rules will be insufficient to render constitutions inflexible. This may seem an obvious point, but it has theoretical significance: supermajority rules presuppose the presence of a heterogeneous decision body, but they are at best ineffective and at worst dangerous when used by a homogeneous society. In his critique of the Weimar Constitution, and of liberal constitutionalism more generally, Carl Schmitt targeted this very vulnerability of the use of supermajority rules to achieve "qualified alterability," or relative inflexibility: "security and stability self-evidently erode when a party or party coalition has the necessary majorities at its disposal and somehow is in the position to satisfy the qualified prerequisites" (Schmitt 2008, 72–73). This was one reason why, for Schmitt, supermajority rules could not adequately entrench constitutional rules, including those protecting minorities.[7]

The constitutionalist may retort that the benefits associated with the stability of outcomes outweigh the potential costs of imperfect but entrenched institutions. Further, she may hold that no institutional arrangement can guarantee such protections. Even "absolutely entrenched" constitutional rules, norms that are formally excluded from amendment by the constitution, can be altered if the amendment clause itself is not entrenched, or if there is sufficient political will to revise the constitution as a whole (Schwartzberg 2007). Supermajority rules do raise the costs of altering the status quo, and effectively stabilize constitutional norms. Yet other mechanisms can secure higher norms without generating the risk that powerful minorities will be able in the long term to block efforts at redistribution.

There are, broadly speaking, two different mechanisms by which a constitution could remain relatively stable without the use of supermajority rules. The first is through the use of constitutional "conventions," a set of informal norms and practices that structure and limit legislative sovereignty. The second is through the presence of institutional powers capable of checking or delaying legislation that might contravene higher law. Although we will primarily focus on the second, the first mechanism deserves comment. The *locus classicus* for the concept of constitutional conventions is Dicey. Dicey certainly did not

[7] Of course, for Schmitt, the real concern was the relativism and instability – the "value neutrality" – of the Weimar Constitution and liberal constitutions more generally. This problem arose in his criticism of the identification of constitutional norms as those that were formally included in the constitution and therefore subject to the "qualified alterability" provisions, rather than by reference to their substantive characteristics. This manifested itself in the "partisan tactics" (Schmitt 2008, 73) used by those who wanted to protect particular provisions from legislative alteration, such as the training of adult education teachers, the importance of religious education in school, and the security of the personal papers of civil servants. (Schmitt 2008, 73; see also Schmitt 2004, 39–40) In fact, for Schmitt, "the introduction of norms that are more difficult to change contains a direct invitation to exploit such premiums and to extend inappropriately the duration of the current majority's hold on power." (Schmitt 2004, 39–40)

believe that England had a hierarchical legal structure ("with us there is no such thing as a supreme law, or law which tests the validity of other laws"); nonetheless, he identified "fundamental or constitutional" laws that "deal with important principles (as, for instance, the descent of the crown or the terms of union with Scotland)". Because such norms were subject to the will of the legislative power, they were not truly "supreme," but Dicey did assert that "the one fundamental dogma of English constitutional law is the absolute legislative sovereignty or despotism of the King in Parliament" (Dicey 1982, 79). Dicey conceptualized constitutional conventions as those constitutional rules that do not have "the coercive power of the Courts" but are nonetheless obligatory (Dicey 1982, 293). Dicey argued that the "obligatory force of constitutional morality is derived from the law itself" (Dicey 1982, 300). Parliamentary sovereignty gives form to the constitution, but the principle of the "rule of law" – that is, the Courts' power to sanction violations – gives it its substance: violations of constitutional conventions necessarily generate legal violations, and these in turn secure the conventions. Hierarchy is maintained from the bottom up. The possibility of punishment for ordinary legal violations provides the anchor for the constitutional conventions, though violations of the latter are not justiciable.

Constitutional conventions, more generally, help explain how a constitution can be self-enforcing. One fundamental question of constitutionalism is why powerful actors with an incentive to "defect" – to try to secure a better bargain for themselves through renegotiating the terms of the constitutional settlement – may nonetheless abide by the constitution. Without an external agent capable of sanctioning violators (as would be necessary to solve a prisoners' dilemma), the constitution has to be self-sustaining. As discussed in Chapter 5, Russell Hardin argues that a constitution must describe, rather than generate, equilibrium. On Hardin's account, the costs of recoordination and the attendant risks of instability vastly outweigh whatever benefits could be accrued by a relevant actor by reneging, stabilizing the constitution. In Hardin's words, "Because it is not a contract but a convention, a constitution does not depend for its enforcement on external sanctions or bootstrapping commitments found in nothing but supposed or hypothetical agreement. Establishing a constitution is a massive act of coordination that creates a convention that depends for its maintenance on its self-generating incentives and expectations" (Hardin 1999, 140). To be sure, the costs of recoordination may be made exorbitant through the use of procedural barriers such as supermajority rules. But these blocks are neither necessary nor sufficient to protect the hierarchy of norms. The work of *preserving* the distinction must be done through non-procedural, self-enforcing means. When actors know that potential violations will be met with resistance and the costs associated with the risk of constitutional collapse outweigh whatever benefits they could gain from acting against the constitution, they will behave accordingly.[8]

So it is possible that at least some of the work of constitutionalism is done through coordination upon conventions rather than through constraint, through the costs of renegotiation rather than through the difficulty of unbinding. Yet the constitutionalist may press the point, holding that supermajority rules themselves do more work in shaping incentives than a purely conventional account suggests. She may argue, for instance, that coordination on a supermajority rule itself is crucially important for individual actors to believe that abiding by the constitution is in their interest, because doing so further raises the costs of recoordination for all agents. If we were to suspect that the constitutionalist was right on this count, then we might also believe that supermajority rules are indispensible simply to define the set of norms on which we coordinate.

Procedural mechanisms constitute the other means by which we can make constitutions more stable than ordinary legislation. Yet while some form of procedural constraints may well be necessary to secure the constitutional order, these constraints need not take the form of a supermajority rule. In evaluating institutional

---

[8] See the literature on "self-enforcing" constitutions, including Ordeshook (1992) and Weingast (2005).

alternatives to supermajority rules to ensure constitutional stability, there are two important questions to ask: Which will induce the desired level of constitutional stability, given the problems of *phronesis*, and which among these options will prove more normatively attractive than supermajority rules?

I take up the latter question in the next chapter, but here let us briefly canvass the empirical evidence concerning rates of constitutional change. The best that can be said is that is the evidence is ambiguous. Even an apparently obvious assertion, that the rigidity of the mechanism of constitutional change affects the rate of amendment, has not been conclusively demonstrated; the more complicated question, of whether moderate or lower rates of amendment improves constitutional durability overall, is especially contentious. The most salient recent work on the subject, however, is unequivocal on the advantages of relatively flexible constitutions, holding that "constitutions endure when they are most like ordinary statutes. Conventional wisdom postulates that constitutions are entrenched, whereas statutes are flexible; constitutions are general, whereas statutes are specific; and constitutional politics exist on a rarified plane in which interest groups will have less influence" (Elkins, Ginsburg, and Melton 2009, 89).

Donald Lutz (1994) sought to demonstrate through the construction of a difficulty index that the rigidity of a constitution reduced the rate of change; John Ferejohn (1997) disaggregated the data, showing that the primary cross-national determinant of amendment rates was legislative complexity, measured in terms of either "special majorities" or separate majorities in different legislative sessions (or bicameralism). Neither referendums nor ratification procedures affected amendment rates. However, examining the data within the U.S. states, Ferejohn also noted that the use of special or sequential majorities did not in fact reduce the amendment rate. In a cross-national study of nineteen Organization for Economic Co-operation and Development (OECD) countries, Rasch and Congleton (2006) also reanalyze Lutz and demonstrate that supermajority rules have no significant effect on amendment rates, although the requirement of multiple bodies for ratification, and especially the use of referendum, does have such an effect. Rasch (2011) suggests that constitutional stability is greatly enhanced by a mechanism that entails multiple decisions with a role for voters (either through intervening elections or a referendum). In fact, constitutions that rely exclusively on a supermajority vote of a legislature are more flexible than those relying on majority voting within the legislature and a referendum or ratification procedure. Countries that do not require a supermajority for amendment include Denmark (parliamentary majority and a majority decision of a referendum that has received the support of 40 percent of the electorate, plus a royal assent); Sweden (with two majority votes of parliament separated by an election, and a referendum with a quorum requirement of more than half of those who voted in the election); Iceland (with two majority votes of parliament separated by an election and a referendum if the status of the Church is altered); Australia (with the involvement of "each State and Territory"); Ireland (with a referendum); and Switzerland (via referendum, with the Federal Parliament's power to declare a proposal invalid according to unity of form/subject matter or international law, or to contrast it with a counterproposal). The least flexible are those that depend on qualified majorities of the legislature (especially in both houses of a bicameral legislature), followed by a supermajority vote of a different body for referendum or ratification, as the United States requires.

It would be wrong to conclude that supermajority rules alone in fact do the fundamental work of stabilizing the constitution. Yet since a unitary model with a simple majority vote of the legislature – as in New Zealand, although even there a referendum is customary – is likely to result in an undesirable degree of flexibility, it is important to consider whether the use of multiple actors might be more attractive. The logic of this alternative is developed in the next chapter. First, however, it is important to ascertain whether supermajority rules can reliably achieve their other ends – of securing consensus support for constitutional amendments and protecting vulnerable minorities. If so, there might still be good reason to support them.

Consensus Support for Constitutional Amendments

It is thought that in the absence of supermajority decision rules for amendment, a narrow and partisan majority could push through amendments that would not reflect the felt needs of the community taken as a whole. The argument runs as follows. Because a bare majority cannot pass amendments, those seeking constitutional change must garner support from other constituencies, and this activity is consensus-promoting. In most cases, the obligation to "cross the aisle" and secure minority party or parties' support will make a proposed amendment more likely to reflect the preferences of a broad constituency.[9] Throughout this work, however, I have challenged the use of an aggregative mechanism to capture consensus. If our aim is to ensure that our rules are compatible with deep and sustained commitments transcending the mere preferences of contemporary citizens – that is, to ensure something like a Rousseauian general will – it is not at all obvious why a particular number of votes over a bare majority should be required. If the citizens or their agents are incapable of moving beyond partisan preferences in enacting constitutional change, the hope of consensus is lost; if they are capable of doing so, however, then the presence of some number of individual judgments above a majority ought to be irrelevant. Likewise, if consensus is reduced to the aggregation of preferences, there is little reason to privilege the vote of the minority over that of the majority. The goal is to design institutions that

---

[9] It is perhaps unnecessary to point out that holds only in cases in which the society is divided in ways that are not mirrored by the supermajority threshold. For instance, if a party commands two-thirds support, sufficient to pass constitutional amendments without requiring the support of the minority party, it is difficult to understand the product of that decision-making process as consensual. Further, the question of the relevant agents again emerges in this context. In federal structures, the supermajority rule frequently targets a consensus of the states rather than of the citizens as a whole. Of course, however, when population is unevenly distributed, an amendment may pass by a supermajority of the states but a minority of the population as a whole, or receive the vast support of the population as a whole but be blocked by states possessing a small fraction of the country's population. This is a familiar objection, but one raised most forcefully and consistently in the important work of Sanford Levinson.

will prevent narrow, partisan majorities, or passionate popular majorities, from enacting fundamental changes to the organization of political life. As Chapter 5 suggested, deliberative institutions hold the greatest promise for our ability to attain any sort of meaningful public consensus on constitutional change.

Scholars of the U.S. Constitution divide on the question of whether consensus around constitutional provisions exists – or existed historically – and, if so, what mechanism might be optimal for identifying such consensus. These scholars ask whether the Supreme Court interprets the Constitution in a fashion that reflects the consensus opinion of the American public. For my purposes, the key issues are how to understand consensus; whether we have good reason to believe there is consensus around constitutional provisions; and then whether a supermajority vote would be necessary to attain it. As Justin Driver has suggested, scholars who seek to explain judicial behavior in terms of the judges' aims to realize "consensus constitutionalism" tend to take public opinion, given by the Gallup Poll, as evidence of the existence of consensus. Alternatively, they may cite the judgments of "We the People," invoking the argument that the Court acts in response to an "emerging consensus" or to a putative consensus that has been created through a feedback loop of judicial responsiveness and public opinion. Transient popular support for a proposal, or support beginning to consolidate for a particular interpretation or potential amendment would presumably fail to justify constitutional change on a consensus model. Instead, if we were committed to the view that constitutional amendments ought to reflect the consensus of the American people, we would want to ground constitutional amendment on the sustained, reflective judgment of the citizens over time.

Yet it is unclear whether Americans have ever reached consensus on fundamental constitutional issues. Since the founding, "Americans have held competing and contradictory conceptions of what the Constitution permits and what the Constitution requires" (Driver 2011, 777). Indeed, as Louis Jaffe once claimed, "How does one isolate and discover a consensus on a question so abstruse as the existence of a fundamental right? The public may value a right and yet not believe it to be fundamental" (Jaffe 1967, 986; cited in Driver 2011, 778). Consensus is at best transient, and perhaps chimerical: more often, citizens deeply disagree about constitutional meaning, although the possibility of "incompletely theorized agreements," in Cass Sunstein's (2001) words, enables constitutions to bind us even in the absence of consensus. Historically, our constitutional politics have been, and will continue to be, grounded in conflict and disagreement rather than rooted in consensus.

Even if we believed that transformations in popular consensus may explain past constitutional transformations, and that amending the constitution to reflect shifting consensus is normatively appropriate, we still might not believe that such consensus ought to be marked by supermajority rules. In his magisterial two-volume work *We the People*, Bruce Ackerman uses the example of Reconstruction to demonstrate the pathologies of the formal supermajoritarian mechanism of Article V. Ten Confederate states were able to serve as a "veto bloc" to the reconstruction amendments. The ensuing constitutional crisis was resolved only because the Republican leadership "refused to allow their opponents' legalistic interpretation of Article Five block Reconstruction. In the face of dramatic challenges by conservatives, they gained popular support to press the established system beyond its breaking point. Only in this way did they finally win the constitutional authority to validate the Fourteenth Amendment in the name of the people" (Ackerman 1998, 16).

Ackerman outlines the mechanisms by which the people have historically, and rightly, acted outside of Article V's provisions. He identifies constitutional moments, the periods in which "political movements generated mobilized popular consent to new constitutional solutions" (Ackerman 1991, 31). What happens at such moments is that "[a]s a result of many electoral victories on many different levels, a broad movement of transformative opinion has now earned the authority to set major aspects of the political agenda" (Ackerman 1998, 409). These movements reflect consensus: "The mark of such periods of constitutional solution is a rare convergence in the language and concerns in the capital and ordinary citizens in the streets. ... [T]here is a broad sense, shared (bitterly) by many opponents, *that the People have spoken*" (Ackerman 1998, 409, italics in the original).

As I shall discuss in a moment, Ackerman's historical claim gives rise to the normative assertion that constitutional change ought not be subject to the strictures of Article V, and his Popular Sovereignty Initiative may constitute one variation of the "complex majoritarianism" scheme that could replace supermajority rule. But we might still want to resist this sort of diffuse logic of consensus – a "rare convergence in the language and concerns" of citizens – for reasons that have been explored throughout this work. Recall that in ancient Athens, acclamation – a consensual device – was used to avoid an "enumerated minority." Likewise, as Jane Mansbridge has written, under consensus decision making, the "minority is, in a sense, eliminated. After it agrees to go along, it leaves no trace. Its objections go unrecorded" (Mansbridge 1980, 170). In contrast, as Bernard Manin has written, majority rule "institutionalizes the admission that there were also reasons not to desire the solution finally adopted" (Manin 1987, 359). Although supermajority rule might similarly enable us to recognize an enduring minority, there is reason to reject any sort of consensus model of decision making – particularly if we defend supermajority rule out of concern for minority voices and interests.

The deliberation indirectly promoted by supermajority rule remains valuable, even if the aim is not to create or capture consensus as such. One important reason for directly implementing deliberation is that it enables the formation of a majority opinion on the basis of reasons, ensures that those in the minority have had an opportunity to have their say, and gives all the members reason to accept the decision as legitimate, even if they hope in the future to reopen discussion. Where deliberation is required – as it is on the complex-majoritarian model sketched in Chapter 7 – there is no reason to bias decision making in favor of the status quo: either the existing norms will have arguments sufficient to convince a majority, or they will not. Further, if deliberation is effective in ensuring that disadvantaged minorities have a voice and that their interests are taken into account during the decision-making process, the subsequent vote need not be deliberately biased in their favor. Finally, if well-designed deliberative mechanisms, those that institutionalize a role for minorities, and aim specifically to give them opportunities to raise concerns about the differential impact of proposed policies on their community, are not sufficient to protect the interests of vulnerable minorities, there is little reason to think that the outcome of any purely aggregative procedure, whether a majority or a supermajority vote, will do so. In political communities where a particular group has historically been subject to the most severe forms of abuse and marginalization, protection of the group's interests may require a departure from strictly democratic procedures.

Constitution Making and Vulnerable Minorities

Political theorists have struggled with the problem of designing institutions to ensure adequate protection and representation for historically marginalized groups for at least two decades. Scholars have looked to supermajority rules because they seem to grant minorities the power to secure their interests through vetoing policies hostile to their interests, perhaps by partnering with other groups. It is surely true that in certain circumstances, supermajority rules may temporarily secure such protections. Will Kymlicka argues that within legislatures, threshold representation ("a number of representatives sufficient to ensure that the group's views and interests are effectively expressed") may be sufficient to protect minority interests under supermajority rules. He describes such rules as a form of compromise decision-making rule (Kymlicka 1995, 147). Even in the legislative context, if a minority group is powerful enough to secure for itself threshold representation, it probably does not require special protections against abuse. Especially in the constitution-making context, a group with sufficient power to veto decisions hostile to its interests is probably a population whose interests are no longer especially vulnerable, or resides in a democratic society already inclined to take their concerns seriously.

In *Democracy and Its Critics*, Robert Dahl argues similarly: in a default majoritarian system, "the protection of minority rights can be no stronger than the commitment of the majority of citizens to preserving the primary democratic rights of all citizens, to maintaining respect for their fellow citizens, and to avoiding the adverse consequences of harming a minority." Likewise, nonmajoritarian (e.g., supermajoritarian) democratic arrangements "by themselves cannot prevent a minority from using its protected position to inflict harm on a majority" (Dahl 1989, 155–156). Yet even as committed a majoritarian as Dahl hesitates to rule out the use of supermajority rules entirely:

A solution might be to combine the advantages of majority rule with the possibilities of supermajorities by using majority rule as a first and last resort. The members could decide in advance, by majority rule, that in certain cases a supermajority rule would be required. These cases might include special issues of great consequence and explosiveness, touching for example on enduring linguistic or religious differences; and they might include voting cycles, if and when they were detected. But the decision as to which issues were to require a supermajority would itself be made by majority rule. (Dahl 1989, 154)[10]

It is not clear why a majority, faced with the choice of either majoritarian or supermajoritarian decision making for "special issues" pertaining to cultural minorities or "explosive matters," would choose to raise the threshold. The problem of majority decision making, from the perspective of a vulnerable minority, ought to be the majority's inclination to ignore its interests. Because Dahl is at pains to emphasize that the majority ought to determine whether the supermajority threshold should be used

[10] We can bracket the issue of cycling in this context, because cycles will typically not emerge insofar as the matter is framed as a binary choice between an amendment and the status quo. It is true, as Nalebuff and Caplin and Nalebuff (1988) have demonstrated, that under certain conditions, a supermajority threshold of 64 percent breaks a cycle and produces a Condorcet winner. Were cycling in fact a major problem for the domains of issues for which supermajority rules are typically defended, we might consider that this would be a strong argument in favor of such rules. Note, however, that the empirical significance of cycles remains in serious question. Gerald Mackie, for instance, has recently examined virtually every salient putative example of a vote cycle in the literature to demonstrate that cycling is at most extraordinarily rare; indeed, Dahl himself noted that that the importance William Riker and others attribute to voting cycles may well be exaggerated (Mackie 2003; Dahl 1989, 154).

in a given circumstance, we might think that (1) either the majority will choose to act tyrannically, and thus not raise the threshold; or (2) the majority will not behave tyrannically, in which case the majority's decision to raise the threshold is at best an unnecessary signal of its good intentions.

Melissa Williams has suggested that supermajority rules may increase the power of a legislative minority insofar as it becomes attractive as a coalition partner, or may join forces with other minorities to block legislation harmful to its interests. Williams notes, however, that supermajority rules can readily lead to legislative paralysis and thus bias decision making toward the status quo, which she recognizes will "almost certainly not favor the interests of marginalized groups" (Williams 1998, 226). As we have seen, from a normative perspective a supermajority rule enables any minority that can achieve the threshold to veto the decisions of a majority, permitting powerful groups to resist efforts at redistribution or renegotiation of the terms by which they secured their interests.

Stephen Macedo recently argued that supermajority rules are of obvious and universal appeal because of their anonymity with respect to minority interests. Among non-majoritarian decision rules he identifies as compatible with political equality, fairness, and inclusivity, perhaps most important are "supermajority voting rules in which minority interests gain special protection: we *all* might prefer these systems given the possibility of finding ourselves in the minority" (Macedo 2010, 1037–1038). But individuals are not equally likely to find themselves in the minority on fundamental questions of political life. In a democracy, in which parties lose elections, every citizen at some point likely finds herself in the minority. Those who are highly advantaged or profoundly disadvantaged are more likely to find themselves at odds with majority preferences – the former against redistribution, the latter against neglect or abuse – and a supermajority rule will be insensitive to the claims of both. Even if we find insensitivity here to be normatively unproblematic, insofar as we wish to improve the terms of real political equality among our citizens, a supermajority rule will not do the work, for reasons we saw in the last chapter. We are not equally likely to wish for a veto

to protect the constitutional status quo; those who have systematically benefited from existing constitutional arrangements are
more likely to resist efforts to change the rules, as the discussion in Chapter 5 of the link between anonymity and neutrality
suggested.

The question of whether a supermajority rule constitutes a
real institutional solution, however, intersects with the question
of what constitutes adequate representation for marginalized
groups – whether proportional representation would be sufficient to empower them, how representatives are chosen given
the heterogeneity of many marginalized groups, and so forth.
Further, as the composition of the legislature changes or, under
proportional representation, group demographics shift the effi-
cacy of a supermajority threshold as a veto will depend on its
placement – a problem, as we have seen, of phronesis. The *ex
ante* indeterminacy of the threshold rule is one problem, but
a further one entails anticipating demographic shifts so that a
minority or (even more complicated) minorities can consistently
reach the veto point even if their population drops. There is no
one optimal solution to the problem of entrenched minorities,
given the diversity among them and the larger societies in which
they exist. Further, because the institutional rules will optimally
remain relatively stable, the stakes are raised in the constitutional context. In the ordinary legislative context, the representation of marginalized groups may remain relatively fluid and
sensitive to demographic shifts, and ongoing deliberations give
members frequent opportunities to reopen debate and press
their challenges to existing policies. The high costs of constitutional change mean that any institutional solution to protect
the interests of marginalized groups must be sufficiently resilient
and specific to ensure that powerful groups cannot easily reap-
propriate it. It must also be flexible enough to accommodate the
dynamic character of all groups. When granted by supermajority or unanimity rule, a veto is indeterminate both in subject and
object: it can be used by anyone, weak or powerful, to block any
action it deems harmful to its interests, fundamental or trivial,
self-aggrandizing or self-protecting, whether for self-regarding
or other-regarding reasons. However, if a veto is targeted both

in subject and in object – it is granted to a vulnerable minority group for decision making over a discrete, well-defined policy domain – it is likely to be effective and potentially attractive (Young 1990, 184).[11]

Thus the question of specification concerns both the agents and the scope of the veto. It cannot be a blanket grant to each distinct interest in a political community, as John C. Calhoun's famous theory of the concurrent majority required. Such a grant would implement, in effect, a unanimity rule. The theory of concurrent majorities raises many of the same concerns addressed in previous chapters such as the fallibility of agents, and their likelihood to exert the veto for purely self-interested purposes. (Of course, Calhoun's own motivation was to protect the interests of Southern slaveholders.) Further, as we have seen, unanimity may generate coercion of dissenters. Calhoun argued that the moral pressure exerted by a unanimity rule was attractive and likely to generate good outcomes: it would generate a focus on the common good, akin to that of a jury. As we have seen, however, it is far from clear that unanimity rules operate in such a fashion even, in that limited context.[12]

---

[11] Note that John Dryzek criticizes this on the grounds that it is possible that one might give Group A the right to veto policy X, while Group B is given the right to veto policy not X. This is of course possible, but it is a relatively remote possibility insofar as the reason for granting the veto is that the matter affects one particularly vulnerable group disproportionately (Dryzek 2002, 61).

[12] Nonetheless, Calhoun's theory has remained influential; it constituted a linchpin of Arend Lijphart's famous theory of consociationalism; Lijphart specifically drew on Calhoun for his argument. Agreeing with Calhoun that majority rule will not generate alternation in office but oppression in divided societies, Lijphart has called instead for governance via a grand coalition and, most importantly for our purposes, the "mutual veto or 'concurrent majority'" rule. Lijphart himself recognized that the success of consociational democracy was in part contingent upon a relatively small number of participants, between three and five. As Read points out, efforts to implement such a rule in contemporary constitutional settings have been unsuccessful. In the 1974 Yugoslavian constitution, each republic possessed a de facto veto, aiming to provide an "effective and fair way to govern a diverse and contentious multinational state" (Read 2009, 214). Certainly Yugoslavia's collapse was not rooted chiefly in its requirement of unanimity, but in Read's words, "it is clear that the consensus process established by the 1974 constitution *failed to prevent* exactly those problems it was intended to resolve" (Read 2009, 215, italics in the original).

One obvious aim in specifying the veto power must be to ensure that a vulnerable group, rather than a powerful one, is protected. However, granting a particular group a veto, and giving such a veto constitutional protection, may reify the group's identity. This is a standard concern for scholars considering the problem of minority group representation: how do we avoid protecting one particular conception of the boundaries of group membership, or privileging one version of the group's understanding of its history and its most important challenges? In assessing Calhoun's theory, Williams correctly holds that "providing a minority veto involves granting new powers to a *particular* social group or section and entrenching those powers in the constitution. As soon as this is done, however, it grants constitutional status to the cleavage itself, and so rigidly defines the parameters of political conflict. Minority protection is purchased at the price of adaptability to changing political circumstances" (Williams 1998, 45).

The problem of reifying group identity must be acknowledged. The targeted veto cannot be a default solution to the problem of underrepresented minorities. When a particular minority group has a long history of marginalization within a given society, however, granting constitutional protection to a veto is surely preferable to either subjecting the group's interests to majority rule or hoping the group will have enough votes to wield a veto via a supermajority threshold. How the group will exercise the veto – in particular, who is empowered to serve as its agent – would require careful institutional specification, though at a minimum group should have power to choose its own representatives.

Let us turn to the scope of the veto. An important objection to Iris Marion Young's proposal to grant such power to marginalized populations was its breadth both in subject and domain, as in her example of providing women with a veto over reproductive rights policy (Young 1990, 184). One might hold, for instance, that both sexes have a vested interest in such policies. Fathers, not just mothers, are affected by decisions over reproduction, even if women bear the costs of pregnancy and nursing, and on average a disproportionate degree of the long-term costs of caring for children. The scope of reproductive rights policy is extremely broad, extending from abortion and contraception to childcare policies. Yet Young's example of land-use policy for American Indian reservations is clearer and closer to the veto power suggested here: American Indians are a particularly vulnerable minority (unlike women, who are a numerical majority), and their interests in land over which they have jurisdictional and territorial sovereignty far outstrip those of other groups (Young 1990, 184). The relevant tribes, land, and policy domains could be clearly and narrowly delineated, and thus providing these groups with a veto over such matters would not generate the same problems of cycling that Dryzek, for instance, fears (Dryzek 2002, 61).

One version of this mechanism is the Belgian "alarm bell" procedure, which constitutes a suspensive veto. Article 54 of the Belgian Constitution provides that a motion signed by 75 percent of the members of one of Belgium's linguistic groups can "declare that the provisions that it designates of a Government bill or private member's bill can gravely damage relations between the Communities." The motion is then suspended within Parliament and referred to the cabinet (in which each linguistic group is represented). The cabinet, which operates under a consensus rule, provides a reasoned opinion on the motion and invites the originating House to reconsider the matter on the basis of the opinion. Although it is true, of course, that such a provision requires a high supermajority proportion of the group members, nothing about the provision hinges upon such a threshold. While the supermajority rule may reduce the frequency with which the suspensive veto is used, its suspensive rather than absolute character and the advisory role of the cabinet reduce the risk that it will be used exploitatively. An absolute, rather than suspensive, veto can generate breakdowns; for instance, the 1960 Cyprus Constitution failed in large part because of the Turkish minority's overuse of it on tax bills (Bogdanor 1997, 81). This affirms the importance of tailoring very narrowly the scope of the topics for which the veto may be deployed. Finally, the susceptibility to breakdown or abuse is a risk of both a supermajority threshold and an absolute veto, perhaps more so if there are numerous minority groups capable of exerting such power.

Regardless, the scope of any absolute veto ought not to extend over to the constitutional context. The risk associated with granting any group a veto over constitutional change is that associated with entrenchment: the need to protect the group's identity and power against any modification, regardless of circumstantial or demographic changes, or fundamental shifts in the configuration of societal cleavages. The constitutionalist may immediately reply that complex majoritarianism leaves these vulnerable minorities subject to tyrannical majorities. However, the deliberative component of the amendment process could easily be designed to promote opportunities for marginalized groups to express their concerns about proposed changes that deem hazardous to their interests. In addition, the constitution could grant representatives of the marginalized group a suspensive veto at the legislative stage, which could generate an advisory opinion from a constitutional court on the likelihood that the group's interests would be harmed by the proposed amendment. This opinion could help guide legislative decisions and potentially shape the public deliberations to follow.

There is, of course, no easy solution to the problem of minority group representation, and this book has not sought to advocate for one particular conception of a representative scheme. However, if contemporary democrats are concerned about the fate of vulnerable minorities under simple-majority rule, the institutional solution should not be supermajority rules. If the implicit or explicit aim of a supermajority threshold is to enable vulnerable minorities to exercise a veto over majority decisions, the more reliable and attractive route actually grant a veto to the truly vulnerable population, rather than risk its use by powerful or dangerous populations. The risk associated with reifying the contours and authority of a historically marginalized minority group, in other words, is less grave than that of authorizing a powerful minority to secure its interests against those of a majority.

Conclusion

The aim in this chapter has been to demonstrate that supermajority rules are unnecessary, and potentially pernicious, even in the "hard case" of constitutionalism. I have challenged the use of supermajority rules in part on the grounds that such rules secure distributive inequalities on an arbitrary basis, and enable those who disproportionately benefit from the status quo to reject efforts at renegotiating the terms of the constitutional bargain. The political inequalities secured by supermajority rule are not a necessary condition of achieving constitutional stability, because such stability does not require supermajority rules. In the next chapter, which sketches a set of complex-majoritarian mechanisms of constitutional amendment, I aim to dispel the concern that abandoning supermajority rule renders democracy subject to popular tyranny. The desiderata of deliberation and time delays indirectly promoted through supermajority rule are given explicit structure and significance under complex majoritarian institutions. But because supermajority rule provides the most vulnerable populations with only a weak hope of vetoing decisions harmful to their interests, and runs the risk of empowering advantaged groups, the limited use of an extremely narrowly targeted veto has been advocated as an alternative to supermajority rules. (As discussed in the next chapter, however, targeted minority vetoes are not complex majoritarian institutions, but derogations from majority rule – indeed, from democratic decision making more generally.)

In conclusion, let us consider one final issue. A perennial question for constitutional scholars and democratic theorists alike is whether constitutionalism is at odds with democracy. There is a canonical set of responses to the question, ranging from the claim that the "dead hand of the past" ought not to govern contemporary majorities, to the rejoinder that constitutionalism secures the conditions of democratic decision making, to the Habermasian defense of co-originality. It should be clear from the foregoing that constitutionalism should, in general, not be conceptualized as antithetical to democratic decision making, as a set of devices designed to prevent majorities from destroying their institutions through their passion or ignorance. There is no necessary connection between constitutionalism and counterma-joritarianism: the capacity to make important democratic com-mitments does not depend on taking power out of the hands of political majorities. As we shall see in a moment, it depends on deliberation and the use of time delays or other devices designed to ensure adequate reflection on important public matters. In so doing, constitutionalism becomes a set of mechanisms designed to elicit the highest-quality judgments from citizens on funda-mental issues for the community. But constitutionalism does not require the use of rules that treat citizens, or their considered judgments, unequally.

A supposed paradox of democracy – that substantive political equality may depend on abandoning formal political equality – has long justified the use of supermajority rules. Indeed, as the discussion of targeted vetoes suggested, there may be highly restrictive contexts in which it is desirable to grant the most vul-nerable members control over public decisions concerning their interests. There is no reason to regard this move as democratic: we should regard it as a derogation from democratic decision mak-ing, regrettably warranted in cases of egregious historical abuse so as to ensure the survival of some citizens and their way of life. This acknowledgment of derogation is importantly different from the argument that the fundamental commitment to demo-cratic equality can only be realized through granting members unequal political power via supermajority rule. As we shall now see, when we disaggregate the use of supermajority rules from the logic of constitutionalism, it becomes clear that only the for-mer poses a challenge to democratic equality. Complex majori-tarianism redeems the promise of constitutional democracy.

7

Constitutionalism under Complex Majoritarianism

Allow me to recapitulate the major deficiencies of supermajority rule, drawing on the arguments of the two preceding chapters. First, supermajority rules bias decisions in favor of one set of judgments, typically those supportive of the status quo. In the context of constitutionalism, supermajority amendment thresholds mitigate risks associated with instability, but introduce the risk of entrenching bad norms that may reflect distributive inequalities and other injustices dating to the framing. Further, the institutional bias in favor of a minority's judgment or interest is introduced on an arbitrary basis, because of the indeterminacy of the threshold choice, and when governing amendment, is only revisable with respect to these same arbitrary strictures. Second, supermajority rules ensure that proposed changes have support above a majority, but do so at the risk of ascribing possibly fictive consensus support to the status quo. Supermajority rules may also reflect a sort of category error, holding that the relevant conception of consensus support is aggregative – reflected by an arbitrarily large number of individuals in favor of an amendment – rather than the sentiment of the community as a whole via the acclamatory or deliberative conception of consensus. Third, the minority granted a veto over the majority through supermajority threshold is at least as likely to be powerful as vulnerable, given the nature of constitutional decision making.

Recall from the opening pages of this book the hypothetical example of a gay couple in California, deprived of their right to marry by a swift majority vote. This example, among countless possible others, gives us reason to hesitate before advocating that barriers to constitutional amendment be swept away, replaced by simple majority referendums or legislative decisions. The perils of partisan and passionate majorities are clear. Yet the alternative to supermajoritarian constitutionalism is not pure populism. A set of institutional arrangements that I have termed complex majoritarianism can replace supermajority rule. Under complex majoritarianism, constitutional stability will be preserved for the right reasons. Decisions rooted in public deliberation, and subject to time delays, capture the desire to ensure that constitutional changes are not merely partisan or whimsical. Deliberative assemblies, optimally, will be sufficient to ensure that minorities are not the objects of tyrannical behavior; at a minimum, such assemblies will enable minority voices to be heard.

Thus the fundamental complicating mechanisms of complex majoritarianism are deliberative assemblies and time delays. These mechanisms reduce predictable causes for concern regarding majority decision making. These institutions could take many different forms, depending on the particular experiences of a given society, its existing institutions, and the challenges it faces. As Chapter 6 suggested, popular constitutionalists have advocated similar proposals, so I will contrast one model of complex majoritarianism with these alternative schemes. The critical difference between complex majoritarianism and supermajority rule is the former rejects the bias in judgment expressly promoted through supermajority rules. Complex majoritarianism does entail a weak status quo bias because of the costs of engaging in constitutional change. But beyond that, it does not presuppose any disjuncture in the wisdom of the framers and today's citizens, or any presumptive view that the status quo reflects an ongoing consensus. Like supermajority rule, it does recognize the risk immediate decision making may pose to minority rights and interests. But it does not generate a bias in favor of just any minority, and in particular it will not benefit powerful minorities.

Complex Majoritarianism: One Proposal

The concept of "complex majoritarianism" is akin to other complex "isms" in political theory. Charles Beitz, for instance, develops a theory of "complex proceduralism" in *Political Equality*. By complex proceduralism, Beitz means to distance himself from purely procedural accounts that define procedural equality to define fair participation; instead, he wants to affirm that the terms of political participation must be ones every citizen could reasonably accept. Beitz also distances his account of proceduralism from outcome-oriented "best result" and "popular will" theories; the former holds that fair terms of political participation are those that produce the optimal result, and the latter produce outcomes that would be identified by a social choice function as the most preferred by the community. Similarly, Norman Daniels has explained Rawls's commitment to democratic equality as a "complex egalitarianism" (Daniels 2003). Rawls's concept of equality is complex because of the interplay among the guarantees of equal basic liberties, the guarantee of fair equality of opportunity, and the difference principle, as well as in terms of the ways in which these three principles can be justifiably promoted and integrated.

What gives the form of majoritarianism here its complexity? The key justification of majority rule rests, as we have seen, on a commitment to epistemic equality – broadly, the presumptively equal capacity of citizens to judge their own interests (and of those agents best suited to represent these interests). Derogations from formal equality within the context of decision-making bodies constitute an affront to the dignity of the agents, in which the presumptively equal capacity to judge among competing alternatives ought to be affirmed. Such derogations are only justifiable in exceptional cases – in those rare cases when a bias in judgment would reduce the risk of grave injustice. An absolute veto over decision making in a particular domain, while perhaps warranted when a political community has proven likely to violate the rights and interests of a historically marginalized population, cannot be justified democratically. Similarly, granting a minority veto over decision making in the form of supermajority rule cannot be justified democratically; even if we believe that the members of the minority may change over time, and will not exclusively be restricted to those who currently benefit from the status quo (as in the constitutional context), supermajority rule systematically treats members of a political community unequally.

The legitimacy of majority decision making in democracies does not derive strictly from the formal equality it mandates. It also requires procedures designed to elicit high-quality judgments, that is, judgments worth aggregating, in the language of Chapter 2. In the weakly epistemic version of majority decision making, described in Chapter 5, majoritarian institutions must be designed with the aim of improving the quality of individual judgments within those domains. It is critical to reduce the risk of whimsical or passionate decision making, promoted through well-structured deliberative institutions and through the use of time delays. Decision makers must have access to high-quality information, as a means of improving their judgments. Even if a large number of citizens do not participate in deliberative assemblies, for instance, this precondition would require an investment of public resources to ensure that citizens receive adequate and balanced information well in advance of votes. Although democratic legitimacy cannot hinge on whether citizens choose to fully inform themselves – through actual deliberation, watching televised debates, or reading briefing materials – legitimate democratic outcomes do depend on procedures that promote the sorts of high-quality individual judgments worth aggregating. The importance of counting these judgments equally derives from the value of respecting the citizens' dignity as judges of their own interest *simpliciter* or as "properly understood."

A Majority Vote within the Legislature

Constitutional amendment would first require a majority vote of the legislature. That the legislature ought to play some role in constitutional change should be relatively uncontroversial. It is the norm empirically, and likely for good reasons: the legislature is most acutely aware of the flaws of constitutional norms, given its responsibility for legislating within constitutional constraints. Further, as representatives, legislators are well positioned to evaluate the validity of voters' calls for constitutional change when they emerge. The more difficult question is the precise mechanism by which the legislature should act. Bicameralism, as many scholars have noted, is in effect a supermajoritarian device. Only in the case of random sorting into an upper and lower house will a motion that would have been supported by a bare majority in a joint house pass a bicameral legislature. The status quo bias of bicameral legislatures has been demonstrated empirically; moreover, there is some empirical evidence that unicameral systems without external veto power (or constitutional review) are not more liable to violate rights or to behave capriciously than bicameral legislatures (Przeworski 2010, 142–144).[1] So there are good reasons to resist bicameralism in general. Where it already exists, however, there is certainly no need to raise the threshold; it is already supermajoritarian enough.

In a unicameral legislature, there might be a reason to consider imposing a quorum requirement in the form of an absolute majority rule, which mandates that a majority of all members eligible to vote approve a measure for passage, rather than merely a majority of those present. The Australian framers, for example, specifically chose not to use supermajority rules for constitutional change, on the grounds that such rules would introduce excessive inflexibility into the constitution. The legislative stage of the amendment procedure instead requires an absolute majority of at least one House of Parliament (optimally two, but after three months without agreement, the Governor-General may submit a version supported by only one House). Legislation, in contrast, requires a simple majority of each house, although in case of deadlock, simultaneous dissolution of both Houses occurs, followed if necessary by a joint sitting of both Houses governed by an absolute majority rule (supermajorities were proposed but rejected at the premiers' conference of 1899) (Aroney 2008,

---

[1] See also McGann (2006).

242). Further, at least some constitutional provisions are governed by an absolute majority rule in Barbados, Greece, Peru, and Sri Lanka.

Absolute majority rules themselves have a status quo bias, inducing inflexibility. Consider the following example, adapted from a proposal by Adrian Vermeule in the most sustained recent discussion of the mechanism. A 100-member voting body has 40 votes in favor, 20 opposed, and 40 absent. Under a simple majority rule, the vote carries 40 to 20; indeed, on a two-thirds rule, it also passes. But under an absolute majority rule, it fails because it does not reach the 51-vote margin. So in this case an absolute majority rule is more effective than a supermajority rule in inducing inflexibility. Absolute majority rules also avoid some of the normative pitfalls of supermajority rules. Cases in which a minority defeats a majority proposal are attributable strictly to absenteeism on the part of the majority. That the majority should bear a cost for high absenteeism, given the salience of a constitutional amendment, is not normatively objectionable. If a majority deems its own proposal insufficient important to appear for deliberation and voting, this constitutes compelling evidence that the amendment is frivolous. To the extent that a minority is highly motivated and a majority is not, as their turnout indicates, the capacity of a minority to veto a majority amendment proposal unproblematic. Further, as Vermeule points out, drawing on Bentham in *Political Tactics*, absolute majority rule enables the majority to avoid "Napoleonic minorities," in which minorities exploit high majority absenteeism to outvote a rump majority and push through legislation or even proposed amendments (Vermeule 2007, 122). But even if an absolute majority rule could work well for a unicameral legislature, it might be less attractive for the popular stage of the amendment procedure; achieving the turnout necessary to satisfy an absolute majority threshold would likely induce complete sclerosis, unless voting were mandatory.

Finally, the amendment procedure could also require two sequential votes of a legislature, perhaps separated by an intervening election. This is a fairly standard feature of amendment procedures in northern Europe. Denmark, Sweden, Finland, and Iceland each require approval from parliaments before and after an election; the Baltic states require repeated decisions in parliament, although an intervening election is not mandated. In Norway, a constitutional amendment must be submitted a year prior to the next election, and then the subsequent parliament votes on the procedure (Rasch and Congleton 2006). Requiring an intervening election directly implements a time delay, of course, but also reduces the chance that amendments will be used for strictly partisan ends through enabling a change of government to occur. This mechanism promotes consensus in the narrow sense of support across the aisle.

Deliberative Assemblies and Public Education

Subsequent to the legislative vote or votes, and prior to any sort of national referendum, deliberative assemblies should be convened. Optimally, in federal systems, these assemblies would be organized at both state and national levels to encourage the widest possible inclusion, given the costs of participating in such assemblies. But assemblies themselves are insufficient; televised national debates, as well as a national education campaign providing materials both for and against proposed amendments, should also be required. The aim, in brief, must be to elicit high-quality discussions about the reasons for and against adopting proposed amendments, while ensuring the greatest possible circulation of these arguments to voters.

Lest a requirement for deliberative assemblies seem naïve or utopian, recall an example with which the book began: the British Columbia Citizens' Assembly on electoral reform. Although technically not a constitutional measure, electoral reform is precisely one of those questions for which one might believe a supermajority would be advisable, on the grounds that otherwise partisan majorities will seek to alter the system to their advantage. The British Columbia example provides an instructive model for the design of deliberative assemblies for constitutional reform – and, perhaps, as a cautionary tale for the use of supermajorities.

In brief, after a number of elections in British Columbia in which the assignment of legislative seats did not track the popular vote, a problem stemming in part from biases associated with the single-member plurality system, citizen groups began to call for substantial electoral reform.[2] Upon taking office in 2000, Liberal BC Premier Gordon Campbell commissioned Gordon Gibson to recommend a process for electoral reform. After wide consultation, Gibson recommended a Citizens' Assembly (CA). The legislative assembly unanimously approved the creation of the CA and established a legislative committee to oversee it; the government provided a $5.5 million budget, which helped provide logistical and administrative support, as well as travel expenses and $150-per-day salaries for members of the CA. CA staff were given 26,500 names randomly drawn from the voter registration lists, and each person was invited to attend a selection meeting; 964 attended, and of these, 158 were drawn by lot (one man and one woman from each of the 79 districts in the province). The chair selected two additional Aboriginal (Nisga'a Nation) members, generating a body of 160 members. The draw was designed to ensure the representation of a range of age groups in addition to geographic and gender parity (it was thus near-random), but the outcome was a diverse socioeconomic group, whose levels of formal education ranged from those without high school degrees to those with PhDs. (Because of the self-selecting nature of the process, members were, relative to the BC population as a whole, whiter, older, better educated, and professional).

The responsibility of the CA was to evaluate "the manner by which voters' ballots are translated into seats in the Legislative Assembly," and, if they desired, to generate a recommendation for an alternative system, formulated as a ballot question, which would be subject to a referendum. After six weekends devoted to educating the members about electoral systems and a workshop on deliberation (some in the form of plenary sessions open to the general public), members attended public hearings around the

---

[2] The explanation of the mechanism is drawn from Warren and Pearse (2008), 8–10.

province. Six more weekends of deliberation, from September to November 2004, followed. The members ranked three of nine goals for the electoral system as most important (electoral local representation; fair results through proportionally translating votes into seats; maximizing voter choice), generating recommendations for two kinds of electoral systems: mixed-member proportional representation (MMP) and single transferable vote (STV). Members voted overwhelmingly for STV over MMP, and then for MMP over the existing system. Ultimately, the CA voted for a version of STV that was modified to reflect the uneven population density of the region, and formulated a recommendation for a ballot measure: "Should British Columbia change to the BC-STV electoral system as recommended by the Citizens' Assembly for Electoral Reform?"

Yet the May 2005 referendum failed. The government had set a double supermajoritarian threshold on the grounds that the recommendation was different from other referendums; it was a quasi-constitutional reform, which thus required the sort of broad-based support ostensibly captured through supermajority rules (Thompson 2008, 39). Thus the threshold was set at 60 percent of the province-wide vote and a majority in 60 percent of the electoral district. It satisfied the latter criterion (seventy-seven of seventy-nine districts) but received only 57.7 percent of the province-wide vote.[3] Further, one primary explanation for the defeat was insufficient attention to public education subsequent to the CA and prior to the vote. Assembly voters were largely left on their own to promote their agenda; 141 of the 160 members joined the "Citizens' Assembly Alumni" to make presentations to interested groups in their district. Failure to devote resources to a public educational campaign led to the decision to hold a second referendum. In advance of the second vote, the government would fund campaigns both in favor of the existing electoral system and the STV proposal, and the Electoral Boundaries

---

[3] A second referendum, held in conjunction with the 2009 municipal elections – long after the Citizens' Assembly disbanded – failed to garner even majority support.

Commission would provide the public with maps indicating the potential constituencies under STV and the existing system (Ratner 2008, 146).

Setting aside the vote threshold, the general outline of the CA may serve as one model for the use of deliberative assemblies for constitutional amendment. Nonetheless, deliberative assemblies will be insufficient to educate the people as a whole without specific resources assigned to improve public education. Thus the assemblies would be only one step in the pre-referendum period. A series of nationally televised debates would help ensure that all citizens have access to arguments for and against the amendments. No doubt other materials could be prepared and circulated to the electorate. Regardless, the aim both of the deliberative assemblies and the broader civic education project must be to improve the judgments of the voters. The time-delaying feature of the deliberative feature alone diminishes the risk of panicked decision making. More important, however, is the role that public deliberation – both within the assemblies and through the various hearings and debates – plays in generating deliberative consensus. Again, we have little reason to believe public discussion will generate substantive agreement. But we do have reason to believe that, at a minimum, minorities will have opportunities to have their say, disseminate arguments against proposals, and raise concerns about threats to their interests. Thus, for reasons discussed in Chapters 5 and 6, deliberation holds out the greatest promise for enabling consensus. The outcome of the procedures can be reasonably inferred to embody commitments of the society as a whole, not merely those of a majority.

A Popular, Majoritarian Referendum

The final stage of the constitutional amendment process would entail a nationwide vote of the electorate. The use of a referendum at a final stage is not uncommon; it may be triggered via mechanisms internal to the legislature (e.g., legislative support below a supermajority, or by request of some portion of the legislature), as in Chile, France, Italy, Spain, and Sweden, or mandated directly, as in Australia, Denmark, Ireland, Japan, Switzerland,

and Venezuela. Structuring the referendum itself would require negotiation; for instance, a federal structure such as Australia requires a majority of eligible voters in a majority of states and a majority of voters nationwide (the "dual referendum"). Given uneven population distribution across states in the United States, however, the requirement of a majority of voters in a majority of states could be tantamount to a supermajority rule, and so there might be good reason to resist the dual referendum mechanism. Instead, we could imagine two sequential national referendums of the citizens as a whole to ensure opportunities for deliberation and education, and to implement the time delays that will discourage passionate and perhaps strictly partisan majorities from forming.

Political theorists and legal scholars have in recent years sketched many such schemes for the reform of Article V, some of which resemble the complex-majoritarian ideal. Akhil Amar, for instance, advocates a mechanism of constitutional change outside of Article V that requires a majoritarian referendum. Amar argues that if a majority of U.S. voters were to petition Congress (or applications from two-thirds of the state legislatures, as specified within Article V), Congress would be obliged to call a convention to propose amendments, which could be ratified by a simple majority of the U.S. electorate. Such a mechanism is less complex than the one advocated here, although Amar does qualify his proposal, suggesting in a footnote that the "[p]eople must in fact deliberate on a proposed amendment rather than reflexively registering exogenous preferences" (Amar 1988, 1064, fn. 79).[4] Similarly, Sanford Levinson advocates a nationwide petition to Congress – or a deliberative poll prior to a national referendum – to call for a constitutional convention to embark upon sweeping constitutional change, not least the modification of the "iron cage" of Article V. Levinson

---

[4] There are other liabilities to such an approach – in part, the claim that Article V does not specify the exclusive means by which constitutional change can occur is tendentious, insofar as we typically believe that where a constitution specifies the means by which an institution should operate, the rule of *expressio unius est exclusio alterius* ought to obtain.

himself invokes the failure of the ERA – an example with which this book began – as evidence of the problematic nature of the supermajoritarian rules for amendment, noting that it is "simply unacceptable, in a modern democratic country, that an amendment can be blocked by only thirteen of the states, and in at least one of those states, Illinois, the ERA had been assented to by one of the two legislative houses, but voted down in the other" (Levinson 2006, 165). Again, although the spirit of the complex majoritarian mechanism for amendment is similar to Amar's and Levinson's, the emphasis both on deliberation and time delays – and, for that matter, on multiple assemblies rather than a convention as such – renders the mechanism less susceptible to abuse.

Both approaches, however, may be distinguished from Bruce Ackerman's recommendation of a Popular Sovereignty Initiative (an amendment being unachievable insofar as it would require states to cede political control over the process). Ackerman's proposal requires referendum, but does so in a way that raises concerns about partisan manipulation and minority dominance. Ackerman describes the mechanism as follows:

Upon successful reelection, the President should be authorized to signal a constitutional moment and propose amendments in the name of the American people. When approved by Congress, such proposals would be sent to the states for ratification. They should be placed on the ballot at the next two Presidential elections, and they should be added to the Constitution if they gain popular approval. (Ackerman 1998, 410)

Ackerman himself recognizes, for instance, the potential risks associated with enabling a president to propose amendments that could be in his personal or partisan interest. But the problem is graver than Ackerman acknowledges. Consider the sort of partisan shifts that could generate both a presidential reelection and a substantial majority of Congress. These changes may indeed signify a constitutional moment, encouraging, in Ackerman's language, "an engaged citizenry to focus on fundamental issues and determine whether any proposed solution deserves its considered support" (Ackerman 1998, 6). But they might also merely signify a shift in ordinary politics. Enabling a president and his party to take temporary dominance to be a mandate for constitutional change encourages the use of constitutional politics for narrow partisan ends. Partisan victory ought to be decoupled from a mandate for constitutional change. When a call for constitutional amendment emerges during electoral campaigns, or in the course of ordinary political life, Congress ought certainly to take the opportunity to propose such amendments if it deems necessary. But the fact of an electoral victory ought to be both unnecessary and insufficient to identify a mandate for constitutional change.

Ackerman notes that the presence of an amendment proposal at the following two elections reduces the risk of purely partisan amendments, suggesting – probably rightly – that "[p]artisan proposals may prove to be political albatrosses five or six years later, embarrassing the party that originally endorsed them" (Ackerman 1998, 411). The delays promoted by two-election requirement for approval should be sufficient to reduce the risks of purely partisan or passionate voting, but Ackerman does not rely on such a mechanism. Perhaps as a means of reducing the risk of purely partisan constitutional change, Ackerman suggests that supermajority rules may be valuable. For instance, he suggests Congress should approve the proposed amendment by a two-thirds vote; Ackerman also wonders aloud if he should use a supermajoritarian threshold for one or both of the referendums (Ackerman 1998, 6).[5] Ackerman also cites the failure of the ERA as a basis for his proposal, noting that the campaign had generated a "far deeper and more considered judgment," with a "strong national majority consistently in its favor" (Ackerman 1998, 6). The ERA, he suggests, teaches us "once again the dangers of allowing a veto by a minority of the states to stifle higher lawmaking in this country" (Ackerman 1998, 6). Ackerman thus ascribes the failure of the ERA to the problems of federalism, not to supermajority rule. But it is difficult to understand why the exercise of power by a minority of states is more problematic

---

[5] He also holds that the initiative itself requires two-thirds Congressional approval, followed by a referendum at the next two presidential elections (Ackerman 1998, 6)

than its exercise by a minority of the citizens. One might expect the complicated nature of state sovereignty under a federalist system to permit the exercise of unequal power and to authorize blocks impermissible under a referendum.

Again, a model of complex-majoritarian constitutional amendment could take many different forms. Recall that what distinguishes complex majoritarianism from ordinary majoritarianism is that the former emphasizes the formation of judgments and not merely its aggregation; hence the importance of deliberation and of time delays. Ancillary institutions such as sequential votes may or may not be required; for that matter, majority votes of state legislatures rather than popular referendums may be permitted (albeit with the attendant risk of treating citizens unequally because of uneven population distributions). The primary aim of complex-majoritarian institutions is to emphasize the presumptively equal capacity for judgment among members of the domain, while ensuring that institutional design emphasizes the formation of high-quality judgments rather than merely aggregate preexisting views.

At this point, the constitutionalist might be willing to concede that this complex- majoritarian mechanism would be sufficiently cumbersome so as to constitute a reasonable barrier to ready alteration, while making amendment more feasible than under the strictures of Article V. That is, she might be willing to recognize that institutional stability is indeed possible under complex majoritarianism. But she might nonetheless ask whether such a model can capture the aims of consensus and minority protection as readily as supermajority rule. So as not to stack the deck, let us imagine substituting supermajority rule for majority rule at the two voting stages of the amendment procedure sketched earlier, while preserving the deliberative assemblies and time delays.

First, what if supermajority rule were to replace (absolute) majority rule at the legislative stage, when constitutional amendments are proposed? The use of a supermajority rule at the legislative stage might have the benefit of reducing the risk that a majority party will introduce a purely partisan amendment. As discussed in Chapters 5 and 6, the goal of consensus on rights and institutional structures spelled out in the Constitution is in many ways attractive, while permitting a dominant political majority to secure policy or purely electoral advantages through the use of constitutional amendment is distinctly unappealing. If opening the amendment process were relatively costless for the dominant party, this might be a serious concern. However, on the model proposed previously, proposing constitutional amendments come with serious costs. These costs are partially financial, the expenses of a sustained process of deliberative assemblies and a major public education campaign. More important are the opportunity costs associated with focusing both legislative and public attention on an amendment campaign, rather than on other features of a political agenda. Further, if citizens deem the amendment frivolous, they will resent the allocation of resources to the agenda, with potential electoral costs for the party. So there are reasons to suspect that the risk of strictly partisan or otherwise trivial constitutional amendments is less severe than one might think under such a scheme.

Would the benefits of supermajority rule, and the risks associated with majoritarianism, outweigh these potential costs? Even setting aside the thorny question of why the filibuster has endured, it remains a highly effective tool of minority obstruction. This, one might claim, is precisely the point: the filibuster enables minorities to block legislation harmful to their or their constituents' interests, and such a capacity is especially important for prospective constitutional changes. But the charge of a partisan or a politicized constitutional amendment, made early and often by the minority party, will reverberate throughout the lengthy process to follow. Because the legislative process is merely the first step in a long and iterated process of deliberation and voting, concerns about majority voting may, surprisingly, be less severe for constitutional amendments than for significant pieces of "ordinary" legislation.

Turning now to the use of supermajority rules at the referendum(s) stage, we might again suggest that raising the threshold mitigates the risk of strictly partisan amendments. As discussed, doing so biases our decision making in favor of the status quo. Given sustained legislative and public deliberation over a period of years, it is not obvious why we ought to bias our judgments systematically in favor of existing norms. Again, if we had reason to believe that the quality of deliberation or the motivations of framers were likely to be superior to those of contemporary legislators and citizens, we might give greater weight to the former. But deliberative institutions ensure that supporters and opponents of the amendment have ample opportunity to persuade each other, and time delays ensure that such judgments are not made hastily. There is little reason to fear that ordinary minorities will be subject to tyrannical behavior from majorities under such a scheme. It is true, minorities will be outvoted, but such a mechanism is no more likely to impair the rights and interests of minority groups than a supermajoritarian scheme.

To see how this might operate, let us consider the course of the Federal Marriage Amendment (FMA), H.J. Res. 56. The amendment would have restricted marriage to heterosexual couples. Article V of the U.S. Constitution, recall, requires the support of two-thirds of each house of Congress and then three-fourths of the states. On July 18, 2006, FMA failed in the House on a vote of 236 (yea) to 187 (nay), where 290 votes would have been necessary for passage. Had proposed amendments required only a majority vote, the measure would have passed the House. The Senate did not vote on the amendment directly, but a cloture vote failed 49 (yea) to 48 (nay) on June 7, 2006, under a cloture rule of 60 votes, and required 67 votes for passage. Without a filibuster or an absolute majority requirement, the measure might have passed the Senate, so let us imagine that the amendment did indeed successfully pass both houses by a simple majority. (Were two Congressional votes required, one following the 2008 elections, the amendment might not have received majority support in both houses, but let us assume for now that only one vote was required.)

The matter then would have proceeded, on the amendment procedure provided earlier, to the deliberation phase. In 2006 national support for same-sex marriage would have been well lower than 50 percent, and one might expect the constitutional

amendment would have passed, were preferences given exoge-
nously and a national referendum held immediately – or perhaps
even at the time of the 2008 election. But the sustained deliberative process prescribed earlier would likely track, if not expedite,
the rapid transformations in public opinion on gay marriage in
the past several years. Some of this change derives strictly from
the substitution of older voters by younger ones who are substantially more supportive of same-sex marriage. But there has
been a shift in public opinion in favor of same-sex marriage, even
across generational cohorts, since 2006. Some of this derives
from the fact that support for other forms of gay rights policies
have empowered more people to disclose their same-sex orientation to their family and friends, which in turn has increased support for marriage rights.

Nationwide deliberations could accelerate this process. One
might expect public hearings and nationwide deliberative assemblies to feature testimony from many same-sex couples and families. National recognition that valuable community members are
in long-term committed same-sex relationships could push for-
ward support for same-sex marriage, or at least decreased opposition to gay marriage. It is true that the effects of deliberation may
be to increase polarization, that is, to push deliberators inclined
in one direction – say, generally against same-sex marriage – to
a more extreme position. (Sunstein 2002) But these effects can
be countered through ensuring that deliberative bodies are relatively diverse, featuring differences both in social identity and in
prior opinions. Randomization combined with a mechanism to
ensure diversity across age cohorts or partisan identification, for
instance, could be an effective means of accomplishing this aim.
Further, public hearings would be constructed so as to ensure the
presentation of opposing points of view. Given national trends,
there is little reason to think that a proposed amendment barring
gay marriage, increasing the salience of the issue and promoting
deliberation, would have generated nationwide opinion majorities *more* hostile to gay rights policy than they were in 2006.
By 2010, a CNN poll indicated that 50 percent of Americans
supported same-sex marriage. We might reasonably expect that

all voters supporting gay marriage would have opposed the amendment, and some voters opposed to gay marriage would also oppose a constitutional amendment preventing it; thus there is good reason to think that by 2012 (a second referendum), the amendment would have failed. (Were a dual referendum – requiring the support of states – also required, the fact that a majority in 2010 supported same-sex marriage in twenty-two states suggests that the state vote would also fail, even if it might have passed in 2008.) We should have confidence in the capacity of majorities to change opinions in a direction more, rather than less, protective of minority interests even in a relatively short period of time. Although it is surely true that in the presence of a supermajority rule Congress would not have passed the FMA in the first place, it is not clear that the cause of same-sex marriage would have been hurt; had the FMA passed and sparked a nationwide debate on same-sex marriage, support for gay marriage might have increased still more rapidly.

Finally, turning from the context of constitutional amendments to ordinary legislatures, if legislatures required supermajority support to pass gay rights legislation, the prospect for many forms of protection would be dim. Across the states, pro-gay-rights opinion majorities do not translate into pro-gay policies, even in the presence of majoritarian institutions, so a supermajority rule would essentially guarantee that protections for housing, health care, and employment were not implemented (Lax and Phillips 2009). Similar findings hold for congressional districts; only in the presence of overwhelming majorities do Republicans vote in favor of such policies (Krimmel, Lax, and Phillips 2011). At least in the context of gay rights policies, supermajoritarian requirements likely hinder the adoption of pro-minority legislation.

More generally, complex majoritarianism is typically unnecessary for legislative decision making outside of the constitutional arena. As discussed, bicameral legislatures are themselves supermajoritarian; they inherently feature sequential voting and associated time delays, elements that optimally promote deliberation. Even in a unicameral legislature, however, there is little reason to have regular recourse to the iterated deliberative and sequential voting requirements that, while improving judgment, necessarily introduce a status quo bias. The most committed advocates of the filibuster do not believe it ought to be used for all legislative decisions, but only for the most important pieces of legislation and to block egregious appointments. Similarly, if legislators could reliably identify categories of decisions that carried grave risks were decision making hasty, outweighing the risks associated with delay and sclerosis, complex majoritarianism might be valuable. The attendant risk of partisan obstruction would be less grave given that a simple majority would still be sufficient to pass legislation, but if the use of delays followed the partisan trajectory of the filibuster, complex majoritarianism could potentially be used to tie up legislative decision making. Complex-majoritarian institutions cannot and should not replace majoritarianism in most instances of political decision making.

A Note on Targeted Vetoes

As suggested throughout the book, supermajority rules constitute at best an unreliable mechanism for protecting the interests of vulnerable minority groups. The blunt instrument of a vote threshold means that any minority can wield the veto generated, and the members most needing protection may not be capable of attaining the threshold. Nonetheless, in circumstances where a historically marginalized group has discrete interests over a particular set of policies, a targeted veto may be justifiable. But granting a targeted veto does necessarily entail derogating from majoritarian decision making. Targeted vetoes are *not* complex-majoritarian institutions; they are full-scale derogations from majority decision making and from the presumption of epistemic equality. No normative triangulation enables us to evade this point. We cannot pretend that ceding judgment over a domain actually firms the capacity of citizens to make decisions in that domain, nor can we assert that it enhances the epistemic equality of members to suspend their capacity to judge certain questions. Removing questions from the domain of judgment may be defensible in such restrictive circumstances, but not on the terms of complex majoritarianism, which aims to enhance the quality of decision making under majority rule.

The use of supermajority rules to bias our judgment may be appropriate in a restrictive set of circumstances, such as the use of a supermajority on a jury to bias against conviction, for instance. Similarly, we could hold that supermajority rules are the optimal solution to persistent failures of judgment with respect to a minority population. But this is the point at which the problems of threshold *phronesis* and misappropriation described earlier have their bite. It is not that supermajority rules might be indefensible for minority protection – it is that they are likely to be ineffective. So we must not only find a normatively defensible mechanism by which to protect vulnerable minorities; we must also ensure that such an institution is likely to be effective, and cannot easily be misused.

This latter condition – its susceptibility to misuse – is important. The targeted veto could be deployed to secure benefits for the vulnerable group that it does not need, and which are harmful to the rest of the community. Again, however, if the scope of the veto is narrowly construed – pertaining to bilingual educational rights or river access, for instance – the capacity for abuse will be diminished. There are additional concerns about the internal composition of the minority: who is authorized to represent the group, and what if the interests of the population diverge? But these questions of representation hold under supermajority rules just as readily as they do under veto power. Construing these groups as entities deserving of rights may also reify them in a particular way and makes them less susceptible to transformation. Under a supermajority rule their protection could depend on their willingness to strike bargains with coalition partners, leading to internal change. But targeted vetoes would be necessary only if the group's survival were at stake – if, historically, the group has suffered such severe abuse that the larger community's judgment is deemed completely unreliable. The internal adaptability of the group is of less serious concern than its capacity to survive. Nonetheless, as Chapter 6 also suggested, it cannot be the case that the veto is entrenched or otherwise immune to reconsideration. The fate of the veto, and of the minority as a whole, will ultimately rest on the community's judgment. But this is true of all institutions: there are no institutional bulwarks against a democracy, or any regime, bent on self-destruction.

So there is an internal complexity to the choice of a targeted veto, both in its relationship to the general presumption of members' equality, and with respect to the conditions under which the veto will be chosen. Constitution makers must recognize that a particular community has been subject to abuse over a discrete set of issues. This recognition cannot strictly derive from pressure on the part of the minority; if it has sufficient political power to secure such a veto, then it probably does not need it. The issue should arise only when there is serious moral concern about the minority at the time of the framing, but either the framers or the community as a whole fear this concern may be fleeting because of historical patterns of recriminations, neglect, and violence. Under these circumstances, a democracy could deem its own judgment to be especially fallible, and cede authority over the relevant domain to the minority group. Yet because the veto cannot be inviolable – it cannot be granted in perpetuity without the possibility of reconsideration – the risk remains that the community will act to remove the veto. Alternatively, and perhaps more hopefully, the community may deem itself able to treat the minority group fairly, and return decision making about that group to the majority vote of the legislature, where optimally it will remain.

Conclusion

Complex majoritarianism thus differs in important ways from supermajority rule. In the first instance, it mandates rather than implies deliberation and time delays for fundamental decisions. Whereas supermajority rules only indirectly promote such mechanisms, complex majoritarianism requires them. But even if supermajority rules were accompanied by obligations of deliberation and delay, the derogation from formal equality would be generally unjustifiable. Although we may wish to raise the costs of altering our fundamental norms through the use of such procedures, biasing our political judgments through supermajority rules entails the view that one set of opinions should be presumed to be superior to another. Respect for members of political bodies – especially those engaging in deliberation – requires us to treat them as bearers of presumptively equal capacities for judgment. We cannot structure democratic decision rules to systematically prefer the judgment of one set of voters.

Ultimately, one set of opinions will prevail. Optimally, however, a majority vote following deliberation will track the relative strength or persuasiveness of the arguments presented, as many scholars have argued.[6] In Manin's words, "The approval of the greatest number reflects, in that context, the greater strength of one set of arguments compared to others. ... The minority (or minorities) also had reasons, but these reasons were less convincing" (Manin 1987, 359). In Habermas's version, "because of its internal connection with a deliberative practice, majority rule justifies the presumption that the fallible majority opinion may be considered a reasonable basis for a common practice until further notice, namely, until the minority convinces the majority that their (the minority's views) are correct" (Habermas 1996, 306). Under a supermajority rule, however, the minority prevails. Recall the plight of the ERA proponent from the beginning of this book; despite sustained deliberation and reason-giving sufficient to persuade an overwhelming majority, a slim minority vetoed the outcome. The better argument did not win; as such, the epistemic validity and – on a Habermasian model, at least – the democratic legitimacy of these outcomes come into question.

The aim of complex majoritarianism is to promote high-quality judgments among the relevant decision makers, through providing forums for argumentation, testimony, and reason-giving, and through reducing the likelihood of panicked, passionate, or ill-considered decisions. In all but the most exceptional circumstances, minority rights remain at least as secure

---

[6] See, for instance, Benhabib (1996), 72.

under complex-majoritarian institutions as under supermajority rules; the primary difference is that these rights do not entail those of veto, except in extraordinary cases where such veto is formally prescribed. Further, institutions remain stable on such a model for good reasons. In Habermas's view, the capacity to change outcomes constitutes an important piece of ground-work for the "reasonable *presumption* that fallible decisions are right" (Habermas 1996, 180). The legitimacy of existing norms depends on their origin in a deliberative process, the capacity of an outvoted minority to reopen debate with the aim of alter-ing the outcome at a later point, and some realistic prospect that such efforts would be successful. If the last condition is not satisfied – as may not occur under a supermajority rule[7] – the epistemic and moral validity of these norms is subject to ques-tion. Under a stringent supermajority amendment procedure, the mere endurance of these norms no longer constitutes evi-dence of their quality or reflects the citizens' judgment that they are worth preserving.

The capacity of complex majoritarianism to promote consen-sus, however, remains for discussion. If consensus arises under complex majoritarianism, it does so as a function of the delib-eration it requires rather than because of any feature of the vot-ing rule as such. Consensus, in either aggregative or acclamatory form, is not mandated by complex majoritarianism, nor is it a clear desideratum. This is because voting rules prize independent and individual judgments, the sort that the consensual institu-tions discussed primarily in the first half of the book sought explicitly to counter. If we wish to capture consensus, we ought to seek non-aggregative means of doing so, as the Conclusion suggests.

---

[7] Habermas (1996, 180) himself mentions in passing that "it is appropriate to qualify the majority, depending on the matter at issue," for instance vis-à-vis basic rights protecting autonomy.

8

Conclusion

The aim of this work has been to challenge the contemporary assumption that supermajority rules are not only normatively unproblematic, but necessary to achieve the desiderata of institutional stability, consensus, and minority protections. Although supermajority rules in the modern era ostensibly aim to reduce the risks associated with political instability, they do so at the cost of introducing new liabilities associated with the biased judgments they generate and secure. Because institutions secure the outcomes of morally arbitrary bargains under the conditions of distributive inequality, to bias future change in favor of these outcomes carries substantial normative risks. Supermajority rule may be defensible in those cases where a bias might be reasonably considered necessary to avoid seriously adverse consequences, but ascertaining the conditions in which this would hold is more difficult than is typically assumed. It is surely not the case that the interests of every minority group, for instance, merit such a bias, and supermajority rules cannot provide a means test.

As the first half of this book suggested, however, supermajority rules do constitute an attractive alternative to unanimity in those rare circumstances when we could expect perfect agreement: for instance, the selection of the true pope by the cardinals or the identification of the general will by citizens of a well-ordered society. When unanimity is not achieved in such contexts, this was thought to constitute evidence of malice, of self-interested behavior, of ignorance, or simply bad judgment on the part of the minority. Historically, the move from unanimity to supermajority rule was justified in order to ensure that erroneous members of the minority could not veto the probably correct outcome, assuming the community were not pathological. As we have also seen, a supermajority rule also reduces the probability of a different sort of human weakness generated by unanimity, namely a tendency toward coercive behavior against lone holdouts. Because contemporary political life is rife with disagreement rather than concord, we might think that these arguments offer purely antiquarian interest. This is partially true: such justifications do not provide valid reasons for adopting supermajority rule as an alternative to majority rule. Yet in certain important circumstances – federations or multinational associations such as the European Union, for instance – unanimity often is still required. However, because unanimity rules so readily lead to breakdown, qualified majority rules are frequently proposed as an alternative, and may be defended on these grounds.

Although supermajority rules do have distinctive liabilities, their use may be justified as a bias against predictable forms of injustice, or as a means of reducing the likelihood of coercion. Even though few blanket conditions emerge from any theory of institutional design, the arguments of this book do generate a set of principles that ought to help us evaluate supermajority rules and indeed the merits of aggregative systems more generally. Social choice theory has for decades dominated our understanding of the normative characteristics voting rules ought to possess. The influence of Arrow's impossibility theorem in particular has generated a remarkable literature in political science on the criteria of unrestricted domain, non-dictatorship, independence from irrelevant alternatives, and Pareto. Examining the history of political thought, and the history of institutional design, reveals a different and at least equally important set of commitments that have guided the selection of voting rules since antiquity. These principles ought to guide the selection of voting rules in different contexts and help citizens evaluate the conditions under which supermajority rules are legitimate and appropriate, and where they ought to be replaced by other thresholds.

The first such principle is *equal epistemic respect*. The right to participate in collective decisions, whatever the form, does constitute an acknowledgment of one's standing in a political community. As we have seen, however, from antiquity, having one's individual vote count served as a marker of the dignity of (some) citizens. Further, as Chapter 5 suggested, the democratic nature of majority rule derives from the fact that it confers this dignity equally upon all citizens, signifying equal respect for their judgments. Although not every decision can or should be made by majority rule, and there are cases in which we should want to bias our judgments to hedge against certain forms of moral and epistemic risks, democracy requires at minimum a commitment to the view that citizens are presumed equally capable of knowing their own interests – of identifying those agents best suited to represent them, and of ensuring that the fundamental constitutional norms governing the society in which they live reflect their core commitments.

The second principle is that of *fallibilism*: the recognition that people and their works are imperfect, and that we may err in our most fundamental beliefs and decisions. Fallibilism constitutes, or ought to constitute, a key commitment for democrats, insofar as it encourages citizens to adopt a critical perspective on even core institutions and fundamental beliefs. The fallibility of those who design institutions is among the most important justifications for enabling the revision of norms (Schwartzberg 2007). In contrast to unanimity, supermajority rule instantiates the principle of fallibilism in two ways. First, it enables a group to make warranted decisions given lapses in judgment or behavior by a few of its members. This capacity is especially important in those circumstances under which we might expect unanimity to be readily achievable, as in identifying a correct answer that should optimally be obvious to the members of a particular body: for instance, the selection of the true pope by the cardinals, as Chapter 3 discussed, and the identification of the general will by the citizens of a well-ordered society, as in the account of Rousseau in Chapter 4. When unanimity is not achieved, this constitutes evidence of malice, of self-interested behavior, or of ignorance on the part of the minority. By weakening the threshold to a supermajority, members of the minority cannot veto that which – barring complete disorder – is clearly the correct outcome. Second, supermajority rules reduce the barriers to revision and enable easier correction of erroneous decisions. Majority rule reduces these barriers further, and has a claim for support on those grounds. However, as discussed in Chapters 4 and 5, where we want to hedge against the risk of one type of error – of convicting the innocent, for instance – supermajority rules may help us mitigate moral and epistemic risk.

The third principle is that of *minimizing coercion*. Coercion can manifest itself both substantively and procedurally. First, from a substantive perspective, unanimity may generate the most coercion, even though it is often assumed to be the least coercive. Under unanimity, one is obliged only to obey decisions to which one has consented; from a contractarian perspective, therefore, unanimity ensures autonomy. However, the loss of freedom does not only result from the imposition of laws with which one disagrees; it may be a consequence of the failure to enact laws when members are not protected from new harms, or the failure to revise old ones when they impose unfair burdens. Circumstantial change, preference transformation, or even fundamental alterations in moral beliefs may erode support for norms enacted even in the relatively recent past. A substantial majority, potentially all but one member, may be forced to abide by decisions that it regards as illegitimate – as no longer beneficial to the community, or not in accordance with contemporary standards of morality. It is true that at the point of initial contract, higher vote thresholds reduce the number of members who must abide by laws with which they disagree. But at moments when there are calls for revisions, the higher the vote threshold, the more members who may be obliged to obey laws they regard as wrong. Second, from a procedural perspective, unanimous decision making generates moral and perhaps even physical pressure on dissenters. Although it is true that members of the majority might seek to coerce minority holdouts at any threshold point, as the conclusion to Chapter 4 discussed, sociological and historical evidence suggests that such coercion is more intense, and the probability of capitulation higher, under unanimity thresholds.

Taken together, the three principles constitute heuristics by which we can assess the normative value of voting rules in distinctive democratic contexts. The primary value these principles instantiate is the capacity to accommodate dissent, both at the moment of the decision and in the future. Unlike unanimity, supermajority and majority rule both permit the existence of what Chapter 2 termed an enumerated minority. This is a merit of an aggregative system more generally, as I have suggested. It records the existence and the size of the minority in opposition for posterity. Vote thresholds below unanimity encourage us not to presume that perfect agreement, real or fictive, is necessary for communal action: instead, they encourage us to recognize that disagreement is inevitable given human fallibility and the diversity of interests.

The best argument for supermajority rules is that they can help us reduce the probability of moral harms through biasing our judgments where we have very good warrant for believing that one alternative is superior to another. In the jury, this amounts to a bias against false conviction. In a constitution, the matter is much thornier. Certainly the majority of constitutional rules prescribing the terms of ordinary politics do not possess any sort of special weight other than their capacity to coordinate us. As the second half of the book argued, however, supermajority rules are not the sole or even the best means of stabilizing political institutions, given the adverse distributive consequences they may both generate and secure. Complex majoritarian institutions would provide the procedural ballast necessary to ensure that alterations are deliberative rather than hasty, without weighing the vote in favor of one set of judgments. The security of expectations does not depend on supermajority rules. It is clear, however, that the capacity to form judgments worthy of epistemic respect – on which the aggregative vote depends – requires norms of free expression and dissent. In those

210 ConclusionConclusion

circumstances where there is some risk that such constitutional rights might be threatened, it may be justifiable to bias our judgments against their alteration through the use of supermajority rules. Most obviously, a set of civil and political rights might be protected in a constitution by a supermajority rule governing amendment, insofar as these rights enable the possibility of ongoing contestation. As noted in Chapter 6, basic liberties are constitutive of high-quality, independent judgments. This does not mean they ought to be entrenched against any change; the formulation of these norms might surely be improved on, or reframed in light of judicial interpretation (Schwartzberg 2007). Nonetheless, because of their constitutive status and, as such, the reasonableness of biasing our judgment in favor of their protection, regulating them through a supermajority threshold might be advisable, if well-framed complex-majoritarian institutions were not in place.

Similarly, as the conclusion to Chapter 4 suggested, supermajority rule might attractively substitute for unanimity rules on criminal jury trials without diminishing the reliability or fairness of the verdict. A supermajority rule does attractively bias jurors against unjust decisions made on the basis of insufficient evidence, and in the context of an asymmetric rule (in which acquittals require only a simple majority), against conviction. Unanimity, by contrast, tends to generate the coercion of holdouts; it does not – and was never designed to – improve the epistemic quality of decision making. A supermajority rule allows jury members to dissent, but more importantly, it offers some evidence to a defendant who believes she has been wrongly convicted that the case was not conclusive. Were dissenting members obliged to provide reasons for their votes, such information could be of critical value for future appeals.

As we have seen, however, only in relatively rare contexts do supermajority rules encourage rather than diminish the likelihood of critical challenge. They weigh members' judgments, including their judgments of their interests, unequally, and in so doing do not realize the first principle of epistemic respect. They introduce a status quo bias, sometimes an exceptionally strong one, into decision making, and encourage us to treat the framers and their products as sacrosanct rather than fallible. They frequently help secure adverse distributive consequences by granting powerful actors a veto over modifications to schemes that support their interests. In so doing, they constrain even substantial majorities of citizens who seek revision and redistribution.

In light of these three principles, let us return to the three cases with which the book began: the ERA advocate, the British Columbia citizens' assembly participants, and the gay couple in California. Are supermajority rules justifiable in any of these contexts? The ERA advocate does have reason to feel that her defeat was both substantively and procedurally unjust. The substantive injustice is easy to understand from the perspective of epistemic respect; she believes that without constitutional protection, she is denied dignity as an equal member of the society, possessing equal capacity for judgment. She objects to the simple fact that a supermajority rule biases popular judgments in favor of treating her unequally. But there are also thornier procedural objections. Even though the amendment clause was ratified long ago and constitutes a social practice, the fact that there were never good reasons, outside of the mere fact of coordination, for the choice of the threshold does weaken its stature. Because its sole basis for legitimacy rests in its *de facto* status, it has no independent basis on which it can withstand criticism. Once the practice is challenged, the only defense available to the supporter of the threshold would be the benefits of predictability or the security of expectations. But insofar as the threshold generates a systematic bias against one set of judgments, there is reason to think that the injustice generated by such bias might reasonably outweigh the putative benefits ascribed to its preservation. However, the same minority that denies the substantive injustice of the defeat of the ERA would need to support changing the amendment clause. Because the amendment clause is self-reflective – it governs the terms of its own alteration – to change it would require a three-quarters majority for alteration at the same time as a new threshold was chosen. This threshold would need to be supported by reasons, even if such reasons can never be strictly dispositive. Thus the ERA advocate finds herself in a double-bind: unable to pass her amendment despite overwhelming support, and unable to alter the threshold without recourse to constitutional revolution.

The members of the citizens' assembly have a different complaint. The electoral scheme they support is of at least equal merit to the existing alternative, given the months spent in consultations and deliberation. Nor is the existing electoral system obviously meritorious in terms of ensuring equal respect for members or securing the capacity for dissent. There is certainly no reason to systematically bias against the judgments of those who think it is worthy. The fact that the electoral system itself is not given constitutional status – as it rarely is – suggests it does not deserve enshrinement. To require that the referendum pass a supermajority threshold grants unequal weight to the judgments of those who prefer the status quo without good reason.

The gay couple in California has yet a different objection; they are angry that a bare simple majority initiative was sufficient to deprive them of court-recognized marriage rights. One might think that because of the moral issues at stake, a supermajority vote would enable a salutary bias against harm to their rights. Note, however, the particular circumstances in which the vote occurred. The California State Legislature passed a law by a wide margin in 1977 restricting marriage to heterosexuals, which was affirmed again as an initiative in 2000 by a vote of 61.4 percent to 38 percent. The California Supreme Court struck down this law, but its verdict was nullified by the passage of the constitutional amendment through Proposition 8. It is surely possible that requiring a two-thirds vote of each house of the Legislature might have prevented the passage of Proposition 8. (Lawsuits challenging Proposition 8 as a constitutional "revision" rather than an "amendment" suggested such a supermajority should have been required.) But requiring a two-thirds vote of the Legislature for its own action on same-sex marriage – which, as advocates suggest, the alteration of a fundamental right ought to require – would likely have failed in the Legislature, protecting the 1977/2000 status quo; in any event, previous legislative efforts to reverse the

1977 law and the 2000 initiative were vetoed by Governor Arnold Schwarzenegger. Similarly, requiring a threshold above 52.47 percent – the margin by which Proposition 8 passed – would have been sufficient to block the rule. Yet one might reasonably suggest that the problem with the initiative process for amendment lies not with the threshold itself, nor even with the use of referendums, but with its lack of complexity. Given the rapid transformations in public opinion on gay marriage, including in California, it is quite possible that subjecting the proposed amendment to sustained deliberative assemblies might have tipped the balance against Proposition 8. The absence of deliberation constitutes the proper objection to the initiative mechanism of California; were the questions placed on the ballot subject to sustained consideration, much of the arbitrariness with which the initiative process is frequently charged would be reduced.

The merit of the deliberative mechanism in the context of an initiative mechanism lies in its capacity to improve the quality of the judgments of individual voters – not, it should be affirmed, to reach any consensus. As Chapter 2 discussed, the value of an aggregative system lies in the dignity it confers on these judgments, including those in the minority. In contrast, the value of an acclamatory, or "consensual," mechanism rests in its capacity to generate the fiction of communal support for collective action. As discussed, however, difficulties arise when aggregative systems seek to capture consensus. In her brilliant *Beyond Adversary Democracy*, Jane Mansbridge argues that the former, which she terms "adversary democracy," is appropriate where interests conflict. The latter, which she terms "unitary democracy," should be used in those contexts marked by the presence of common interests. She makes this point syllogistically:

Its first premise ... is that the larger the polity, the more likely it is that some individuals will have conflicting interests. Its second premise ... is that the more individual interests come in conflict, the more a democracy encompassing those interests must employ adversary procedures. These two premises demand the conclusion that democracies as large as the modern nation-state be primarily adversary democracies. (Mansbridge 1980)

The consensual ideal of "unitary democracy" fails once interests conflict because it becomes an "individual veto over the actions of the majority," even in small groups (Mansbridge 1980). In nation-states, exhilarating acclamatory decisions (as sketched in the discussion of Athens) quickly become "social or institutional coercion on a national scale" (Mansbridge 1980). In her view, danger lies in creating unitary institutions in conflictual circumstances.

Following this lesson of *Beyond Adversary Democracy*, this book has examined the use of supermajority rules to capture consensus, a task for which it is ill-suited. The goal of consensus constitutes a reason – if, I have suggested, not a compelling one – for the use of supermajority rules for constitutional amendments, and, as discussed at the conclusion of the first half, for decision making in international institutions. Reminiscent of Mansbridge's discussions of consensus making in late 1960s and 1970s New Left collectives, supermajority rules today substitute for consensus in major contemporary social movements, including the Occupy Movement. As in the collectivities explored by Mansbridge, the Occupy Movement adopts consensus decision making, rather than majority rule, as an ostensible means of avoiding the conflictual nature of politics and the generation of winners and losers. At General Assembly Meetings, consensus depends on a facilitating team to help organize deliberation. A proposal is introduced and facilitators lead a discussion in which attendees take turns asking questions, suggesting amendments, or making general points; the proposers respond in turn. The facilitator periodically checks the "temperature" of the proceedings by asking the participants for hand signals indicating their stance. If there is widespread agreement, the facilitators ask whether consensus has emerged, and individuals are given the opportunity to formally block the proposal. If there are no blocks, the proposal passes.

The difficulty of attaining consensus does mean that there is a risk of coercion – of the exclusion or browbeating of recalcitrant members – and there is some anecdotal evidence to suggest that this occurs. More generally, the requirement of perfect agreement – not merely the general spirit of the body, but of una-nimity – means that General Assembly attendee who clings to a different perspective is able to block a decision. Chapter 3 took up this problem in the context of papal elections. The solution – as in the medieval context – has been to weaken the threshold, generating a "modified-consensus" rule, a nine-tenths superma-jority rule designed to allow for a few blocks by members who believe the decision to be fundamentally wrong. Naturally, the nine-tenths rule entails that a very narrow minority can block decisions preferred by the overwhelming majority. It is hard to view this outcome as less coercive than a majority decision rule. The egalitarian ethos of the Occupy movements is real-ized through the deliberative mechanism – not the decision rule, which betrays this commitment.

More generally, when the aim is consensus, the use of a counted vote will necessarily be problematic, as the Athenians knew well. In *Political Tactics*, Jeremy Bentham wrote, "to say that anything has passed by acclamation, is to wish to make it be believed that it has passed unanimously; but if this unanimity were real, more would be gained by proving it by distinct voting" (Bentham 1999, 149). Yet, as we have also seen, when voting is both public and preceded by deliberation, even unanimous out-comes may not constitute evidence of unanimity. Where the aim is to signal widespread agreement and speak univocally – whether in the Athenian assembly or in the EU Council – the language of consensus may have the merits of transparency, or, one might say, deliberate opacity. Where we want to secure extraordinary sup-port for a proposal, a consensus rule, the decisiveness of which rests on the silence of dissenters, is preferable to either quali-fied majority or unanimity, simply because it does not pretend to derive from an aggregation of members' individual judgments.

However, in contemporary democratic life, we rarely confront a pressing need to speak with one voice and to suppress disagree-ment. Although agreement may always be desirable, in pluralistic societies it may be impossible to generate widespread agreement on even the most fundamental of questions. If one knows that disagreement is inevitable, then the use of a supermajority vote threshold will always, and inevitably, generate contention. It will bias the decision toward one set of judgments, typically those supporting the status quo or inaction. It will necessarily empower a minority, whether powerful or vulnerable, to veto. Its losers will justly lament that they have more than majority support on their side, and that they were not defeated, either by might in the form of the opposition's greater support or by right through the force of the better argument. In sum, if the core of democracy is a set of institutions designed to resolve disagreement, then the democratic threshold must be majority rule.

References

Abraham, Henry J. 1992. *Justices and Presidents*. New York: Oxford University Press.

Ackerman, Bruce. 1991. *We the People: Foundations*. Cambridge, MA: The Belknap Press of Harvard University Press.

   1998. *We the People: Transformations*. Cambridge, MA: The Belknap Press of Harvard University Press.

Aeschylus. 1977. Eumenides. In *The Orestia*. New York: Penguin Books.

Affeldt, Steven G. 1999. The Force of Freedom: Rousseau on Forcing to Be Free. *Political Theory* 27 (3): 299–333.

Allen, Danielle S. 2000. *The World of Prometheus: The Politics of Punishing in Democratic Athens*. Princeton, NJ: Princeton University Press.

Amar, Akhil. 1988. Philadelphia Revisited: Amending the Constitution Outside Article V. *University of Chicago Law Review* 55 (4): 1043–1104.

Aristotle. 1992. *Nicomachean Ethics*. Translated by D. Ross. Oxford: Oxford University Press.

   1995a. *Politics*. Translated by E. Baker. Oxford: Oxford University Press.

   1995b. *Rhetoric*. Translated by W. R. Roberts. Edited by J. Barnes. Princeton, NJ: Princeton University Press.

   1996. The Constitution of Athens. In *The Politics and the Constitution of Athens*, edited by S. Everson. Cambridge: Cambridge University Press, 209–263.

Arneson, Richard. 1993. Democratic Rights at National and Workplace Levels. In *The Idea of Democracy*, edited by David Copp, Jean Hampton, and John Roemer. Cambridge: Cambridge University Press.

Aroney, Nicholas. 2008. *The Constitution of a Federal Commonwealth*. Cambridge: Cambridge University Press.

Austen-Smith, David and Jeffrey S. Banks. 1996. Information Aggregation, Rationality, and the Condorcet Jury Theorem. *American Political Science Review* 90 (1): 34–45.

1999. *Positive Political Theory I: Collective Preference*. Ann Arbor: University of Michigan Press.

Baker, Keith Michael. 1975. *Condorcet*. Chicago: The University of Chicago Press.

Balasko, Yves and Hervé Crès. 1997. The Probability of Condorcet Cycles and Super Majority Rules. *Journal of Economic Theory* 75:237–270.

Baldwin, Marshall. 1968. *Alexander III and the Twelfth Century: The Popes through History*. New York: Newman Press.

Banks, Jeffrey S. 2000. Buying Supermajorities in Finite Legislatures. *The American Political Science Review* 94 (3):677–681.

Baron, David P. and John Ferejohn. 1989. Bargaining in Legislatures. *American Political Science Review* 83 (December):1181–1206.

Barry, Brian. 1965. *Political Argument*. London: Routledge and Kegan Paul.

Beatty, John and Alfred Moore. 2010. Should We Aim for Consensus? *Episteme* 7 (3):198–214.

Beck, Deborah. 2006. *Homeric Conversation*. Cambridge, MA: Harvard University Press.

Beitz, Charles R. 1989. *Political Equality*. Princeton, NJ: Princeton University Press.

Benhabib, Seyla 1996. Toward a Deliberative Model of Democratic Legitimacy. In *Democracy and Difference*, edited by S. Benhabib. Princeton, NJ: Princeton University Press, 67–94.

Benson, Robert L. 1968. *The Bishop-Elect: A Study in Medieval Ecclesiastical Office*. Princeton, NJ: Princeton University Press.

Bentham, Jeremy. 1999. *Political Tactics*. Oxford: Oxford University Press.

Binder, Sarah A. and Steven S. Smith. 1997. *Politics or Principle?: Filibustering in the United States Senate*. Washington, DC: The Brookings Institution.

Black, Duncan. 1958. *The Theory of Committees and Elections*. Cambridge: Cambridge University Press.

Boegehold, Alan. 1963. Toward a Study of Athenian Voting Procedure. *Hesperia* 32 (4):366–374.

Bogdanor, Vernon. 1997. Forms of Autonomy and the Protection of Minorities. *Daedalus* 126 (2):65–87.

Borgeaud, Charles. 1887. *Histoire de Plébiscite*. Geneva: H. George.

Brennan, Geoffrey and Loren Lomasky. 1993. *Democracy and Decision: The Pure Theory of Electoral Preference*. Cambridge: Cambridge University Press.

Brennan, Geoffrey and Philip Pettit. 1990. Unveiling the Vote. *British Journal of Political Science* 20:311–33.

Buchanan, James and Gordon Tullock. 1962. *The Calculus of Consent: Logical Foundations of Constitutional Democracy*. Ann Arbor: University of Michigan Press.

Burns, James Henderson, ed. 1988. *The Cambridge History of Medieval Political Thought c. 350–c. 1450*. Cambridge: Cambridge University Press.

Butters, H. C. 1985. *Governors and Government in Early Sixteenth Century Florence 1502–1519*. Oxford: Clarendon Press.

Caplin, Andrew and Barry Nalebuff. 1988. On 64%-Majority Rule. *Econometrica* 56 (4):787–815.

Cartledge, Paul. 2001. *Spartan Reflections*. London: Duckworth & Co.

Christiano, Thomas. 1996. *The Rule of the Many: Fundamental Issues in Democratic Theory*. Boulder, CO: Westview Press.

   2000. Waldron on Law and Disagreement. *Law and Philosophy* 19:513–543.

   2008. *The Constitution of Equality*. Oxford: Oxford University Press.

Cicero. 1928. *On the Republic and on the Laws*. Translated by C. W. Keyes. Cambridge, MA: Harvard University Press.

Coggins, Jay S. and C. Federico Perali. 1998. 64%-Majority Rule in Ducal Venice: Voting for the Doge. *Public Choice* 97:709–723.

Cohen, Joshua. 1986. An Epistemic Theory of Democracy. *Ethics* 97:26–38.

Coleman, Jules L. and John Ferejohn. 1986. Democracy and Social Choice. *Ethics* 97:6–25.

Colomer, Joseph M. and Iain McLean. 1998. Electing Popes: Approval Balloting and Qualified-Majority Rule. *Journal of Interdisciplinary History* 29 (1):1–22.

Condorcet, Marie Jean Antoine Nicolas Caritat, Marquis de. 1785. *Essai sur l'Application de l'Analyse à la Probabilité des Décisions Rendues à la Pluralité des Voix*. Paris: Imprimerie Royale.

   1968. *Oeuvres: Nouvelle impression en facsimilé de l'édition Paris 1847–1849*. Edited by e. M. F. A. a. A. C. O'Connor. 12 vols. Stuttgart- Bad Cannstatt: Friedrich Frommann.

Crimmins, James E. 1996. Contending Interpretations of Bentham's Utilitarianism. *Canadian Journal of Political Science* 29 (1): 751–777.

Dahl, Robert A. 1989. *Democracy and Its Critics*. New Haven, CT: Yale University Press.

Daniels, Norman. 2003. Democratic Equality: Rawls's Complex Egalitarianism. In *The Cambridge Companion to Rawls*, edited by S. Freeman. Cambridge: Cambridge University Press, 241–276.

Dasgupta, Partha and Eric Maskin. 2008. On the Robustness of Majority Rule. *Journal of the European Economic Association* 6:949–973.

Daston, Lorraine. 1988. *Classical Probability in the Enlightenment*. Princeton, NJ: Princeton University Press.

De Ste. Croix, G. E. M. 1972. *The Origins of the Peloponnesian War*. London: Duckworth.

Demosthenes. 1949. Against Neaera. In *Demosthenes [59]*. Cambridge, MA: Harvard University Press.

Dicey, A. V. 1982. *Introduction to the Study of the Law of the Constitution*. Indianapolis, IN: Liberty Classics.

Downs, Anthony. 1957. *An Economic Theory of Democracy*. New York: Harper and Row.

Driver, Justin. 2011. "The Consensus Constitution." *Texas Law Review* 89, 755–832.

Dryzek, John S. 2002. *Deliberative Democracy and Beyond*. Oxford: Oxford University Press.

Dworkin, Ronald. 1996. *Freedom's Law: The Moral Reading of the American Constitution*. Oxford: Oxford University Press.

Eisgruber, Christopher L. 2002. Democracy and Disagreement: A Comment on Jeremy Waldron's Law and Disagreement. *Journal of Legislation and Public Policy* 6 (1):35–47.

Elkins, Zachary, Tom Ginsburg, and James Melton. 2009. *The Endurance of National Constitutions*. Cambridge: Cambridge University Press.

Elster, Jon. 2000. *Ulysses Unbound*. Cambridge: Cambridge University Press.

   2007. The Night of August 4, 1789: A Study of Social Interaction in Collective Decision-Making. *Revue Européenne des Sciences Sociales* 45:71–94.

   2009. *Alexis de Tocqueville, The First Social Scientist*. Cambridge: Cambridge University Press.

Estlund, David M. 2008. *Democratic Authority: A Philosophical Framework*. Princeton, NJ: Princeton University Press.

Estlund, David M., Jeremy Waldron, Bernard Grofman, and Scott L. Feld. 1989. Democratic Theory and the Public Interest: Condorcet and Rousseau Revisited. *American Political Science Review* 83 (4):1317–1340.

Farrand, Max, ed. 1966. *Records of the Federal Convention of 1787*. Revised ed. 3 vols. New Haven, CT: Yale University Press.

Ferejohn, John. 1997. The Politics of Imperfection: The Amendment of Constitutions. *Law and Social Inquiry* 22:501–531.

Finley, M. 1979. *The World of Odysseus*. New York: Penguin.

Foreville, Raymond. 1965. *Latran I, II, III et Latran IV, Histoire de conciles oecuméniques VI*. Paris: Editions de l'Orante.

Forrest, W. G. 1980. *A History of Sparta 950–192 B.C.* London: Duckworth.

Fry, Timothy. 1981. RB 1980 in Latin and English with Notes. Collegeville, MN: Liturgical Press.

Gaudemet, Jean. 1960. Unanimité et majorité (Observations sur quelques études récentes). In *Études historiques à la memoire de Noël Didier*. Paris: Montchrestien.

Gilbert, Margaret. 1987. Modelling Collective Belief. *Synthese* 73 (1):185–204.

Glotz, Gustave. 1929. *The Greek City and Its Institutions*. London: Kegan, Paul, Trench, Trubner, and Co., Ltd.

Goodin, Robert. 2003. *Reflective Democracy*. Oxford: Oxford University Press.

Greenberg, Joseph. 1979. Consistent Majority Rule over Compact Sets of Alternatives. *Econometrica* 47 (3):627–636.

Grofman, Bernard N. and Scott L. Feld. 1988. Rousseau's General Will: A Condorcetian Perspective. *American Political Science Review* 82 (2):567–76.

Groseclose, Tim and James M. Snyder. 1996. Buying Supermajorities. *American Political Science Review* 90 (2):303–315.

Groseclose, Tim, and James M. Snyder, Jr. 2000. Vote Buying, Supermajorities, and Flooded Coalitions. *The American Political Science Review* 94 (3):683–684.

Guicciardini. 1994. *Dialogue on the Government of Florence*. Translated and edited by Alison Brown. Cambridge: Cambridge University Press.

Guinier, Lani. 1995. *The Tyranny of the Majority: Fundamental Fairness in Representative Democracy*. New York: Free Press.

Guinther, John. 1988. *The Jury in America*. New York: Facts on File Publications.

Gutmann, Amy. 1980. *Liberal Equality*. Cambridge: Cambridge University Press.

Habermas, Jurgen. 1996. *Between Facts and Norms: Contributions to a Discourse Theory of Democracy*. Cambridge, MA: MIT Press.

Hacking, Ian. 1990. *The Taming of Chance*. Cambridge: Cambridge University Press.

Hallinger, Kassius. 1965. Das Wahlrecht der Benediktusregula. *Zeitschrift für Kirchengeschichte* 76:233–245.

Hansen, Mogens Herman. 1991. *The Athenian Democracy in the Age of Demosthenes*. Oxford: Blackwell.

Hardin, Russell. 1982. *Collective Action*. Baltimore: Johns Hopkins University Press.

   1991. Hobbesian Political Order. *Political Theory* 19 (2):156–180.

   1999. *Liberalism, Constitutionalism, and Democracy*. Oxford: Oxford University Press.

Hart, H. L. A. 1994. *The Concept of Law*. Oxford: Oxford University Press.

Hastie, Reid, Steven D. Pernod, and Nancy Pennington. 1983. *Inside the Jury*. Cambridge, MA: Harvard University Press.

Held, Allison, Sheryl L. Herndon, and Danielle M. Stager. 1997. The Equal Rights Amendment: Why the ERA Remains Legally Viable and Properly Before the States. *William & Mary Journal of Women and the Law* 3 (1):113–136.

Hobbes, Thomas. 1985. *Leviathan*. Edited by C. B. Macpherson. London: Penguin.

Holmes, Stephen. 1995. *Passions and Constraint*. Chicago: University of Chicago Press.

Homer. 1990. *The Iliad*. Translated by R. Fagels. New York: Penguin.

   1996. *The Odyssey*. Translated by R. Fagels. New York: Viking.

Jaffe, Louis. 1967. Was Brandeis an Activist? The Search for Intermediate Premises. *Harvard Law Review* 80: 986–1003.

Jonakait, Randolph. 2003. *The American Jury System*. New Haven, CT: Yale University Press.

Jones, Philip. 1997. *The Italian City-State: From Commune to Signoria*. Oxford: Clarendon University Press.

Kalven, Harry and Hans Zeisel. 1966. *The American Jury*. Chicago: Chicago University Press.

Kantorowicz, Ernst H. 1946. *Laudes Regiae: A Study in Liturgical Acclamations and Mediaeval Ruler Worship* (University of California Publications in History, xxxiii). Berkeley and Los Angeles: University of California Press.

Kelsen, Hans. 1989. *Pure Theory of Law*. Translated by M. Knight. Gloucester, MA: Peter Smith.

Kendall, Willmoore. 1965. *John Locke and the Doctrine of Majority-Rule*. Urbana: University of Illinois Press.

Kishlansky, Mark. 1986. *Parliamentary Selection: Social and Political Choice in Early Modern England*. Cambridge: Cambridge University Press.

Knight, Jack. 1992. *Institutions and Social Conflict*. Cambridge: Cambridge University Press.

Knight, Jack and James Johnson. 1994. Aggregation and Deliberation: On the Possibility of Democratic Legitimacy. *Political Theory* 22 (2): 277–296.

2011. *The Priority of Democracy: Political Consequences of Pragmatism.* Princeton: Princeton University Press.

Konopcyznski, Ladislas. 1930. *Le Liberum Veto: etude sur le development du principe majoritaire.* Paris: Librarie Ancienne Honore Champion.

Krimmel, Kate, Jeffrey R. Lax, and Justin Phillips. 2011. Public Opinion and Gay Rights: Do Members of Congress Follow Their Constituents' Preferences. Typescript.

Kymlicka, Will. 1989. *Liberalism, Community and Culture.* Oxford: Oxford University Press.

Kymlicka, William. 1995. *Multicultural Citizenship.* Oxford: Oxford University Press.

Lagerspetz, Eerik. 1986. Pufendorf on Collective Decisions. *Public Choice* 49 (2):179–182.

Lanni, Adriaan M. 1997. Spectator Sport or Serious Politics? Hoi Periestekotes and the Athenian Lawcourts. *Journal of Hellenic Studies* 117:183–199.

2006. *Law and Justice in the Courts of Classical Athens.* Cambridge: Cambridge University Press.

Laplace, Pierre Simon. 1814. *Essai philosophique sur les probabilités.* 14 vols. Vol. 7, *Oeuvres completes.* Paris: Académie des Sciences.

Larsen, J. A. O. 1949. The Origin and Significance of the Counting of Votes. *Classical Philology* 44 (3):144–181.

Lax, Jeffrey R. and Justin Phillips. 2009. Gay Rights in the States: Public Opinion and Policy Responsiveness. *American Political Science Review* 103 (3):367–386.

Leibniz, Gottfried Wilhelm. 1951. Preface to the Universal Science. In *Leibniz Selections*, edited by P. P. Wiener. New York: Charles Scribner's Sons.

Levinson, Sanford. 1995. *Responding to Imperfection.* Princeton, NJ: Princeton University Press.

2006. *Our Undemocratic Constitution.* New York: Oxford University Press.

Lewis, David. 1969. *Convention.* Cambridge, MA: Harvard University Press.

Lienhard, Joseph T. 1975. *Sanius Consilium*: Recent Work on the Election of the Abbot in the *Rule* of St. Benedict. *The American Benedictine Review* 26 (1): 1–15.

Lintott, Andrew. 1992. *Judicial reform and law reform in the Roman Republic.* Cambridge: Cambridge University Press.

1999. *The Constitution of the Roman Republic.* Oxford: Oxford University Press.

List, Christian. 2004. On the Significance of the Absolute Margin. *British Journal for the Philosophy of Science* 55:521–544.

Livy. 1960. *The Early History of Rome.* Translated by A. de Selincourt. New York: Penguin.

Locke, John. 1988. *Two Treatises of Government.* Edited by P. Laslett. Cambridge: Cambridge University Press.

Loraux, Nicole. 1997. *The Divided City.* New York: Zone Books.

Lutz, Donald. 1994. Toward a Theory of Constitutional Amendment. *American Political Science Review* 88:355–370.

Macedo, Stephen. 2010. Against Majoritarianism: Democratic Values and Institutional Design. *Boston Law Review* 90 (2):1029–1042.

Mackie, Gerry. 2003. *Democracy Defended.* Cambridge: Cambridge University Press.

Manin, Bernard. 1987. On Legitimacy and Political Deliberation. *Political Theory* 15 (3):338–368.

　1997. *The Principles of Representative Government.* Cambridge: Cambridge University Press.

Mansbridge, Jane. 1980. *Beyond Adversary Democracy.* New York: Basic Books.

　1986. *Why We Lost the ERA.* Chicago: University of Chicago Press.

Mansbridge, Jane, et al. 2010. The Place of Self-Interest and the Role of Power in Deliberative Democracy. *The Journal of Political Philosophy* 18 (1):64–100.

McGann, Anthony J. 2006. *The Logic of Democracy.* Ann Arbor: University of Michigan Press.

McGinnis, John O. and Michael B. Rappaport. 2002. Our Supermajoritarian Constitution. *Texas Law Review* 80 (**March**): 703–805.

McLean, Iain, and Fiona Hewitt. 1994. *Condorcet.* Aldershot: Edward Elgar Publishing Limited.

Mill, John Stuart. 1998. On Liberty and Other Essays. Oxford: Oxford World Classics.

Monahan, Arthur P. 1987. *Consent, Coercion, and Limit: The Medieval Origins of Parliamentary Democracy.* Leiden: E. J. Brill.

Montesquieu, Charles de Secondat. 1992. *Spirit of the Laws.* Translated by A. M. Cohler, B. C. Miller, and H. Stone. Cambridge: Cambridge University Press.

Morris, Colin. 1991. *The Papal Monarchy: The Western Church from 1050 to 1250.* Oxford: Oxford University Press.

Moulin, Léo. 1958. Sanior et maior pars. Note sur l'evolution des techniques électorales dans les orders religieux du VIe au XIIIe siècles. *Revue historique de droit française et étranger* 4th series (36):368–397 and 491–529.

Najemy, John M. 1982. *Corporatism and Consensus in Florentine Electoral Politics 1280–1400.* Chapel Hill: University of North Carolina Press.

Nederman, Cary J. 2009. *Lineages of European Political Thought.* Washington, DC: Catholic University of America Press.

Novak, Stéphanie. 2010. Decision Rules, Social Norms and the Expression of Disagreement: The Case of Qualified-Majority Voting in the Council of the European Union. *Social Science Information* 49: 83–98.

Ober, Josiah. 1989. *Mass and Elite in Democratic Athens.* Princeton, NJ: Princeton University Press.

2005. *Athenian Legacies: Essays on the Politics of Going Together.* Princeton, NJ: Princeton University Press.

2008. *Democracy and Knowledge: Innovation and Learning in Classical Athens.* Princeton, NJ: Princeton University Press.

Ogden, Daniel. 1997. *The Crooked Kings of Ancient Greece.* London: Duckworth.

Ordeshook, Peter C. 1992. Constitutional Stability. *Constitutional Political Economy* 3 (2):137–175.

Padua, Marsilius of. 2005. *The Defender of the Peace.* Translated by A. Brett. Cambridge: Cambridge University Press.

Pausanias. 1918. *Description of Greece.* Translated by W. H. S. Jones and H. A. Ormerod. Cambridge, MA: Harvard University Press.

Peterson, John and Elizabeth Bomberg. 1999. *Decision-Making in the European Union.* Basingstoke: Palgrave-MacMillan.

Peltzer, Jörg. 2008. *Canon Law, Careers and Conquest: Episcopal Elections in Normandy and Greater Anjou, c. 1140–c. 1230.* Cambridge: Cambridge University Press.

Plato. 1970. Laws. Translated by Trevor J. Saunders. New York: Penguin Books.

1975. Apology. In *The Trial and Death of Socrates.* Indianapolis, IN: Hackett.

1996. Protagoras. Translated by C. C. W. Taylor. Oxford: Oxford University Press.

Plutarch. 2001a. *Agis.* Translated by J. Dryden. Edited by A. H. Clough. Vol. 2, *Lives.* New York: Modern Library.

2001b. *Lycurgus.* Translated by J. Dryden. Edited by A. H. Clough. Vol. 1, *Lives.* New York: Modern Library.

Post, Gaines. 1950. A Roman Legal Theory of Consent, *Quod Omnes Tangit*, in Medieval Representation. *Wisconsin Law Review (January)*: 66–78.

1964. *Studies in Medieval Legal Thought: Public Law and the State, 1100–1322.* Princeton, NJ: Princeton University Press.

Przeworski, Adam. 2010. *Democracy and the Limits of Self-Government.* New York: Cambridge University Press.

Putterman, Ethan. 2005. Rousseau on the People as Legislative Gate-Keepers, Not Framers. *American Political Science Review* 99 (1):145–151.

Quillet, Jeannine. 1988. Community, Counsel, and Representation. In *Cambridge History of Medieval Political Thought*, edited by J. Burns. Cambridge: Cambridge University Press, 520–572.

Raaflaub, Kurt A., Josiah Ober, and Robert W. Wallace. 2007. *Origins of Democracy in Ancient Greece*. Berkeley: University of California Press.

Rae, Douglas W. 1969. Decision-Rules and Individual Values in Constitutional Choice. *American Political Science Review* 63 (1): 40–56.

Rae, Douglas W. 1975. The Limits of Consensual Decision. *American Political Science Review* 69:1270–1294.

Rasch, Bjorn Erik. 2011. Veto Points, Qualified Majorities, and Agenda-Setting Rules in Constitutional Amendment Procedures. In *2nd International Conference on Democracy as Idea and Practice*. Oslo, Norway.

Rasch, Bjorn Erik and Roger Congleton. 2006. Amendment Procedures and Constitutional Stability. In *Democratic Constitutional Design and Public Policy: Analysis and Design*, edited by R. C. a. B. Swedenborg. Cambridge, MA: The MIT Press, 319–342.

Ratner, R. S. 2008. Communicative Rationality in the Citizens' Assembly and Referendum Processes. In *Designing Deliberative Democracy: The British Columbia Citizens' Assembly*, edited by Mark E. Warren and Hilary Pearse. Cambridge: Cambridge University Press.

Read, James H. 2009. *Majority Rule versus Consensus: The Political Thought of John C. Calhoun*. Lawrence: University of Kansas Press.

Rhodes, P. J. 1981. Notes on Voting in Athens. *Greek, Roman, and Byzantine Studies* 22 (2):125–132.

Rhodes, P. J. and David M. Lewis. 1997. *The Decrees of the Greek States*. Oxford: Oxford University Press.

Risse, Mathias. 2004. Arguing for Majority Rule. *Journal of Political Philosophy* 12 (1):41–64.

Robinson, I. S. 1990. *Papacy 1073–1198: Continuity and Innovation*. Cambridge: Cambridge University Press.

    2004. The Institutions of the Church, 1073–c.1198. In *Cambridge Histories Online*, ed. D. Luscombe and J. Riley-Smith. Cambridge: Cambridge University Press. http://dx.doi.org.ezproxy.cul.columbia.edu/10.1017/CHOL9780521414104.012 (accessed August 20, 2010).

Rossiter, Clinton, ed. 1961. *The Federalist Papers*. New York: Penguin Books.

Rousseau, Jean-Jacques. 1997. *The Social Contract and Other Later Political Writings*. Edited and translated by Victor Gourevitch. Cambridge: Cambridge University Press.

Rubinstein, Nicolai. 1997. *The Government of Florence under the Medici (1434 to 1494)*. 2nd ed. Oxford: Oxford University Press.

Ruffini Avondo, Edouardo 1925. Il principio maggioritario nella storia del Diritto Canonico. *Archivio Giuridico Filippo Serafini* IX.

Saks, Michael J. 1998. What Do Jury Experiments Tell Us about How Juries (Should) Make Decisions. *Southern California Interdisciplinary Law Journal* 6:1–53.

Schelling, Thomas C. 1960. *The Strategy of Conflict*. Cambridge, MA: Harvard University Press.

Schmitt, Carl. 2004. *Legality and Legitimacy*. Translated by J. Seitzer. Durham, NC: Duke University Press.

2008. *Constitutional Theory*. Translated by J. Seitzer. Durham, NC: Duke University Press.

Schuessler, Alexander A. 2000. Expressive Voting. *Rationality and Society* 12:87–119.

Schwartz, Bernard. 1983. *Super Chief: Earl Warren and His Supreme Court – A Judicial Biography*. New York: New York University Press.

Schwartz, Edward P. and Warren F. Schwartz. 2000. And So Say Some of Us … What to Do When Jurors Disagree. *Southern California Interdisciplinary Law Journal* 9:445–447.

Schwartzberg, Melissa. 2003. Rousseau on Fundamental Law. *Political Studies* 51 (2):387–403.

2007. *Democracy and Legal Change*. New York: Cambridge University Press.

2008. Voting the General Will: Rousseau on Decision Rules. *Political Theory* 36 (3):403–423.

Scott, John T. 2005. Rousseau's Anti-Agenda-Setting Agenda and Contemporary Democratic Theory. *American Political Science Review* 99 (1):137–144.

Shapiro, Ian. 2003. *The State of Democratic Theory*. Princeton, NJ: Princeton University Press.

Shaw, Christine. 2001. Counsel and Consent in Fifteenth Century Genoa. *English Historical Review* 116 (468):834–862.

Sherwin-White, A. N. 1982. The Lex Repetundarum and the Political Ideas of Gaius Gracchus. *Journal of Roman Studies* 72:18–31.

Simon, H. A. 1957. *Models of Man: Social and Rational*. New York: Wiley.

Solt, Stephanie. 2011. Vagueness in Quantity: Two Cases from a Linguistic Perspective. In *Understanding Vagueness: Logical, Philosophical and Linguistic Perspectives*, edited by C. G. F. Petr Cintula, Lluis Godo, and Petr Hajek. London: College Publications, 5–23.

Staveley, Eastland S. 1972. *Greek and Roman Voting and Elections*. Ithaca, NY: Cornell University Press.

Steiner, Gilbert Y. 1985. *Constitutional Inequality: The Political Fortunes of the Equal Rights Amendment*. Washington, DC: Brookings.

Sunstein, Cass R. 2001. *Designing Democracy: What Constitutions Do*. New York: Oxford University Press.

Sunstein, Cass R. 2002. The Law of Group Polarization. *Journal of Political Philosophy* 10 (2): 175–195.

Tanner, Norman, ed. 1990. Decrees of the Ecumenical Councils, vol. 1. Washington, DC: Georgetown University Press.

Taylor, Lily Ross. 1966. *Roman Voting Assemblies*. Ann Arbor: The University of Michigan Press.

Thier, Andreas. 2001. Hierarchie und Autonomie. Regelungstraditionen der Bischofsbestellung in der Geschichte der kirschlichen Walhrechts bis 1140 Ludwig-Maximilians-Universität, Munich.

Thompson, Dennis F. 2008. Who Should Govern Who Governs? The Role of Citizens in Reforming the Electoral System. In *Designing Deliberative Democracy: The British Columbia Citizens' Assembly*, edited by Mark E. Warren and Hilary Pearse. Cambridge: Cambridge University Press 20–49.

Thucydides. 1972. *History of the Peloponnesian War*. Translated by R. Warner. New York: Penguin Books.

Tocqueville, Alexis de. 2000. *Democracy in America*. Translated by H. C. a. D. W. Mansfield. Chicago: University of Chicago Press.

Tsopanakis, Agapētos G. 1954. *La Rhètre de Lycurgue-l'Annexe-Tyrtée*. Thessaloniki: Hellenika.

Tuck, Richard. 2008. *Free Riding*. Cambridge, MA: Harvard University Press.

Ullmann-Margalit, Edna and Sidney Morgenbesser. 1977. Picking and Choosing. *Social Research* 44:757–785.

Urbinati, Nadia. 2004. Condorcet's Democratic Theory of Representative Government. *European Journal of Political Theory* 3 (1):53–75.

    2006. *Representative Democracy: Principles and Geneaology*. Chicago: University of Chicago Press.

Vaahtera, Jyri. 1990. Pebbles, Points, or Ballots: The Emergence of the Individual Vote in Rome. *Arctos* 24:161–177.

Vermeule, Adrian. 2007. *Mechanisms of Democracy: Institutional Design Writ Small*. New York: Oxford University Press.

Voltaire. 2000. *Treatise on Tolerance and Other Writings*. Cambridge: Cambridge University Press.

    2009. *Oeuvres Completes de Voltaire*. Vol. 80B. Oxford: Voltaire Foundation.

Waldron, Jeremy. 1995. The Wisdom of the Multitude: Some Reflections on Book 3, Chapter 11 of Aristotle's *Politics*. *Political Theory* 23:563–584.

    1999. *Law and Disagreement*. Oxford: Oxford University Press.

2002. *God, Locke, and Equality: Christian Foundations in Locke's Political Thought.* Cambridge: Cambridge University Press.

Waley, Daniel. 1988. *The Italian City-Republic.* 3rd ed. London: Longman.

Wallace, Helen, Mark A. Pollack, and Alasdair R. Young. 2010. *Policy-Making in the European Union.* Oxford: Oxford University Press.

Wallace, Robert W. 1989. *The Areopagus Council, to 307 BC.* Baltimore: Johns Hopkins University Press.

Warren, Mark E. and Hilary Pearse, ed. 2008. *Designing Deliberative Democracy: The British Columbia Citizens' Assembly.* Cambridge: Cambridge University Press.

Waters, Nicole L. and Valerie P. Hans. 2009. A Jury of One: Opinion Formation, Conformity, and Dissent on Juries. *Journal of Empirical Legal Studies* 6 (3): 513–540.

Watson, Alan. 1985. *The Digest of Justinian.* Philadelphia: University of Pennsylvania Press.

Wawro, Gregory and Eric Schickler. 2006. *Filibuster: Obstruction and Lawmaking in the U.S. Senate.* Princeton, NJ: Princeton University Press.

Weingast, Barry. 2005. Self-Enforcing Constitutions: With an Application to Democratic Stability in America's First Century. *Working paper.*

Weirich, Paul. 1986. Rousseau on Proportional Majority Rule. *Philosophy and Phenomenological Research* **XLVII** (1):111–126.

Whitman, James Q. 2008. *The Origins of Reasonable Doubt: Theological Roots of the Criminal Trial.* New Haven, CT: Yale University Press.

Williams, Melissa S. 1998. *Voice, Trust, and Memory: Marginalized Groups and the Failings of Liberal Representation.* Princeton, NJ: Princeton University Press.

Winroth, Anders. 2000. *The Making of Gratian's Decretum.* New York: Cambridge University Press.

Young, Iris Marion. 1990. *Justice and the Politics of Difference.* Princeton, NJ: Princeton University Press.

Index